DIGITAL INFLUENCE MERCENARIES

DIGITAL INFLUENCE MERCENARIES

PROFITS AND POWER THROUGH INFORMATION WARFARE

JAMES J. F. FOREST

NAVAL INSTITUTE PRESS
ANNAPOLIS, MARYLAND

Naval Institute Press
291 Wood Road
Annapolis, MD 21402

© 2022 by The U.S. Naval Institute
All rights reserved. No part of this book may be reproduced or utilized in any form or by any means, electronic or mechanical, including photocopying and recording, or by any information storage and retrieval system, without permission in writing from the publisher.

Library of Congress Cataloging-in-Publication Data
Names: Forest, James J. F., author.
Title: Digital influence mercenaries : profits and power through information warfare / James J. F. Forest.
Description: Annapolis, MD : Naval Institute Press, [2022] | Includes bibliographical references and index.
Identifiers: LCCN 2021052292 (print) | LCCN 2021052293 (ebook) | ISBN 9781682477229 (hardcover) | ISBN 9781682477526 (epub)
Subjects: LCSH: Internet marketing—Corrupt practices. | Information warfare.
Classification: LCC HF5415.1265 .F672 2021 (print) | LCC HF5415.1265 (ebook) | DDC 658.8/72—dc23/eng/20211109
LC record available at https://lccn.loc.gov/2021052292
LC ebook record available at https://lccn.loc.gov/2021052293

♾ Print editions meet the requirements of ANSI/NISO z39.48-1992 (Permanence of Paper).
Printed in the United States of America.

30 29 28 27 26 25 24 23 22   9 8 7 6 5 4 3 2 1
First printing

CONTENTS

	Preface	vii
	Acknowledgments	xi
	List of Abbreviations	xiii
1	The Diverse Landscape of Digital Influence Mercenaries	1
2	Digital Influence Methods	31
3	Fear and Uncertainty	58
4	Comforting Falsehoods and Conspiracies	82
5	Overconfidence and Confirmation Bias	103
6	Collective Identity and Conformity	123
7	Echo Chambers and Filter Bubbles	138
8	Confronting the Future Challenges of Digital Influence Mercenaries	155
	Notes	171
	Selected Bibliography	219
	Index	235

PREFACE

My first book on influence warfare, published in 2009, examined propaganda, psychological operations, and disinformation, especially how websites, blogs, email, online videos, digital magazines, and other such things were used to shape beliefs, attitudes, and behaviors. The central theme of that book was how governments were competing with terrorists for influence and support in the public domain, and particularly on the Internet. More recently, my research has focused on how nation-states (like Russia, China, Iran, and the Philippines) have embraced new forms of online information operations against foreign and domestic audiences, often in pursuit of political goals. But I also found many perpetrators of influence operations that were neither states nor terrorists. Some were merely individuals who had found a way to profit from disseminating disinformation and provoking emotions via social media platforms, while others were teams, or even formal companies with expertise in data analysis and online marketing. In the end, as with many journeys of intellectual exploration, I discovered that what I've been calling influence warfare is far more complicated than I had originally envisioned.

Digital forms of influence warfare encompass much more than state-sponsored meddling in U.S. elections, terrorist movements seeking to inspire and indoctrinate new recruits, or political parties seeking to provoke and deceive target audiences. There is a massive profit-making enterprise, built to function upon (and take advantage of) an even larger profit-making enterprise created by social media platforms with hundreds of millions of users worldwide. Throughout this enterprise there are clear and recognizable strategies and tactics used to manipulate the perceptions and behaviors of others. The mercenary's arsenal of methods and tactics include deception (including information deception, identity deception, and engagement deception), emotional provocation, and outright attacking the target (including bullying, hacking, exposing embarrassing information online, etc.). The first several chapters of this book will examine these methods (as well as the underlying economics of this industry), with many examples to illustrate what is meant by the term "digital influence mercenaries," what they do, and why.

Digital influencing involves people exploiting other people, using the tools and platforms of social media as a means to an end. But these operations are not only about technology—automated fake accounts, data algorithms, deepfake videos, and so forth. As reflected in the chapters of this book, this arena of activity involves the intersections of human behavior, beliefs, preferences, technology, power, and profit. The targets of these digital influence operations are you, me, and the billions of other people worldwide who are providing free and unfiltered access to themselves by posting photos and personal revelations, telling people where they are at a given moment, publicly declaring their likes and dislikes, and showcasing who their friends and family are. Further, because of the profit models that pervade the attention economy, Internet firms track a user's patterns of behavior so they can formulate the right kinds of advertising campaigns. Just as every click and keystroke can be monitored, recorded, and used for analysis that generates advertising profits for the Internet companies, the same data inform the strategies and tactics of digital influence.

There are also important psychological dimensions to the effectiveness of digital influence efforts, as we'll explore in chapters 3 through 7. For example, successful mercenaries understand that human beings typically have a strong desire to avoid uncertainty. We adopt a wide range of decisions and behaviors that are meant to reduce uncertainty and mitigate its effects. Unfortunately, these decisions and behaviors create opportunities that digital influence mercenaries can exploit for their own purposes. For example, we know that exploiting uncertainty and fear is a powerful way to grab attention and to provoke emotional or behavioral responses among the targets of an influence effort. There are also ways to manufacture uncertainty where there once was none—such as spreading false information about scientific evidence linking smoking and health risks.

At the same time, when we have strong beliefs or confidence about the world around us (and our place within it), we tend to prefer only information that bolsters our confidence, while avoiding or rejecting information that contradicts what we believe. We like to see things that support our beliefs, as this makes us feel good about choices we have made. But this also creates opportunities that digital influence mercenaries can exploit for their own purposes. For example, influence operations can use provocation tactics to challenge our beliefs, compelling us to defend our conviction about something we feel strongly about.

Provoking a reaction is a cornerstone of digital influence operations, because it generates online engagement (e.g., getting us to click on a link, post some sort of comment, reply to a message that offends us, etc.), and that engagement can generate revenue for the mercenary. They may be paid to do such things, but they can also focus their efforts on luring people to an ad-heavy website, where visitors will see loads of bias-confirming information, while the mercenary watches their ad revenues increase. Further, mercenaries are increasingly able to exploit media outlets, some of which will repeat false narratives while others attempt to counter those with fact-checking and condemnation—in both cases, amplifying the original disinformation by providing it more exposure.

Confronting the efforts of digital influence mercenaries will require a whole-of-society effort, as we'll discuss briefly in the concluding chapter. Social media platforms have already begun tagging disinformation with warning labels, while coordinated inauthentic behavior is being identified and blocked. Websites, Facebook pages, and YouTube channels are being shut down, and social media accounts are being suspended, often permanently. Governments in Europe and North America have launched numerous investigations, and in some cases have brought criminal charges (like the United States did against individuals involved in attempts to influence the 2016 presidential election). More forceful measures have also been taken—for example, in 2018, the U.S. Cyber Command conducted a series of operations to undermine the capabilities of Russian digital influence mercenaries seeking to influence the midterm elections that year.

Overall, there is much greater attention to the digital influence threats to security and society than there were a decade ago. A flurry of new research articles, reports, and books have shed light on the problems of fake social media accounts, troll farms, fake news, manipulated photos and videos, and the threats these and other things pose to the health and prosperity of a democratic society. But each of us also has an important role to play in recognizing and repelling digital influence efforts by taking personal responsibility for critical thinking and self-reflection about our biases and prejudices, while also thinking carefully before sharing or spreading information that benefits the digital influence mercenaries at our own expense.

ACKNOWLEDGMENTS

I owe a great debt of gratitude to literally thousands of people who have significantly influenced my intellectual journey into the sordid world of digital influence mercenaries. First, I need to express my appreciation to Jacob Shapiro and J. M. Berger for their feedback and advice along the way. I have also benefited greatly from the hard work and publications of researchers like Olga Belogolova, Kate Starbird, Marc Owen Jones, Claire Wardle, Clint Watts, Barb McQuade, Cass Sunstein, Camille Francois, Carl Miller, Caroline Orr, Thomas Rid, Cindy Otis, Phil Howard, Samantha Bradshaw, Samuel Woolley, Peter Pomerantsev, Emma Barrett, Nathaniel Gleicher, Emma Briant, Erin Gallagher, Jay Rosen, Joan Donavan, Judd Legum, Natalia Antonova, Nick Carmody, and Yael Eisenstat. If you like the contents of this book, you will find the work of these people most enlightening, in addition to the hard-working folks at the Oxford Internet Institute's Computational Propaganda project, the Global Network on Extremism and Technology, the Centre for the Analysis of Social Media, the RAND Corporation's Truth Decay project, Graphika, and the Stanford Internet Observatory. Weekly publications like *First Draft*, *Popular Information*, and *The Source* (published by the Atlantic Council's Digital Forensic Research Lab) are also strongly recommended.

I sincerely thank the Naval Institute Press, particularly senior acquisitions editor Padraic "Pat" Carlin and director Adam Kane, for agreeing to work with me in molding this manuscript into publishable material. I also thank the peer reviewers who assisted the Press with identifying deficiencies in this manuscript that needed to be remedied before it was ready for public consumption. Their feedback certainly helped strengthen the quality of the final product. Any errors in facts or conceptual explanations remaining in this book are mine alone. And finally, I thank Alicia, Chloe, and Jack for always being a positive influence in my life.

JAMES J. F. FOREST, PhD
Lake Winnipesaukee, New Hampshire
May 1, 2021

ABBREVIATIONS

AI	artificial intelligence
API	American Petroleum Institute
BLM	Black Lives Matter
CFCs	chlorofluorocarbons
CISA	Cybersecurity and Infrastructure Security Agency
DDos	distributed denial-of-service
DoS	denial-of-service
FIE	foreign influence effort
IP	Internet protocol
IRA	Internet Research Agency
MMR	measles, mumps, and rubella
NATO	North Atlantic Treaty Organization
NSC	National Security Council
OII	Oxford Internet Institute
OPSEC	operational security
PR	public relations
RICO	Racketeer Influenced and Corrupt Organizations (Act)
SEO	search engine optimization
TIRC	Tobacco Industry Research Council
UNESCO	(United Nations Educational, Scientific, and Cultural Organization)

1

THE DIVERSE LANDSCAPE OF DIGITAL INFLUENCE MERCENARIES

The attention economy has spawned a rapidly growing online influence industry. The work of many service providers in this industry is perfectly legal. Online marketing firms, search engine optimization consultants, and many others have found highly profitable ways to help companies, politicians, and celebrities maximize the benefits of their online presence. But this book focuses on the more malicious types of online activity—including deception, provocation, and other dirty tricks—conducted by what I call digital influence mercenaries, a term inspired by a recent Soufan Center analysis describing the global diversity of "disinformation-fueled social media campaigns waged by trolls and virtual mercenaries."[1] Basically, these are individuals (or teams and groups with resources and strategic direction) who have particular skills and knowledge that can be applied in a digital influence campaign. These mercenaries can be located anywhere with an Internet connection—Brazil, Macedonia, Zimbabwe—and the targets of their influence operations can be virtually anyone. They can do this for state governments that are willing to pay, and that often provide targeting instructions (usually in support of foreign policy objectives) while trying to mask official involvement in the influence operations launched on their behalf. Non-state actors, including corporations and political parties, can also pay for these kinds of digital influence services as well. These state and non-state "clients" may have specific metrics by which they will assess the mercenaries' performance, and may even provide bonus incentives for exceptional work. And in addition to being paid for services rendered, digital influence mercenaries also have a prime opportunity for a secondary profit source, simply by manipulating the targeted advertising algorithms used by social media platforms.[2]

For example, a completely fake story published online in July 2016—"Pope Francis Shocks World, Endorses Donald Trump for President"—blasted across American social media networks like wildfire.[3] Although it was quickly proven false, including by a stern denial from Pope Francis himself,[4] three times as many Americans read and shared it on their social media accounts as they did that week's top performing article from the *New York Times*. This "fake news" story was created by a few young Internet entrepreneurs in Macedonia who had previously built up a following of Trump supporters on social media through a variety of popular (and completely false) news stories on the dozens of websites they operated, including the claim of "proof" that President Obama was born in Kenya. Their purpose behind this effort was not political, but profit-oriented: they were able to reap thousands of dollars in revenue by driving traffic to their ad-heavy websites using disinformation.[5]

In fact, a significant amount of fake news (also called "junk news") during the 2016 U.S. election came from the Balkans and other parts of eastern Europe, including a struggling university student in Tbilisi, Georgia, who was trying to make some cash from Google ads.[6] Like many others, he found that provoking Trump supporters was more profitable than any other target audience, so he focused on negative stories about Hillary Clinton and favorable ones about Trump, making thousands of dollars as a result. His most lucrative story was pure fiction: that the Mexican government had announced they would close their border if Trump won the White House.[7] In Macedonia, a BBC reporter interviewed teenagers earning thousands of euros a day from advertising revenue generated by spreading fake news on Facebook. One, a nineteen-year-old with a very expensive designer watch, boasted about how "the Americans loved our stories and we make money from them.... Who cares if they are true or false?"[8] In late 2016, stories in *Wired*, the *Guardian*, the *New Yorker*, and *Buzzfeed* revealed that Veles, Macedonia (population 55,000), was the registered home of at least one hundred pro-Trump websites, many of them filled with sensationalist, utterly fake news—and where the "sites' ample traffic was rewarded handsomely by automated advertising engines, like Google's AdSense."[9] Between August and November of that year, one young entrepreneur had earned nearly $16,000 off his two pro-Trump websites (while the average monthly salary in Macedonia was $371).[10]

Another report about Veles by the Organized Crime and Corruption Reporting Project found that the first U.S. political fake news website, USA Politics Today, was launched there in September 2015.[11] Headlines promoted by the site included a lot of provocative right-wing conspiracy clickbait, such as "Obama's Ex-Boyfriend Reveals Shocking Truth That He Wants to Hide from America," and "HUGE Scandal—Chelsea Isn't Bill Clinton's Daughter?" In at least one instance, the site republished an article from the satirical website the *Onion*, presenting it as real news. "By the summer of 2016," the report notes, "Veles was home to a cottage industry of U.S. politics sites," including USA Politics Insider, USA Daily Politics, Guerrilla News, Read Conservatives, New Conservatives, and Conservative Army.[12] Nearby, in Kosovo, another BBC reporter interviewed a so-called "fake news merchant" who "could get his content to nearly a million pairs of eyeballs and he turned those clicks into ad revenue—both within the social media platform and on external sites. He earned about 600 euros a day."[13]

Elsewhere, in June 2019, a few days after Sudanese soldiers massacred pro-democracy demonstrators in Khartoum, an obscure digital marketing company (New Waves) in Cairo launched a covert operation to praise Sudan's military on social media. The Egyptian company, run by Amr Hussein—who retired from the Egyptian military in 2001 and describes himself on his Facebook page as a "researcher on internet wars"—paid individuals "$180 a month to write pro-military messages using fake accounts on Facebook, Twitter, Instagram, and Telegram. Instructors provided hashtags and talking points."[14] According to a Facebook report, New Waves and an Emirati company with a near-identical name "worked together to manage 361 compromised accounts and pages with a reach of 13.7 million people. They spent $167,000 on advertising and used false identities to disguise their role in the operation."[15]

And of course, there are several examples of digital influence mercenaries based here in the United States. For example, Jestin Coler originally founded his company Disinfomedia (based in California) to show how easily fake news spreads. "The whole idea from the start was to build a site that could kind of infiltrate the echo chambers of the alt-right, publish blatantly . . . fictional stories and then be able to publicly denounce those stories and point out the fact that they were fiction."[16] For example, one fake story described how customers in Colorado marijuana shops were using food stamps to buy pot, which then led a state legislator to propose "actual legislation to prevent people from using their food stamps to buy marijuana, based on something that had just never happened."[17] However, when the stories spread, Coler began making some serious money from the ads on his websites—perhaps as much as $30,000 per month. One of his company's more successful fake news stories—"FBI Agent Suspected in Hilary Email Leaks Found Dead in Apparent Murder-Suicide"—was shared on Facebook more than half a million times. Coler told NPR that he enjoys "the game" of spreading disinformation, and that he and his writers "tried to do similar things to liberals" but those efforts didn't go viral the way stories aimed at Trump supporters do.[18] For the "FBI agent" fake news story, he noted that "the people wanted to hear this. . . . Everything about it was fictional: the town, the people, the sheriff, the FBI guy. And then . . . our social media guys kind of go out and do a little dropping it throughout Trump groups and Trump forums and boy it spread like wildfire."[19]

According to a *PBS Newshour* report, one of the most prolific distributors of politically volatile fake news in recent years is Cyrus Massoumi, a northern Californian responsible for some of the most hyperbolic headlines and politically provocative "news" imaginable—which also happened to be among the most successful at generating user engagement. His two largest efforts were the Facebook page Truth Examiner, focusing on liberal-leaning topics, and another page Truth Monitor, with a much more conservative audience. Massoumi discovered that "anger is what generates likes, and conservative stories were more lucrative. Conservatives are angrier people. . . . You ever seen a Trump rally on TV?"[20] Meanwhile, a Trump supporter named Cameron Harris found a similar path to profit by posting fake news online. In one instance, he posted a story with the headline "Tens of Thousands of Fraudulent Clinton Votes Found in Ohio Warehouse" to his Christian Times website. For this story, as Lee McIntyre explains, "Harris invented a janitor, copied a picture of British ballot boxes from the Internet, and cooked up the whole thing right from his kitchen table," which was then shared with 6 million people and earned him $5,000 in ad revenue.[21]

In another example, Adam Rahuba discovered ways to make money by provoking people through a number of social media hoaxes, including an incident on July 4, 2020, when he spread rumors of a planned burning of the American flag at the Gettysburg National Military Park in Pennsylvania. The rumor was covered in news broadcasts by Fox News, Gateway Pundit, and Breitbart, which then provoked hundreds of bikers and members of right-wing militias, the Ku Klux Klan, and other white supremacist groups—many with guns—to show up to confront the nonexistent flag burners. "Controversy creates cash," he said, noting that he made $3,000 in a week from one of his websites. "One of the best ways you can generate traffic to your website, to generate attention to anything, is by pissing a lot of people off."[22]

And a final example is Christopher Blair, a middle-aged blogger who developed a Facebook page in 2018 called America's Last Line of Defense.[23] A lifelong Democrat, Blair began posting a series of fictional "news" stories that were so ludicrous they would be seen as a practical joke among his friends. His political satire was meant to make fun of the many conservative-oriented fake news websites that had become so popular since the election of Donald Trump to the White House. He made up stories about California instituting sharia, former president Bill Clinton becoming a serial killer, undocumented immigrants defacing Mount Rushmore, and former president Barack Obama dodging the Vietnam draft when he was nine. But to Blair's surprise, his page became one of the most popular on Facebook among Trump-supporting conservatives over fifty-five. Even the fourteen disclaimers on his page—including one that reads "Nothing on this page is real"—did not deter thousands of people on Facebook from clicking "like" and then "share." Their engagement helped generate considerable income for Blair—on a good month, up to $15,000.[24]

Supply and Demand: The Rise of the Digital Influence Mercenaries

These are examples of what I have begun calling digital influence mercenaries. Many more will be provided throughout this book. Others who conduct research in this area have used similar terms, like "disinformation mercenaries" and "disinformation firms" to describe profit-seeking individuals and entities engaged in this kind of activity.[25] A report by Craig Silverman describes a "worldwide industry" of "troll farms" and "black PR" firms "ready to deploy fake accounts, false narratives, and pseudo news websites for the right price."[26] A recent UNESCO report describes how today's social media platforms have become fertile ground for "computational propaganda" activities involving "sock-puppet networks" and "profiteering troll farms."[27] Whatever we want to call them, there is clearly a global market for what they offer. One research study found that by 2018, digital influence operations were in play in forty-eight countries, with significant amounts of money being spent on research and development in public opinion manipulation.[28]

As a recent NATO report noted, "The size of the social media manipulation industry is troubling. We have identified hundreds of providers. Several have many employees and significant revenue. It is clear that the problem of inauthentic activity is extensive."[29] Public relations firms, marketers, news media, politicians, social activists, and many others are all trying to master the tools and techniques of data-driven targeting and online campaigning. In 2018, the Oxford Internet Institute (OII) explored the "tens of millions of dollars being spent on computational propaganda and social media manipulation."[30] According to their report, "There is a growing industry of non-legitimate businesses that use fake social media accounts, online trolls and commentators, and political bots to distort conversations online, help generate a false sense of popularity or political consensus, mainstream extremist opinions, and influence political agendas."[31] The digital influence industry encompasses firms of various sizes as well as individual freelancers. I consider them mercenary in that the profit models they pursue have no relation to any particular belief in why they are doing it or whom they are doing it for. Unlike government operatives, vigilantes or true believers, mercenaries typically do not believe in the information they are posting; it only serves a purpose (i.e., to deceive and disinform, sow confusion, provoke emotional responses, etc.) for which they aim to be compensated either through fee-paying clients or via advertising. Throughout human history, different kinds of conflicts have attracted mercenaries, individuals looking to generate personal wealth by using their talents in the service of at least one of the combatants, so in a sense this is just a new form of mercenary activity, adapting to the digital age.

The rise of the digital influence mercenary can be explained by the simple economic forces of supply and demand. There is a market for specific kinds of social media manipulation skills, so individuals with those skills can find profitable work. According to Alex Stamos, formerly the chief security officer at Facebook and currently director of the Stanford Internet Observatory, "The truth is, the vast majority of political disinformation is coming from semi-professionals who are making money pushing disinformation. . . . It's their career. There are hundreds of times more people doing that than there are working in professional disinformation campaigns for governments."[32] Further, individual freelancers in this industry appear to be assisting each other in ad hoc ways. Research by Carl Miller discovered individuals selling "Facebook pages with hundreds of thousands of likes . . . others sold fake likes, or fake accounts, or offered advice on how to get around Facebook's enforcement. . . . We even found a 'fake news starter pack' for a beginner, complete with a collection of Facebook pages to gather an audience, along with websites to monetize your activity. This was a service sector economy for misinformation."[33]

According to NATO, "The scale of the 'black market' infrastructure for developing and maintaining social manipulation software, generating fictitious accounts, and providing mobile proxies is vast."[34] And perhaps more troubling yet, "rather than a shadowy underworld, it is an easily accessible marketplace that most web users can reach with little effort through any search engine."[35] Different kinds of information serve as the core elements of the profit models pursued by these mercenary firms and freelancers. Social media users produce tons of information about themselves and each other. Algorithms use this information to identify targets best suited for achieving the strategic goals of an influence effort, and to determine what kinds of content would be most effective in trying to influence those targets. As Philip Howard explains, "The successful business model of these firms is to connect users algorithmically to content that is relevant to them individually, and target them with personalized advertising using systems in which political actors can 'pay to play.' The information users produce about themselves online helps craft the computational propaganda they are subsequently sent and the algorithmic allocation of peer influence."[36]

As mentioned earlier, there are two primary models for generating revenue within this industry, both of which can be pursued simultaneously. One is a straightforward "fee for service" contract, where the firm's social media accounts and automated botnets are used to achieve a paying client's strategic influence objectives. This is the model represented by New Waves (the firm in Cairo), and by the Internet Research Agency in Russia (notorious for its efforts to influence the 2016 presidential election, which we'll discuss later). Meanwhile Coler, Harris, Blair, and the other entrepreneurs described above exemplify the model of generating revenue through advertisements, where the more social media traffic you can drive to your website, Facebook page or YouTube channel, the more views your ads will receive, and the more money the advertising sponsors will pay. Again, both of these profit models can be (and often are) pursued in tandem by a diverse array of firms and freelancers.

A CLIENT-SERVICES PROFIT MODEL

Mercenaries can sell their abilities to virtually anyone willing to pay. Researchers from the NATO Strategic Communications Centre of Excellence found that anyone can purchase computerized "user engagement" (e.g., to get more likes, comments, and clicks) from various online companies that have thousands of automated fake accounts at their disposal.[37] A majority of companies in the so-called "for-hire manipulation industry" are in Russia, and they "advertise openly on major platforms." They found several "manipulation service providers" offering fake social media engagement at prices like $330 for roughly 3,500 comments, 25,000 likes, 20,000 views, and 5,000 followers.[38] According to Philip Howard, the industry has grown "with firms competing to offer increasingly aggressive services."[39] Companies like Cambridge Analytica and the Psy-Group have offered services such as data mining, negative campaign strategies, political entrapment, bribery, and using social media to expose or amplify division among rival campaigns and factions.[40]

By far the best-known Russian firm in recent years has been the Internet Research Agency (IRA), based in St. Petersburg, which was featured prominently in Senate Intelligence Committee reports, the U.S. Special Counsel Investigation (the Mueller Report), and many other official documents.[41] Corporate ownership of the IRA, which was established in 2013, has been traced back to the Concord holding company owned by Russian billionaire Yevgeny Prigozhin, a friend of President Vladimir Putin who made his fortune through lucrative government contracts.[42] As Thomas Rid notes, Russia has increasingly sought to subcontract a range of disinformation and influence operations "to dedicated third-party services providers,"[43] and the IRA has largely been at the forefront of those efforts.[44]

In late 2013, a Russian journalist began publishing an exposé about what she called a "troll factory," and this was followed by news articles published by several other undercover reporters.[45] In February 2015, a major story included photos, videos, and copies of "technical tasks" given to the trolls.[46] While these and other accounts shed light on IRA operations,[47] it took a couple more years before the U.S. government truly recognized the extent of their influence attempts against American targets. A report published in January 2017 by the Office of the U.S. Director of National Intelligence describes how "third-party intermediaries and paid social media users" tried to influence the 2016 presidential election, and states "the likely financier of the so-called Internet Research Agency of professional trolls located in Saint Petersburg is a close Putin ally with ties to Russian intelligence."[48]

On February 16, 2018, Deputy Attorney General Rod Rosenstein announced that the United States was indicting thirteen Russian nationals (including Prigozhin) and three Russian companies (including the IRA) "for committing federal crimes while seeking to interfere in the United States political system, including the 2016 presidential election."[49] The U.S. Special Counsel Investigation uncovered a network of Russian trolls who had created thousands of fake accounts, groups, and messages, posing as genuine Americans representing a wide array of political backgrounds, from nationalist gun-loving Trump supporters to black civil rights campaigners who promoted the idea that his rivals weren't worth voting for.[50] According to one research report, "Over 30 million American users, between 2015 and 2017, shared the IRA's Facebook and Instagram posts with their friends and family, liking, reacting to, and commenting on them along the way."[51]

Despite the various attempts to confront and curtail the IRA's digital influence efforts, the company (now under a new name) has continued to pursue a broad range of operations. In October 2019, Facebook announced it had uncovered and suspended several networks of Russian accounts that were attempting to interfere in the domestic politics of eight African countries, including Mozambique, Cameroon, Sudan, and Libya. These accounts were connected to Yevgeny Prigozhin.[52] Unlike past influence campaigns from Russia, the networks targeted several countries through Arabic-language posts. According to the Stanford Internet Observatory, which collaborated with Facebook to unravel these networks and their influence operations, the volume of activity seen in this instance was at times larger than what was seen during the 2016 U.S. presidential elections. "While the Kremlin-backed Internet Research Agency posted on Facebook 2,442 times a month on average in 2016, one of the networks in Africa posted 8,900 times in October alone."[53] And a December 2020 report found that the same tactics—franchising page ownership to locals, creating front media organizations—were replicated in more attempts to target individuals in Libya, Sudan, Syria, and the Central African Republic.[54] On December 15, 2020, Facebook announced the takedown of 126 pages, 16 groups, 211 profiles, and 17 Instagram accounts linked to those efforts.[55]

In addition to the IRA, Russia also employs several online media companies that serve as proxies for influencing various targets. One of the most prominent of these is called RT (formerly "Russia Today"), which publishes its digital content in six languages: English, Arabic, French, Spanish, German, and of course Russian. As of 2018, it had more YouTube subscribers than BBC or Fox News.[56] A 2016 report by the Office of the U.S. Director of National Intelligence refers to RT as an "international propaganda outlet" clearly funded by Russian authorities, while also describing how its U.S.-based affiliate RT America TV "has positioned itself as a domestic U.S. channel and has deliberately sought to obscure any legal ties to the Russian Government."[57] Specifically, "RT America formally disassociates itself from the Russian Government by using a Moscow-based autonomous nonprofit organization to finance its U.S. operations. According to RT's leadership, this structure was set up to avoid the Foreign Agents Registration Act and to facilitate licensing abroad."[58]

Another "independent and alternative" quasi-media outlet based in the United States, called *Southfront*, was proven to have direct links to Russia.[59] The main objective of these and other Russia-based media outlets is to spread anti-Western (and pro-Russian) narratives while trying to appear as objective, independent news organizations. Russian authorities have also sponsored operations in other countries, including a news organization operating in the Baltics—with websites posing as domestic Lithuanian, Latvian, and Estonian sources—that consistently received instructions from Moscow about what and when to publish.[60] And in March 2020, investigators discovered a Prigozhin-linked group funding a Libyan broadcast media outlet.[61] Essentially, Russia pays well to have a variety of digital influence mercenaries—including the IRA and online media outlets—penetrate the information ecosystems of their adversaries, often looking to sow chaos and confusion. As Clint Watts noted in his 2017 testimony before Congress, "Russians are investing heavily in online troll farms, cyber hacking units and other means by which they can continue these efforts using the most modern tools available to them."[62]

Of course, there are also domestic providers of "social media engagement" services here in the United States. For example, in October 2020, Facebook permanently banned Rally Forge, a marketing firm accused of running a domestic "troll farm" through which Facebook and Instagram users—many of them teenagers in the Phoenix, Arizona, area—were hired to post comments largely sympathetic to Trump and other conservative causes across social media. The participants in this campaign were paid to establish fake personas that they used (in addition to their personal accounts) to post information provided to them on a shared document, and they would score bonuses if their activity spurred higher engagement. In addition to glorifying Trump and demonizing Democratic candidate Joe Biden, they spread false information about COVID-19, and cast doubt on the integrity of mail-in ballots.[63] The pages and accounts removed by Facebook had developed a following of nearly 400,000 people. Twitter also acted against the Rally Forge operation, suspending 262 accounts involved in "platform manipulation and spam." However, the social media platforms decided not to punish the funding sources that paid Rally Forge for these operations, including the conservative pro-Trump youth organization Turning Point Action, led by Charlie Kirk.[64]

Essentially, there is a robust private sector in which digital influence mercenaries will do the dirty work of online public perception manipulation on behalf of the highest bidder, which could be political parties, corporations, dictators, individual politicians and CEOs, or even government agencies. In a fascinating report published in mid-2019, Princeton University researchers Diego Martin and Jacob Shapiro presented a database of 53 "foreign influence efforts" (FIEs). Among their findings was that during the previous six years, FIEs had targeted twenty-four different countries, but that the United States had been the target more than a third (38 percent) of the time.[65] Most often, the entities engaged in state-based digital influence warfare were not government agencies, but were doing so on behalf of a country's government. They would typically have some sort of contractual relationship with a government agency or its leader(s), and while seen as largely autonomous they were likely to receive some kinds of strategic direction from their sponsors.

Martin and Shapiro's research found that within the six-year time span of their study, private companies were responsible for 47 percent of the documented FIE incidents in their database, followed by media organizations (39 percent) and intelligence agencies (22 percent).[66] While several attempts to polarize public opinion were documented among these incidents, the more common approaches had focused on amplifying, creating, or distorting information. Moreover, "99% of the cases use creation of original content, 78% amplification of preexisting content, and 73% distortion of objectively verifiable facts."[67] Half of the attacks they studied had included the use of automation to spread their message, and similarly, just over half of the FIEs had used fake accounts. Most often, combinations of different strategies were used together, while a collection of different social media platforms, video services, and news outlets were the means by which the messages were disseminated. Hashtag hijacking and other digital tools and influence methods (which we'll explore in the next chapter) were also prominently represented among the strategies and tactics identified in their research.

As detailed in a 2018 NATO report, "There is a large, vibrant online market for buyers and sellers of tools and services for social media manipulation."[68] Many of the service providers offer social metrics manipulation (likes, comments, shares, views, followers, etc.) for all major platforms, as well as "trending content" services on platforms such as YouTube. "Some suppliers also offer manipulation of specified targets such as web panels, surveys, or recommendation sites in order to manipulate the outcome of a political survey or smearing a business competitor, etc."[69] In March 2018, Andrew Gully—the research manager of Jigsaw (a subsidiary of Alphabet, which also owns Google)—led his team in an experiment to test how easily and cheaply social media disinformation campaigns (or "influence operations") could be bought in the shadier corners of the Russian-speaking web. After negotiating with several underground disinformation vendors, the team at Jigsaw agreed to pay $250 for one to attack a politically oriented website that the team had created as a target. The experiment demonstrated how private individuals could easily arrange their own forms of online disinformation campaigns. In his description of their research, Gully explained how "we wanted to see if we could engage with someone who was willing to provide this kind of assistance to a political actor . . . to buy services that directly discredit their political opponent for very low cost and with no tooling or resources required. For us, it's a pretty clear demonstration these capabilities exist, and there are actors comfortable doing this on the Internet."[70]

Similarly, the Insikt Group (a unit of the threat intelligence firm Recorded Future) published a report in October 2019 illustrating how disinformation services are publicly available on underground forums (some blatantly criminal) and are highly customizable to meet the client's needs, with costs ranging from a modest investment to hundreds of thousands of dollars. The providers of these services have "the ability to publish articles in media sources ranging from dubious websites to more reputable news outlets," coupled with "the ability to create and maintain social media accounts in bulk, while using a combination of both established and new accounts to propagate content without triggering content moderation controls."[71] Similar to the Jigsaw example described earlier, the research team created their own target—this time, a fake company. Then "they paid one Russian group $1,850 to build up its reputation and another $4,200 to tear it down."[72] Their report also describes the costs of other services offered by a firm in Russia, including "$15 for an article up to 1,000 characters; $8 for social media posts and commentary up to 1,000 characters; $10 for Russian to English translation up to 1,800 characters; and $1,500 for search engine optimization (SEO) services to further promote social media posts and traditional media articles, with a time frame of 10 to 15 days."[73]

Disinformation service companies studied in this report claimed to employ "a network of editors, translators, search engine optimization specialists, hackers, and journalists, some of them on retainer, as well as investigators on staff who could dig up dirt and had experience working on targets in the West. One firm even offered to lodge complaints about the company for being involved in human trafficking. It also offered reputation cratering services that could set someone up at work, counter a disinformation attack, or 'sink an opponent in an election.'"[74] The researchers concluded their report on a sobering note: "We predict that disinformation as a service will spread from a nation-state tool to one increasingly used by private individuals and entities, given how easy it is to implement."[75]

According to Clint Watts, a senior fellow at the Foreign Policy Research Institute and *NBC News* security analyst, "This trolling-as-a-service is the expected next step of social media influence after the success of the Internet Research Agency. . . . There's high demand for nefarious influence and manipulation, and [for] trained disinformation operators who will seek higher profits."[76] This demand is being met by thousands of what Michael Erbschloe calls "social media warfare mercenaries," who may assume a variety of roles on behalf of their clients including "surrogates, supporters, friends, fans, imposters, antagonists, protagonists, advocates or adversaries. Basically, social media warfare mercenaries can take on any role they need to in order to participate in social media events, conversations, and interactions."[77] When playing this role, they will use all the usual attributes expected of an online profile, including a photo and descriptions of their professional background and personal interests. Further, he explains, "the difference between an effective social media warfare mercenary and a less effective one is how skillfully they play their role in social media—that is, how effectively they can pass themselves off as regular social media users," thus making it exceedingly difficult to determine whether the individual you encounter online is real or contrived.[78]

Today's social media platforms have become a multibillion-dollar competitive arena in which companies and individuals get paid for trying to influence us. And of course, significant amounts of money can be made in this industry. The Arizona-based marketing firm Rally Forge, mentioned earlier in this chapter, received $221,349 from Turning Point Action in 2020, according to the Federal Election Commission.[79] In 2016, the firm received nearly $120,000 from a political action committee supporting Republican candidate Kelli Ward, and an additional $50,000 in 2018 when she ran again. And the firm received more than $300,000 in 2016 from another political action committee, RallyPAC, in order to conduct a pro-Trump meme campaign on a Facebook page called I Love My Country.[80]

According to Philip Howard, those engaging in online disinformation today are not amateurs: "There is a new professionalism to the activity, with formal organizations that use hiring policies, pay scales, performance evaluations, bonus incentives, organizational hierarchies, office politics, and paperwork."[81] And like many other service-based organizations, there will be a range of positions within the firm, including social media manager, recruiter, marketer, information technology support staff, human resources and payroll manager, security guard, and so forth. If a country's digital influence industry is well developed, these jobs are openly advertised.[82] For example, "online job ads for the IRA in Russia detailed the pay and range of activities for potential new employees: preparation of thematic posts, developing mechanisms to attract new audiences, and monitoring target groups."[83]

Digital mercenary firms and individuals see themselves as merely offering a service for hire, much like military contractors, temp workers, consultants, and others employed through short-term arrangements. Some firms rely on a staff of hundreds who maintain hundreds of thousands of social media profiles. Sometimes, the operation consists of loose affiliations of small, specialized businesses and freelance workers who live near one another.[84] Some firms and individuals will be subcontractors to other firms, perhaps providing "social media optimization" to a firm specializing in "political strategy consulting."[85] Philip Howard describes how "there is an interesting diversity in how these firms operate. . . . Sometimes they look like newsrooms. Sometimes they evolve out of military units that have been retasked with manipulating public opinion. In their day-to-day operations, their organizational behavior usually mimics that of a tech start-up or telemarketing firm."[86]

And similar to what you would find in Silicon Valley, the most talented individuals in this digital influence industry can transport their skills from one firm to another, and are in high demand. However, the main tasks of a digital influence mercenary can be fairly tedious and monotonous, yet stressful. In 2019, an investigative journalist in Poland went undercover at a "troll farm" for six months, and then reported what life was like as an employee at one such company. She described how she was first instructed to establish a user account (using a fake identity) for sharing "social and political content," and then, after attracting a minimum of five hundred followers, she would receive guidance and instructions on "what issues to engage with, who to promote, and who to denigrate. The accounts produced both left-wing and right-wing content, attracting attention, credibility, and support from other social media users, who could then be rallied in support of the company's clients."[87] In a similar account, P. W. Singer and Emerson Brooking have described how a Russian employee of the IRA would begin the workday by assuming a series of fake identities (known as "sockpuppets," described more fully in chapter 2), and begin writing a steady stream of social media posts. Through hundreds of these messages each day, the goal was to hijack online conversations and spread lies, all to the benefit of the Russian government. Evidence of social media engagement (including likes, shares, and retweets) and attracting large numbers of followers would be rewarded. Those who proved to be adept at communicating to foreign audiences could get paid substantially more than those communicating to domestic audiences.[88]

Another type of work involves creating and managing "legends," described by Philip Howard as "the biographical background, supported by a stream of photos, comments, and online activity, that makes an account appear to represent a genuinely social, real person."[89] One company in Poland has created more than 40,000 legends, each of which has multiple accounts on various social platforms and portals. The creator of a legend will use unique Internet addresses consistently so that the fabricated user appears to be from the same part of the world. By posting stories, liking and sharing content from real users, and joining online groups, the legend gives the appearance of an account belonging to a real, active person. This network of fake legends across multiple platforms gives the company an ability to interact with citizens of countries around the world.[90]

The firm rents out these legends to their clients, in order to meet the strategic objectives of a so-called "guerilla marketing" campaign. Many firms will use terms that hide the reality of the disinformation work they are doing. For example, according to one expert, they "use the terms 'supplemental pages' and 'digital support workers' to describe what is otherwise known as 'fake news sites' or 'paid trolls' when they pitch their services to prospective clients. This lends an aura of respectability to the transaction and—crucially—gives politicians a level of plausible deniability."[91] Legends used for an influence campaign will usually be made to appear from the same locale as the citizens they are trying to influence. The controllers of the legends post original comments, rather than copying and pasting the same material to multiple accounts (which could enable social media platforms to identify shared content as a sign of coordinated inauthentic behavior).[92]

Of course, the use of legends is much more labor-intensive than controlling tens of thousands of automatic accounts, and access to these human-curated fake users is a premium service, costing much more than it would to simply rent botnets.[93] As a Chinese digital influence mercenary recently noted, automation and artificial intelligence "can quickly generate traffic and publicity much faster than people."[94] Clients of this mercenary include companies, brands, political parties, and candidates in Asia who—as Craig Silverman explains—are "purchasing an end-to-end online manipulation system, which can influence people on a massive scale—resulting in votes cast, products sold, and perceptions changed."[95] And there is now a worldwide market for this type of influence manipulation. In the Philippines, as Jonathan Corpus Ong observes, "disinformation production within the PR [public relations] industry has become so financially lucrative that they have moved from shady black market transactions to the professional respectability of the corporate boardroom."[96] In Ukraine, the PR firm Pragmatico employed dozens of young, digitally savvy people to pump out positive comments on fake Facebook accounts about clients. An Israeli firm called the Archimedes Group created networks of hundreds of Facebook pages, accounts, and groups around the world, boasting on its website that it would "use every tool and take every advantage available in order to change reality according to our client's wishes."[97]

To sum up, there are professional firms and freelancers around the world who will work for virtually anyone willing to pay them to spread disinformation, influence targets, and attack opponents. Some use human-curated fake accounts that look real to the casual observer, while many others use (less expensive) forms of automation. As the social media platform of choice for billions of people, Facebook has become the most popular venue for these kinds of mercenary activities, and has increased its efforts to identify and shut down what it calls "coordinated inauthentic behavior." But as we'll describe in later chapters of this book, Facebook is often playing a cat-and-mouse game with firms like these, who continually find new and creative ways to deceive and influence large numbers of users. And meanwhile, there is also another prominent model of profit generation that can be (and often is) pursued simultaneously by these digital influence mercenaries, one in which the social media platforms themselves play a vital facilitating role.

AN ONLINE ADVERTISING PROFIT MODEL

While mercenaries can be paid by clients to try and influence specific targets, they can also use data about those targets to make money via advertising. In fact, advertising revenue is a major source of income for purveyors of fake news and disinformation. The most common approaches involve ads placed on either websites or on social media platforms. In terms of the former, according to a 2020 report by the OII, "The overwhelming majority of junk news ad disinformation domains rely on major advertising platforms to monetize their pages, and 61 percent of junk news and disinformation sources used Google ads."[98] So, the goal in this approach is to drive as much visitor traffic to your ad-heavy website [as possible], because the more people who view the ads, the more money the advertising sponsors will pay you.[99] On the other hand, ads on social media platforms are targeted to users of the platform according to a range of profile information—including location, demographic background, stated interests, patterns of browsing, likes and shares, followers, and so forth. Virtually anyone can sponsor these kinds of ads, which are usually displayed in the sidebar of the social media platform (like a Facebook page) as the user scrolls through their information feed.

Both kinds of digital influence efforts are, as a recent UNESCO report notes, "designed to reap internet advertising profits via gullible consumers who click and share."[100] And in both approaches, revenues are earned by the digital influence mercenary as well as the Internet advertiser (e.g., Google ads) or the social media platform (e.g., Facebook), who are paid by the original ad sponsor (e.g., a corporation like Dell, Nike, or Sony; a political campaign; an online university; and many others). This can be quite a lucrative endeavor. As a 2019 NATO report explains, "Social media manipulation and disinformation generate significant ad revenue . . . inauthentic influencer marketing is a $1.3 billion per year problem."[101]

Let's use a hypothetical example of a digital influence mercenary named "Jill" to further illustrate the fake news website approach (chapter 2 will discuss this in much greater detail). First, Jill will need to identify her target audience, gather as much information as she can about them, and devise a strategy for infiltrating whatever sources of influence they seem to pay attention to most (e.g., their Twitter, Instagram, or Facebook information feed). If she detects signs of a fairly robust digital echo chamber (a walled-off virtual community of like-minded users),[102] that will be a particularly favorable environment in which to pursue her strategy, because these tend to reinforce and replicate an accepted narrative, no matter how false. Her fake news distribution strategy then proceeds with the purchase of inexpensive web hosting space, and registering a domain name that sounds vaguely authentic, like "DailyNews45.com." Next, she will develop a realistic-looking news website, using real websites as a model to follow (mercenaries often "scrape" the code from real websites for this purpose). There are lots of tools available today that allow even a beginner to build a website, but if necessary she can always subcontract this out to someone more technically and artistically inclined. As an alternative, she can also launch her own Facebook page or YouTube channel, which essentially serves the same function of providing information to visitors, but the advertisements are arranged by the social media platform. Her site will want to provide emotionally provocative, even outrageous information, in order to attract the amount of attention and traffic needed to generate ad revenues. Once the website is established, Jill will arrange for her advertisement revenue stream. There are a wide variety of companies that will facilitate "pay for clicks" advertising arrangements, and once in place, she is ready to start driving traffic to her site.

At this point, Jill will create a flurry of social media accounts, which can be used to manufacture the illusion of "social proof" (a type of perceived endorsement discussed in chapters 5 through 7) by liking, sharing, and retweeting messages containing links to her fake news website.[103] But when creating these accounts, she will be sure to craft their profiles to conform with the accepted values of her target audience. These accounts should also be used to like, share, and retweet messages posted by authentic users within the network, demonstrating the kind of "alikeness" that will lead the target audience to accept her profile as "one of them." These accounts can be programmed to do these things automatically, or she can choose the more labor-intensive route of controlling the accounts manually. The most successful digital influence campaigns devote considerable attention to cultivating engagement, establishing connections with real users on the social media platform in order to have those connections at the ready when they are needed to amplify the influencer's message. Further, an effective way to drive traffic to a fake news website is by provoking engagement—for instance, by providing a link to a "news story" that offers fuel to a rumor or conspiracy circulating among other users, or provides some kind of reinforcement about deeply held biases or animosity toward whomever the target audience considers to be the "other" (see chapters 6 and 7). The advertisements on the fake news site will generate revenues based on the number of people who view them, so the more traffic Jill can drive to her ad-heavy website, the better.

So, how will she inspire or provoke people to visit her website? We'll review a number of tactics and tools in the next chapter, but in general she will use the social media accounts at her disposal (whether automated or human-curated) to target users with various messages that are most likely to generate the desired response. For example, a pro-Trump target is likely to click on a link to a pro-Trump fake news headline because they want to read a story that they expect will reaffirm their support for Trump. The same holds true for a fake news headline that is clearly negative about someone known as anti-Trump, where the enticement is reading something that will reaffirm the user's hatred of anyone perceived as a Trump adversary. Similarly, if the target is anti-Trump, she will want to use messages that contain an anti-Trump fake news headline that target is likely to click on, in order to read a story that reaffirms their anger about Trump. And headlines that seem favorable toward others who are anti-Trump may also entice the user to click.

So, if the target has indicated a strong opinion about the Black Lives Matter movement, or NASCAR, or anti-immigration policies, or a ban on public displays of affection—virtually any number of topics—Jill's fake news headline can be tailored accordingly to increase the likelihood the target will click through to her website. In addition, to ensure her messages are contextually relevant to her target audience, she may also use humor (a proven means of garnering attention) or outrage as part of her provocation strategy. Naturally, the messages don't need to be true to be believed. In fact, research by Craig Silverman on the top election news-related stories during the 2016 U.S. presidential election found that fake news stories received more engagement on Facebook than the top stories from all the major traditional news outlets combined.[104]

The more emotionally provocative her messages are, the more likely Jill will trigger a response among her target audience. Uncertainty, fear, the desire for affirmation or confirmation of one's beliefs, even the natural human desire for stimulation all contribute to the effectiveness of provocation strategies. In a sense, the demand for disinformation (people want to deceive, and people want to be deceived) is being met by the supply of disinformation by social media manipulators. The implications of this in terms of what people believe—and how they act on those beliefs—are striking. If greater revenues on social media come from higher levels of engagement, and if engagement is more likely via fake news than from true information, it creates a profit incentive for more disinformation in the future. And while provoking emotional responses about what people believe (or want to believe) has been a long-standing strategy for profit, social media platforms make it much easier to capture people's attention and engage them, provoke a response, and influence their behavior—particularly because so many millions of people worldwide view these platforms as their primary (or sole) source of information today.

Further, there is a particular benefit from engaging in this kind of effort through social media accounts that inhabit a digital echo chamber. For example, as described at the beginning of this chapter, digital influence mercenaries like Jestin Coler, Christopher Blair, and Cameron Harris found success spreading disinformation (particularly of the provocative kind) among Trump supporters.[105] They discovered that the favorable stories about Trump were getting many more clicks than the favorable ones about Hillary Clinton—and that the *negative* stories about Clinton were getting the most clicks of all. So, if Jill's assessment leads her to conclude that greater revenues will come from generating more fake news of a particular political orientation, her profit motive tells her how to proceed.[106]

This is why in 2016, according the OII, "The largest botnet . . . of the Trump supporter network was more than three times the size of the largest network of highly automated accounts promoting Clinton."[107] According to Philip Howard, "Trump-supporting bot-networks were more active and expansive than the Clinton-supporting ones. There were more of them, they generated more content, and they were more interconnected."[108] Further, "Facebook's algorithms distributed false news favoring Trump thirty million times and distributed false news stories favoring Clinton eight million times."[109] Overall, the research concludes that in 2016, "the audience for misinformation was primarily Republican voters who supported Trump."[110]

In fact, political orientation is an important attribute to keep in mind when choosing targets for an influence effort. There are central reasons why Trump supporters have proven far more vulnerable to digital influence and manipulation. Essentially, liberal audiences tend to rely on multiple sources of information, and have somewhat egalitarian views about diversity and equality. These things make it more difficult for digital influence mercenaries to target them effectively, particularly with the typical "othering" narratives commonly used for provocation tactics. In contrast, researchers have consistently found that conservatives prefer a much smaller menu of information sources and tend to wholly reject information from sources not on that menu. Further, there is a much stronger and deeper strain of "othering" found among political conservatives, where animosity (even overt hostility) is aimed at non-heterosexuals, immigrants, and a broad range of others who don't conform to the idealized image of what political conservatives want to see in their world. As a result, digital influence campaigns targeting political conservatives have distinct advantages, much the same way as radio talk show host Rush Limbaugh discovered that by provoking listeners with his opinionated vitriol, he gained more attention, more listeners, and greater advertising revenue.[111]

The unique advantages of a talk radio show include being able to repeat a narrative in multiple ways (regardless of whether it's true) and to provoke emotional responses among listeners without giving them any real opportunity to address those emotions. The talk radio host can simply refuse to air anyone's opinion or evidence that contradicts what the listeners believe or want to hear. If a caller tries to question the merits or veracity of a statement or narrative, the host can just hang up on them, even follow up with a barrage of derogatory insults that serve the dual purpose of delighting the true-believer listeners (and reinforce their solidarity of "belonging" in the influence silo) and clearly demarcating the boundaries of what is to be considered unacceptable information or behavior. Through this type of forum, Limbaugh was able to spread an incredible amount of provocative rumors, distortions, innuendos, unsupported claims presented as the truth, and even outright fake news disinformation. Those who disliked what they heard would simply turn away from the radio channel and choose some other source of information, leaving a much more homogenous audience of listeners, among which the percentage of those agreeing with the host naturally increased over time. In the end, Limbaugh established a radio-based influence silo in which Americans who shared his opinions and his anti-liberal sentiments became very loyal listeners, allowing him to build up a sizable following.[112]

The incentives to be as provocative as possible are also now a central feature built into the digital information (or disinformation) ecosystem. The segment of the population who harbor political views that are not encouraged by the mainstream press or moderate media outlets want confirmation of their beliefs and endorsement of their "othering" animosity toward people who do not share these beliefs. As we will examine more fully in chapter 5, people are inclined to favorably view information that conforms to what they already believe, creating a kind of tacit trust and perceived legitimacy that fuels the spread of disinformation. And if the target audience for a digital influence campaign is already primed to believe the worst possible things about others outside their echo chamber, this makes for a prime profit-generating opportunity for the mercenary.

Provoking engagement in the attention economy generates revenue, because money flows to those who can provide the most "eyeballs" for advertisers. Professional influence mercenaries who pursue this type of profit-seeking strategy range from the individuals described at the beginning of this chapter to huge enterprises like TheSoul Publishing, a company run by Russians based in Cyprus that is linked to thirty-five YouTube channels and twenty-five Facebook pages. According to a report by Lisa Kaplan, its largest channels have millions of subscribers and billions of views, and it funds itself with ad revenues from YouTube and Google worth tens of millions of dollars.[113] In addition to its popular nonpolitical content (like instructions for do-it-yourself projects), TheSoul Publishing also posts videos about history, often with a noticeably political (and overtly pro-Russian) orientation. One video published on its YouTube channels claims that Ukraine is part of Russia, while another speculates about several countries (including the United States) "That May Not Survive the Next 20 Years."[114]

THE SPECIAL CASE OF YOUTUBE

Before we continue, it should be noted that not all social media platforms function in the same way. Facebook, Instagram, and Twitter generate revenues through targeted advertisements shown to their users based on sophisticated algorithms. Individual users of these social media platforms can generate profits by having other users click on links, contained in messages, that take them to someplace else (e.g., a website, blog or YouTube video). YouTube is a different kind of platform, dominated by content producers and content consumers. Similar to the other platforms, YouTube makes money by selling advertising space to companies who want those ads put in front of viewers (the content consumers). And just like Facebook, Twitter, and Instagram, the content that draws users to the platform is provided by other users—in this case, they create videos that are then uploaded and hosted on the YouTube site. But here's a key difference: through its revenue-sharing model, YouTube provides money to these content creators once they have begun attracting enough viewers to begin showing advertisements in their videos. In this way, YouTube "stars" can generate substantial incomes, in some cases enough so that creating YouTube content becomes their full-time occupation.

However, this also results in a significant incentive for creating emotionally provocative, stimulating content that may or may not have any connection to reality. For some, this means creating the most outrageous or unique material, even if (or perhaps especially if) it is racist or homophobic. For others it means promoting conspiracy theories that play on people's fears and uncertainty. The notorious Alex Jones and his InfoWars channel (which YouTube eventually banned in 2018) is a prime example of this. But as described earlier in this chapter, people are often drawn toward information that confirms their biases, prejudices, and beliefs. In a way, YouTube videos can be used to reinforce the narratives within an echo chamber and deepen an audience's animosity toward "others." And YouTube is willing to pay you to do this, from the comfort of your own home (or home studio).

On this platform, a different sort of strategy emerges for our hypothetical digital influence mercenary. First, she will need to identify her target audience and make a list of issues they care deeply about. Next, she will create a YouTube channel with a name and description that is likely to resonate with her target audience. Then she will need to produce whatever shocking, emotionally provoking videos she has in mind that will have high salience for that audience, and upload them to her YouTube channel. Next, she will use her social media account(s) to drive traffic toward those videos. Once her visitor traffic has reached YouTube's threshold for viewer advertising, they will begin inserting ads and Jill can begin to profit from their revenue-sharing arrangement.

Further, YouTube has its own incentive to allow the kinds of videos on its platform that are likely to draw crowds of viewers (the more viewers, the more they can charge companies to display their ads). So, in essence there is a dual incentive to create and host videos that may become popular regardless of whether they are abhorrent or even offensive to certain audiences. One slight note of caution, however: companies that are paying YouTube for ad placement may or may not want to be associated with certain videos. For example, when videos posted by a skinhead group attract a significant viewership, the ads begin appearing, and then YouTube splits the advertising revenue with the content creator, meaning advertisers risk directly funding creators of hateful, misogynistic or terrorism-related content. Such was the case in March 2017, when AT&T, Johnson & Johnson, and other deep-pocketed marketers announced that they would pull their ads from YouTube because they were displeased about their brands appearing next to offensive material, including hate speech.[115]

Videos containing false information can also be posted to the site. This was the centerpiece of much public debate when in late 2019 a Trump campaign ad attacking Democratic candidate Joe Biden was posted online. While the *New York Times*, the *Washington Post*, and many other news outlets assessed the video and concluded that it was making completely false allegations, and CNN refused to air it, the video was hosted on a YouTube channel.[116] Google, which owns YouTube, has policies in place that would not allow a user to post politically oriented videos that can be proven fraudulent. For example, stating that people can vote via text message, or providing the wrong time or location for casting your vote on election day, or making easily debunked claims about a particular candidate—these would all be disallowed on the platform. But when a video provides tidbits of true information melded together with falsehoods or carefully edited inferences and allegations that are more difficult to prove false, such a video apparently can be allowed.

For the digital influence mercenary, the implications are fairly clear: making money on YouTube could in some ways be easier than going through all the steps of the fake news distribution strategy discussed earlier in this chapter. Myriad video-editing software options are available throughout the Internet, some of them free (or even prepackaged on your laptop and smartphone). Sometimes all that's required is the ability to alter the speed of a video clip to make it look like a political leader is slurring her words.[117] And sophisticated deepfake video creation tools, using artificial intelligence (AI) to seamlessly integrate misleading alterations, are making it increasingly difficult to determine whether a video is authentic or not.

Summary

Essentially, as the OII explains, "Advertising plays an important role in monetizing and economically incentivizing the junk news and disinformation ecosystem."[118]

The online advertising profit model allows the digital influence mercenary to leverage the business model of social media platforms, where profit and share value are determined by ad revenue and the number of user accounts. The tactics, tools, and technologies available for spreading disinformation (which we'll discuss in the next several chapters) are diverse and often disappointingly effective. A prominent type of the digital influence mercenary involves a collective (a group, team, firm, etc.), and they may have an advantage over individual mercenaries in terms of attracting high-paying clients who are concerned about risk avoidance and return on investment. Yet both firms and individual freelancers (really, anyone with the right technical skills) can also generate profits through this advertising model. Additionally, instead of working within the confines of a firm, freelancers have much more autonomy and can pursue self-interests in a way similar to academic researchers. And the community of digital influence freelancers also appears to be helping each other to some degree. Overall, the global Internet infrastructure has facilitated the rise of digital influence mercenaries—tech-savvy individuals in Macedonia, Russia, Brazil, and anywhere else who are finding ways to make money with relatively little investment.

Other Forms of Digital Influence Mercenary-Type Activity

While the predominant forms of activity described in this book involve either client-based fees for services, or generating revenue from ads, ordinary individuals can also profit simply by serving as a proxy within a particular digital echo chamber. This is a unique form of mercenary activity—paying someone to influence others on your behalf. As Davey Alba explains, "In addition to using fake accounts, perception manipulation can also involve accounts belonging to real people, where individuals are paid a small amount of money for liking or sharing posts."[119] According to research by Ryan Holiday, certain individuals with large numbers of followers on their social media can be incentivized to post prewritten messages and endorse products.[120] A recent UNESCO report about the "industry of public relations companies under contract to political or commercial actors" describes how "countless bloggers, Instagram 'influencers' and YouTube stars promote products and politicians without disclosing that they are paid to do so."[121]

Researchers have found evidence in several countries that local individuals have been paid to use their social media accounts as a means for disseminating information as requested by Russian authorities. In some instances, these individuals have even allowed others to take control of their social media accounts. For example, disinformation researcher Jakub Kalenský describes evidence of mercenaries "paying Ukrainian citizens to give a Russian agent access to their personal pages" as a way "to circumvent Facebook's new safeguards."[122] Not only does this effectively launder the source of Russia's disinformation narratives, obscuring its foreign origins, it also provokes both domestic consumption and domestic redistribution while amplifying the exposure and perceived legitimacy of those narratives. This is a unique form of "paying a fee for service" in order to achieve specific digital influence goals.

In addition to a broad range of deception and provocation tactics, digital influence mercenaries may also be contracted for orchestrating direct attacks against specific targets (including harassment, cyberbullying, hacking and defacing websites, and Internet service disruptions). However, I should note that digital influence mercenaries are not to be confused with vigilantes or other provocateurs who use their technical skills and tools to manipulate perceptions on behalf of a political or ideological agenda but not for monetary benefit. For example, consider Anonymous, a hacker collective that may harass (by naming and shaming) their targets, break into computer systems to shut down Web servers and accounts, and try to influence public perceptions about the target of their attacks. Michael Erbschloe calls them "social media warfare rangers" who are "motivated by social justice causes" and "have been credited with hacking actions against various governments, corporations, and even ideological networks like the Ku Klux Klan, the Westboro Baptist Church, the Islamic State, and child pornographers."[123] They have also stolen files from computers and uploaded them to public Web servers like Wikileaks, which itself represents another type of digital influence and provocation that we'll examine later in this book. By releasing secret or classified documents (or other information that was not intended for public consumption) into the public domain, Wikileaks has influenced the ways in which millions view the U.S. government, offshore banking (e.g., the Panama Papers), senior leaders of the Democratic party, and many others.

There are some similarities between mercenaries and digital vigilantes or "true believers." For example, digital vigilantes typically have the same set of technical skills as digital influence mercenaries, and many of them would certainly love to have the ability to shut down a specific voice online, perhaps even delete that target's account and all of its followers. Some have successfully hacked into the social media accounts of their targets and used them to disseminate disinformation, or even post messages intended to undermine the reputation of those individuals. They engage in a broad range of tactics discussed in this book, including trolling, distributing fake news, provoking emotions and behavior, sowing confusion and uncertainty, shaping beliefs, promoting conspiracy theories, and so forth. What they have in common with the mercenaries is the underlying goal of wanting to influence, but often that goal is related to something they believe in, rather than the mercenaries' focus on generating profit.

The core difference is that while the mercenaries always want to get paid, the digital vigilantes and "true believers" do not seem motivated by revenue generation or profit seeking. Some may be true believers in a specific cause, but not necessarily a single, coherent ideology. Others may be advocates of a particular extremist group or narrative. For example, most of the online propaganda produced by jihadist terrorist groups like al-Qaeda and the Islamic State is redistributed by various ideological believers in different parts of the world who may have no connection to (or even knowledge of) each other. White supremacists and other right-wing extremists also engage in the same kind of online messaging distribution, seeking to both spread and defend their narratives about non-whites, Muslims, immigrants, and so forth. Other individuals may be true believers in a political party or even a specific individual. Trump advocates, for example, will spend countless hours trolling and provoking anyone deemed a suitable target due to their criticism of Trump.

Another type of true believer is the intentional provocateur who seeks to sabotage the message of their opponent. Jack Posobiec is one of these. At a 2017 anti-Trump protest in Washington, D.C., he infiltrated the crowd and briefly held up a provocative sign—with the words "Rape Melania"—just long enough for one of his colleagues to take a photo of it, and then posted the photo online. From there, through engagement with his network of alt-right social media users, and coverage by the Russian media outlet RT, the image went viral. As Singer and Brooking note, "Tens of thousands of Twitter users all screaming at the same nonexistent adversary" is what the image was meant to provoke—first by creating controversy about a "violent left," and then when the hoax was discovered and reported, engaging in a new battle of words about the rights of free speech.[124] Through it all, the one thing that was completely overshadowed was the anti-Trump protest and their cause. By hijacking the entire incident in this way, one can use digital influence warfare to deflect and redirect attention away from what the influencer doesn't want you to see, hear, or discuss.[125]

Digital vigilantes and true believers have been responsible for some significant digital influence campaigns. However, we have also seen some instances where an ideologically motivated individual discovered that handsome profits could be made from the kinds of provocation they were engaging in, and subsequently transformed into the type of money-making mercenary described in this book. For example, earlier in this chapter I described the October 2020 incident in which an online marketing firm called Rally Forge was hired by Charlie Kirk and his pro-Trump youth organization Turning Point Action to spread conservative-leaning disinformation across social media platforms. Kirk has actually founded a number of online pro-Trump organizations, and by regularly provoking outrage was able to attract more than a million followers. He would use his social media account to distribute messages like: "Breaking: Legal group finds hundreds of double voting cases, thousands of deceased voters on rolls in Palm Beach County. A new discovery shows 24,000 instances of irregularities among the voter rolls in Palm Beach County, Fla., according to a new report. Voter fraud is real."[126] However, he would provide no sources or links with this message, nothing for people to click on that would lead them (for example) to a site where he could generate revenue from advertisements. Instead, merely stoking the fires of this particular conspiracy would ensure an emotional response among large numbers of his followers as well as attract new followers. And the amount of visibility this kind of provocation activity brings can also help Charlie sell more copies of his book, so his profile conveniently offers a link to it on Amazon.com. Sebastian Gorka and several others have followed a similar path, demonstrating how provocative online antics can become a way to make some serious money.

One of the more sophisticated examples of profit seeking through ideologically motivated forms of digital influence was reported in December 2019, when a team of researchers discovered a coordinated effort "to create a commercial enterprise that harvests Islamophobic hate for profit."[127] The group behind this effort was "using its 21-page network to churn out more than 1,000 coordinated faked news posts per week to more than 1 million followers," funneling audiences to a cluster of ten nearly identical ad-heavy websites masquerading as news sites (with generic titles like *The Politics Online* and *Free Press Front*) and "milking the traffic for profit.... Ad-heavy and poorly designed, the websites feature 'stories' that usually combine slabs of copied text intermingled with unsourced opinion and graphic imagery."[128] Through at least 165,000 posts (which attracted 14.3 million likes, shares or comments), the group largely focused on inciting "deep hatred of Islam across the western world . . . amplifying far-right parties such as Australia's One Nation and vilifying Muslim politicians such as the London mayor, Sadiq Khan, and the U.S. congresswoman Ilhan Omar."[129]

Essentially, the pursuit of profit can dovetail nicely with racial hatred and political polarization. And of course, it should also be noted that different kinds of activities and actors may sometimes intersect. For example, there have been numerous instances where Russia's paid trolls have collaborated with individuals in the target countries who support their activities for a wide range of personal and idiosyncratic reasons.[130] While the mercenaries can profit monetarily from the disinformation they spread, their local collaborators can gain a sense of personal satisfaction from convincing others about the righteousness of their sociopolitical views, sharing their indignation and prejudices, nurturing a shared antipathy toward some type of "other," and reinforcing the comforting certainty of their chosen in-group identity. And all of this is made possible—encouraged, even—by social media.

Conclusion

Many years ago, terrorism expert Cindy Combs observed how terrorists and the media had a kind of symbiotic relationship, in which the terrorists needed the attention provided by the media, and the media needed dramatic events to attract readers and viewers (which included acts of terrorism).[131] Today we see a similar kind of symbiotic relationship between social media platforms and digital influence mercenaries (as well as their clients). In the attention economy, profit is derived from users viewing and engaging with the information provided online. The profit model embraced by the proliferation of social media platforms is built primarily on promoting engagement. And the most successful digital influence mercenaries are those who are able to orchestrate the kind of attention and engagement that generates profits for both them and the social media platforms.

Meanwhile, politicians and corporations are willing and eager to pay for viral digital content that attracts attention to their political platform and name brand (while also spreading disinformation about their peer competitors or adversaries).

Governments and nation-states (like Russia) are also paying digital influence mercenaries to conduct a broad range of malicious operations against perceived adversaries, both foreign and domestic. And to aid in all these efforts, social media platforms collect massive amounts of information on their users that can be used to craft targeted digital influence operations in ways that help achieve the specific goals and objectives described above.[132]

Essentially, this symbiotic relationship is driven by the forces of supply and demand that one finds in any service industry. In this case, the digital influence mercenaries are providing the supply to meet the demand from clients willing to pay for their services. But there is an additional twist here that seems unique to the world of social media: with the advertising revenue generation model, framed by the attention economy, a secondary form of demand comes from individuals who *want to be influenced*. This type of demand for the services of digital influence mercenaries is coming from us, the users of social media, who want to be stimulated and deceived in ways that confirm our closely held beliefs and biases about something we want to believe is true. Our thirst for certainty and confirmation bias, and our desire to avoid the discomfort of uncertainty, are vulnerabilities that can be exploited by these mercenaries. We now live in a world where the supply of deception is meeting the demand for deception, and the supply of provocation is meeting the demand for stimulation.

According to a 2019 NATO report, "The tools and methods developed and funded to scam the advertising industry are also used for political and national security interference."[133] However, many of today's professional social media manipulators are more interested in cash than politics. In fact, the social media business model encourages the digital influence mercenary to generate significant profits by "weaponizing" information and disinformation. The political impacts of exacerbating societal divisions and polarization are often side effects that are of no real concern to the mercenary.[134] While fake news propagated during the 2016 presidential election evolved from clickbait to disinformation, and morphed from a vehicle for financial gain to one for political manipulation, this was not the main intention of the digital influence mercenaries.[135]

Meanwhile, the future outlook for the business of digital influence mercenaries is unfortunately quite promising. This is now a growth industry, with freelancers generating revenue through advertisements and profit-seeking "social media consulting" companies developing strategies to obtain clients within the market for digital influence services, and even showcasing specific kinds of performance metrics, in order to convince prospective clients of the potential return on their investment. As this industry grows, we will see increasing competition for profit and reputation among various firms and freelancers, who will market themselves as being the best at what they do. The most effective mercenaries can provide unique advantages to those who employ them, particularly through the strategic and technical prowess they bring to any digital influence efforts. When employing the methods described in chapter 2, savvy digital influence mercenaries can amplify uncertainty and fear, exploit overconfidence and confirmation bias, and manipulate perceptions in order to gain power and profit.

2

DIGITAL INFLUENCE METHODS

One of the first things that successful digital influence mercenaries will need to do is gain an understanding of their potential targets, in order to then devise the most effective ways to deceive, provoke, and manipulate them. As Jarol Manheim notes, "The single most important key to success in an information and influence campaign is good intelligence. . . . Any well-crafted campaign will incorporate in its overall planning and implementation a significant strategic research component."[1] This makes intuitive sense: rather than trying to influence someone you know nothing about, you would want to maximize the use of your time and resources by focusing your attacks against people whom you are most likely to influence. Fortunately for the mercenary, there are ample data available about anyone who regularly uses the Internet, which makes targeting relatively straightforward.

The Internet encourages us to share information about us and our lives in ways that are unprecedented. Every day people are providing online a variety of personal revelations, including photos and videos of themselves along with friends, family, pets, celebrations, and notes about other people, events or things they care about. This reflects the "privacy paradox" described by Susan Barnes—while most people understand privacy issues, they are posting tons of information on their social media accounts and personal websites.[2] Further, the transparency of a social media user's account information and activity lends itself to an environment that is rich for gathering data to inform influence efforts. Each account contains data—followers, likes, shares, group memberships, demographics, and so forth—that offer visual indicators of that person's potential value as a target. So, an important first step in pursuing a digital influence effort involves harvesting (or "scraping") these data. I won't go into the specific details in this book about how to do this, but the aspiring digital influence mercenary can find plenty of instructional guides, YouTube videos, and tools to assist with this kind of activity.[3] Further, some tools don't even require any knowledge of coding programs; they have been set up as ready-to-use resources for the collection of data from social media accounts and websites.

Other data sources that reveal an Internet user's preferences and behavior include complaints (or compliments) posted in the comments section of a website, or product reviews posted on shopping websites. Our affiliations are also useful data, including relationships with educational institutions, political and social organizations, family members, friends, businesses, financial institutions, religion, and much more. And then there's the information about our online activities that we produce involuntarily. Internet and social media platforms routinely track our website visits, the terms we search for, the videos we watch, the things we download or upload and send to others, and much more. Additionally, Internet service providers can also gather a lot of information on visitors to websites they host, providing insights for website owners about where their website visitors come from, how they find the site, how long they stay at the site and what they do (i.e., what they read, click on, search for, etc.)—data that can be used by digital influence mercenaries to identify an audience whose members have shown interest in the subject matter of that website.

Overall, a combination of data analysis and algorithms will reveal specific identity attributes about individuals that can then aid in devising an appropriate targeting set in support of the mercenary's influence goals.[4] These attributes can include a person's education, hobbies, friends and associates, occupation, favorite sports teams, movies, and music. In addition to examining the kinds of messages they post or share online, and what these messages indicate about interests, concerns, preferences, likes and dislikes, we can also determine when that person is most likely to be online and for how long. Especially revealing are patterns of an individual's behavior—for example, if they show a pattern of frequently favoring information posted online by specific individuals or organizations, news media, websites, and so on. We can also determine what kinds of previous images and videos have provoked some type of interaction or response. While this is clearly not an exhaustive list, it illustrates the rich terrain that can be mined by the digital influence mercenary looking for targets most likely to respond to information in ways that will benefit their goals.

In sum, targets can be identified by a broad range of data, including IP (Internet protocol) addresses. Data analytics establish patterns of behavior, especially patterns of preference for and reactions to online information that can be captured, stored, and analyzed.[5] These data are also used to inform algorithms (usually proprietary to each social media platform) that play a role in many kinds of user experiences, from determining the ads and other information we see to recommendations for other accounts we might want to follow. Google uses algorithms to determine what search engine results will be displayed, and what ads are shown in Gmail users' accounts. Amazon uses algorithms to make suggestions about what we might like to buy. Some people tend to bestow magical qualities on algorithms because they misunderstand what these things are all about, but as Carl Miller explains, algorithms are fairly simple: they involve input, a process, and output.[6] The higher the quality of the data you input, and the more sophisticated and elegant the process, the better the overall outcome will be. So, this means algorithms are extremely dependent on ensuring the highest quality data. And this, in turn, means that the higher the quality of data the digital mercenary has at their disposal, the more success they will enjoy.

The Essential Importance of Targeting Data

The importance of rich data on the intended targets of digital influence efforts can also be seen as a means of revenue generation. One of the key selling points of digital influence mercenary firms is that they can help their clients identify targets that will be most likely to respond in ways that meet the client's strategic influence objectives. Several of the digital influence firms described in the previous chapter have their own in-house data gathering and analysis capabilities. Other firms may focus primarily or even exclusively on this specific area of the digital influence industry. I call those kinds of firms "influence data miners," drawing from the definition of data mining as "the process of monitoring and examining large volumes of data by combining tools from statistics and artificial intelligence to recognize useful patterns."[7] Data mining allows the mercenary to develop strategies for microtargeting, a process of preparing and delivering customized digital messages to voters or consumers. According to Philip Howard, contemporary microtargeting involves preparing and delivering a message that is tailored specifically for particular individuals using their data, social ties, cognitive biases, and big data records, often in ways that are unsupervised, untraceable, and unknown to the individuals.[8] For example, the Trump campaign's digital director in 2016 (and for a while director of Trump's 2020 reelection campaign) once described how they used Facebook's advertising tools to microtarget potential supporters with customized ads, making some fifty to sixty thousands ads a day, continually tweaking language, graphics, even colors, to try to elicit a favorable response.[9]

One of the most prominent examples of these activities is seen in the case of (the now bankrupt) Cambridge Analytica, which (alongside Psy-Group, Colt Ventures, the Internet Research Agency and others) gained infamy following an investigation into the 2016 U.S. presidential election.[10] It all began in 2014, when executives of the London-based political communications firm SCL Group (short for Strategic Communications Laboratories) persuaded conservative billionaire Robert Mercer to provide funding for a new "data science" company called Cambridge Analytica. The vision for this company involved developing psychological profiles of millions of American voters, and its efforts would be supervised by Mr. Mercer's daughter, Rebekah, and by Steve Bannon, who later became chief executive of Donald Trump's presidential campaign, and then chief strategist in the Trump White House.[11] SCL had spent nearly twenty-five years in political communication, helping presidents and prime ministers with their election campaigns and influence efforts. To them, data was a means to an end, and they recognized that mining the huge amount of data being amassed by social media and Internet platforms would be a tremendous asset.

The central goal of Cambridge Analytica was to harness the power of behavior predictability for the purpose of winning elections.[12] To do this, however, required a massive amount of data—which they acquired by contracting with Aleksandr Kogan (a senior research associate at Cambridge University) to harvest millions of Facebook profiles, without the users' knowledge or permission. As *Guardian* investigative reporter Carole Cadwalladr explains, "Psychologists at Cambridge University had previously harvested Facebook data (legally) for research purposes and published pioneering peer-reviewed work about determining personality traits, political partisanship, sexuality, and much more from people's Facebook 'likes'. And SCL/Cambridge Analytica contracted Kogan to harvest new Facebook data . . . [which became] the source of the psychological insights that enabled Cambridge Analytica to target individuals."[13] Here's how it worked, according to a *New York Times* exposé published in April 2018.[14] First, a Facebook user was invited to take an online survey. Before doing so they were asked to give the survey application access to the user's Facebook account. Once that access was granted, the app would harvest all of the user's data as well as data from the profiles of all their Facebook friends. "Their names, birth dates, and location data, as well as lists of every Facebook page they had ever liked, were downloaded—without their knowledge or express consent."[15]

By 2015, the central aspect of the company's work was described as targeted audience segmentation, microtargeting, and other such terms. There were peer competitors in this marketplace, like the microtargeting firm Targeted Victory,[16] so Cambridge Analytica had to offer something unique in order to attract potential customers. To that end, the company offered tools that it claimed could identify the personalities of American voters and influence voter behavior,[17] and sold its data science and analytical capabilities to campaigns that wanted to "boost engagement," resulting in an increasing number of lucrative contracts.[18] Their first major impact was contributing to the outcome of the UK vote over whether to stay or leave the European Union (commonly known as "Brexit"). On June 23, 2016, a small majority of eligible voters voted to leave the EU, confounding expectations of most pollsters and political commentators. Research by Emma Briant revealed that Cambridge Analytica provided mostly strategic consulting on data collection and analysis methods, helping the far-right Leave.EU campaign identify the most important issues (which included the impact of immigration on housing, schools, and overcrowding) to be amplified during their influence campaign.[19] In testimony to the House of Commons on March 27, 2018, Christopher Wylie (a former Cambridge Analytica employee turned whistleblower) stated that the company's exploitation of personal data had swung the results of Britain's 2016 referendum on leaving the European Union.[20] In a separate interview, Wylie explained how "we exploited Facebook to harvest millions of people's profiles . . . and built models to exploit what we knew about them and target their inner demons. That was the basis the entire company was built on."[21]

During the 2016 U.S. presidential campaign, Cambridge Analytica used its advanced data analysis and manipulation techniques for Republican candidates, first Ted Cruz and then Donald Trump. During one period, the Cambridge Analytica data team divided the GOP voter target data into "Core Republicans," "Reliable Republicans," "Turnout Targets," "Priority Persuasions," and "Wildcards." From this segmentation they would devise different messaging strategies on issues ranging from national security to the economy and immigration.[22] A recent book by Brittany Kaiser, another whistleblower who worked for nearly four years at Cambridge

Analytica, exposed the ways in which the firm exploited vulnerabilities in Facebook's massive collection of user data, and then used those data to manipulate the online behavior of millions.[23] Its so-called "psychographic modeling" techniques, which were built in part with the data harvested from Facebook, underpinned Cambridge's work for the Trump campaign. Google played a major (and profitable) role as well, selling search result placement and ads to the Trump campaign, including on the home page of YouTube.com—a highly coveted and very expensive piece of digital real estate.[24]

On December 11, 2015, the *Guardian* published an exposé about Cambridge Analytica and the campaign of Ted Cruz. The allegations were that Cambridge Analytica had obtained data from Facebook in violation of the social media site's terms of use. As Kaiser explains, "The data was the private information of some thirty million Facebook users and their friends, and most of those individuals had not wittingly agreed to share it." Moreover, "Cambridge was using that data as a weapon to affect the outcome of the Republican primaries and make Ted Cruz the GOP nominee."[25] In May 2018, the Senate Judiciary Committee learned that Steve Bannon had directed Cambridge Analytica to use "voter disengagement tactics" to "discourage or demobilize certain types of people from voting"—specifically, African Americans. Robert and Rebekah Mercer ultimately shut down Cambridge Analytica in May 2018 after the company came under FBI scrutiny for harvesting private data from 50 million Facebook users without their consent or knowledge.[26] By then, the Mercers had already fallen out with both Bannon and Trump as well.

In January 2020, more than 100,000 Cambridge Analytica documents, relating to work in sixty-eight countries, were leaked by the Twitter account @HindsightFiles.[27] The documents were revealed to have come from Brittany Kaiser, and were the same ones subpoenaed by Robert Mueller's investigation into Russian interference in the 2016 presidential election. Kaiser said the Facebook data scandal was part of a much bigger global operation that worked with governments, intelligence agencies, commercial companies, and political campaigns to manipulate and influence people.[28] In its own investigation after the election, Facebook revealed that the data of up to 87 million people may have been shared improperly with Cambridge Analytica, which used this information to help create tools designed to predict and influence voter behavior.

I had originally planned to spend a good deal more time in this chapter describing the antics of Cambridge Analytica, but instead I encourage readers to take a look at Brittany Kaiser's book *Targeted*,[29] as well as Emma Briant's forthcoming book *Propaganda Machine*.[30] But this should serve as a useful example of the crucial intersections of data mining and the strategies of digital influence mercenaries. Naturally, the same strategies used by political campaigns to identify the voters most likely to support their candidate's ideas are also used to identify individuals most susceptible to disinformation, and most likely to share it with others. As Singer and Brooking explain, "The best predictor for whether something posted online will become influential is not the accuracy or even the compelling value of the content: it is the number of friends and followers who share the content first. They are more likely to believe what it says, and then to share it with others who, in turn will believe what they say; it is all about us, or rather our love of ourselves and people like us."[31] As Wojciech Cieśla of Investigate Europe (a consortium of European investigative reporters) observes, "Once you have won someone's trust by reflecting their own views back at them, you are in a position to influence them."[32] So, an essential part of digital influence efforts involves infiltrating online communities with credible online personas.

Crafting Credible Fake Online Personas

For most of the remaining parts of this chapter, let's describe a hypothetical digital influence mercenary named Jack, in order to illustrate a broad range of tactics and strategies in a simple, straightforward way. As described earlier, one of the first things digital influence firms and freelancers will need is data. So, let's assume Jack has already accumulated the necessary data about his targets and is now creating accounts that he will use to interact with them. These could be automated "bots," computer-generated accounts on social media platforms that are programmed to do specific things autonomously and automatically. Typically, these fake social media accounts are built with software or code designed to mimic human behavior online and are designed to generate posts and engage with content on a particular social media platform.[33] And as noted in chapter 1, there is a Dark Web market online where Jack can purchase fake accounts, Facebook pages, even a "fake news starter pack" for beginners.[34] According to a study published in 2017, "Russian marketplaces have do-it-yourself (DIY) kits in the form of software that can perform activities such as automated social media spamming."[35]

Another study published in 2017 suggested that as many as 48 million Twitter accounts aren't real people, and Facebook has admitted to finding tens of millions of "bots" on its platforms.[36] And as Sara Fischer observed in her 2017 Axios report, more than half of all Internet traffic involves bots, in part because the push by social media platforms to provide open access worldwide "means the barrier to entry on these platforms isn't just low for users, but for bots and bad actors as well."[37] Basically, mercenaries want the target to believe these bots are real people, writing messages or doing other things that normal people do. A collection or network of bots that communicate across multiple devices to perform tasks is called a "botnet."[38] They act in coordination, typically controlled by one person or group, and can be used to create a buzz around a certain person, issue, or topic; push a point of view or agenda; or even manufacture the appearance of popularity for products or posts.[39] Commercial botnets can include tens of thousands of bots[40] and can be hired and used by a variety of clients. As Philip Howard observes, "The market for deceitful robots is a competitive one. The people who build and maintain such networks must create visually pleasing and sufficiently entertaining stories of political intrigue, hidden agendas or malfeasance. The stories must contain enough realism about the situation that users accept the claims enough to click through, read more, and retain a few details and doubts."[41]

Software used for creating and using large armies of bots can be found online, and there are plenty of instructional guides for those who want to program and control a collection of bots on their own.[42] However, there are also companies that Jack could pay to provide him with trained professionals who can program the fake accounts, help him identity target audiences, and manage as many accounts as he wants. Fake news perpetrators create fake stories that are often amplified by a network of bots that automatically like, share, or comment on the content. Algorithms on the social media platforms elevate content that is popular, further amplifying the effect. Bots can even be used to manipulate online polls and surveys.

The most sophisticated social media "bots" are those that are programmed to give other people the impression that lots of people agree with a certain position or argument you are making. Jack can have thousands of fake accounts programmed to like, share, and retweet one of his posts, in order to manufacture the illusion of broad support for what he said. Repetition can be automated, and sheer repetition and volume of a falsehood can lead to a perception of it being credible, something that marketing professionals, propagandists, and many others know well.[43] Automated bot accounts can also be programmed to interact with other people's social media accounts in a variety of ways that generate forms of reciprocity and in-group identity affiliation.

However, automated bots and scripts can only do so much, and advances in artificial intelligence are providing social media platforms with better tools to monitor and catch this type of "coordinated inauthentic behavior."[44] So, many digital influence mercenaries employ real humans in their efforts, who modify the posts and interactions slightly in order to avoid automated detection. These could be human-curated "legends"—accounts that appear to represent a real person[45]—like those described in chapter 1. Sometimes this kind of fake account is called a "sock puppet," a term used to describe an alias or "fake persona created by social media users to masquerade as someone or something else on the Internet."[46] As Peter Pomerantsev observes, this kind of fake identity is designed specifically to deceive others, and is particularly useful for infiltrating an online community and then manipulating it from the inside.[47] For example, consider the case of "Melvin Redick," whose Facebook account described a fairly ordinary, middle-aged family man from Harrisburg, Pennsylvania. His profile photo showed him in a baseball cap alongside his young daughter. On June 8, 2016, Redick urged his friends and followers to view a link to the website "DCLeaks.com," where he claimed they would discover "the hidden truth about Hillary Clinton, George Soros and other leaders of the US."[48] However, "Redick" was a fabricated account. A search of Pennsylvania records found no evidence of Redick's existence, and the person shown in his profile photo was actually a man in Brazil.[49] Investigators concluded that whoever was posing as Redick was likely a Russian, perhaps even a contractor.

According to Robert Walker, "The false nature of the sock puppet allows them to make controversial or offensive comments while taking sides on a particular issue without the risk of exposing their real identity. Sock puppets have also been known to post commentary on content that they might have produced themselves under a different identity."[50] In October 2019, Facebook announced it had suspended a network of Instagram accounts operated from Russia, with "links to the Internet Research Agency" that targeted Americans with divisive political messages ahead of the 2020 U.S. presidential election, with operators posing as people within the United States.[51] According to a report by Graphika, "The operators went to great lengths to hide their origins, prioritizing operational security (OPSEC) over audience growth. . . . They claimed to represent multiple politically active US communities: black activist groups, advocates speaking out against police violence, police supporters, LGBTQ groups, Christian conservatives, Muslims, environmentalists, gun-rights activists, southern Confederates, and supporters of Senator Bernie Sanders and President Donald Trump."[52] In March 2020, Facebook and Twitter disabled a sophisticated Russian-linked operation designed to stoke racial tensions among African Americans in the United States.[53] In August 2020,

Facebook removed a Romanian network of one hundred accounts masquerading as African American Trump supporters.[54] And in October 2020, as described in chapter 1, an investigation by Facebook uncovered a coordinated network of individuals who "attempted to conceal their identities and coordination" and were linked to "Rally Forge, a US marketing firm, working on behalf of Turning Point USA and Inclusive Conservation Group."[55]

Digital influence efforts could also involve paying a social media influencer (one who has a large online following) to retweet your posts. For example, investigations by Facebook have uncovered disinformation operations linked to Russia in which locals in a target country were employed to post anti-Western messages via their own accounts.[56] Jack could also persuade individuals to allow him (usually for a fee) to control their social media account, at least temporarily. The tactics of using proxies to disseminate disinformation and propaganda are not new, but now Jack can hire virtually anyone with a social media account, have them post whatever kinds of information are part of his influence campaign, and then have other individuals—using their own authentic user accounts—signify their agreement and support for that information by liking and sharing it.

Whichever identity-manipulation approach the digital influence mercenary chooses to carry out, the central objective is to establish a presence on whatever social media platforms are used by the target. Having complementary accounts for the same persona on multiple platforms helps reinforce the perceived credibility of the fake persona and also provides a means to amplify disinformation across multiple social media platforms. One thing that helps the fake account seem more authentic is consistency. For example, if the fake persona is that of a right-leaning American, they should be sure to always post or endorse information that aligns with that political agenda. Accounts linked to the Internet Research Agency in Russia—active on Facebook, Twitter, Instagram, Stitcher, YouTube, and other platforms—have masqueraded as American citizens and organizations from a wide variety of political orientations or from no obvious political orientation at all.[57]

Another, less common method used by digital influence mercenaries involves hijacking the social media account of someone who has a sizable number of followers. As with many kinds of cyberattacks, the first step is to acquire the person's login information, something made easier by people who are careless when it comes to their personal cybersecurity. Once the perpetrator has accessed the social media account targeted, they can use it to disseminate whatever information they desire, including messages that may be meant to embarrass or discredit the account's true owner.

The mercenary can also create Facebook groups or other collective entities, focusing on specific topics or ideas that may appeal to a large audience. Once the group has been created, Jack can populate it with hundreds or thousands of fake accounts (human or automated) who seemingly share a common set of views about the topics at hand.[58] This, in turn, provides the illusion of social validity, a psychological motivator of behavior that we'll discuss later in this book. In the end, ordinary social media users who feel strongly about a particular topic will be attracted to groups whose members appear to have views and values that are aligned with their own. A best-case scenario is that a group Jack creates becomes the exclusive go-to source of information for its members, allowing him to provoke and deceive them at will without having to worry about them being exposed to competing or contradictory sources of information. These digital echo chambers can be highly effective means for manipulating perceptions, as we'll discuss in chapter 7.

To sum up, connections with others—an underlying motivation of many Internet users—can provide a cornerstone for the success of digital influence efforts. By knowing the target's connections, the mercenary can work to influence some of them. As a result of seeing your friends embrace a certain narrative, you are more likely to embrace it yourself. Basically, our online connections can serve as a means of exerting peer pressure on each other's views and behaviors. This digital influence approach exploits the ties that bind people together, and is sometimes referred to as "affinity fraud," taking advantage of people's tendency to trust others with whom they share similarities, such as religion or ethnic identity, in order to gain their trust and then influence them.[59] This trust, in turn, enables the mercenary to pursue various kinds of deception, provocation, and manipulation strategies.

From Deceptive Identities to Deceptive Information

The terms "misinformation" and "disinformation" are frequently used in referring to "fake news," but the terms in fact mean different things. Misinformation is defined as the unintentional spread of information that is wholly or partly false, "contested information that reflects political disagreement and deviation from expert consensus, scientific knowledge, or lived experience."[60] In contrast, while misinformation is initially provided without the direct intention to deceive,[61] disinformation involves the intentional dissemination of information that is completely (or partly) false, exaggerated, biased, or presented in manipulative and misleading ways. Most often, fake news websites are forms of disinformation—efforts to intentionally deceive the visitors to the website, and usually also to provoke some sort of behavior.

Establishing a fake news website is fairly straightforward, and as described in chapter 1, there are many ways to go about it. One approach starts with choosing a name that reflects a location—like *Denver Guardian*, the site Jestin Coler used to publish his highly lucrative "FBI Agent Suspected in Hilary Email Leaks Found Dead in Apparent Murder-Suicide" fake news story.[62] People outside the region would be unlikely to know that there is no actual media outlet in Denver by that name, so links to "news stories" on that site would project a certain type of perceived credibility. Also, a programmer could reproduce the look and feel of a truly professional media website; with the right mix of headline banners, reporters' bylines, images and so forth, an average visitor to the fake news site can be easily duped into believing the site is credible.

Naturally, Jack will also want to establish social media accounts that carry the same name as the fake news website. Sometimes, it may be useful to maintain an appearance of political neutrality—for example, a variety of digital influence operations have involved accounts that presented themselves as U.S. local news aggregators and had descriptive names such as @OnlineMemphis and @TodayPittsburgh.[63] A mercenary may do this temporarily, in order to accrue followers, then switch to more politically oriented material. Once the website and social media accounts are set up, the next step involves signing up the website to one of the ad networks (there are literally hundreds of ad networks to choose from), so that when Jack begins attracting visitors he can generate revenues.

Jack's fake news website can provide information in a variety of formats, including images and videos. Today's technology enables virtually anyone to modify these things as part of a disinformation effort. Slightly altered photos, audio, and video clips are often called "cheapfakes," and examples of this include a photo that has been enhanced to make someone look younger (or older), or an audio or video clip that has been edited or slightly slowed down to make it appear the speaker is slurring their words, possibly even inebriated. Sometimes the nuances of these alterations are more difficult to spot than an outright forgery. In contrast, "deepfakes" are fabricated media produced using artificial intelligence (AI). By synthesizing different elements of existing video or audio files, AI enables the creation of "new" content, in which individuals appear to speak words and perform actions that are not based on reality.[64]

Today, massive amounts of highly plausible fabricated video and audio material are being disseminated in order to reduce the target society's confidence in a shared reality and intensify their loss of faith in institutions (and each other). In addition to popular social media platforms like Facebook and Twitter, there are many online community sites where users have been prolific in the creation and sharing of deepfake images and videos, "memes" or other viral content. These include Reddit, 4chan, MetaFilter, and Tumblr. Further, recent years have seen the rapid transmission of deepfake technologies from the research lab to user-friendly applications. What started in 2017 with the FakeApp software has now evolved to an open-source version called Faceswap, and the code for accomplishing face swaps is now openly available as a software package called DeepFaceLab.[65]

In a recent *Foreign Affairs* article, Robert Chesney and Danielle Citron argue that "deepfakes will become better and cheaper, and democracies will have to learn resilience and how to live with lies."[66] As Michael Mazarr and his colleagues noted in a recent RAND report, "Simply put, the ability to manufacture seemingly tangible reality from scratch has now become commonplace."[67] In December 2020, as a warning about the dangers of this technology, Britain's Channel 4 created a deepfake video featuring the queen of England delivering an "alternative Christmas speech" in which she cracks jokes and performs a TikTok dance routine.[68]

To sum up, anyone with at least a modest degree of computer literacy can now engage in many forms of digital deception, with software and tools for image and video manipulation widely available online. The strategy here for Jack, the digital influence mercenary, is to identify the kinds of deception that will be most appealing to the audience being targeted. As noted earlier, this is where data collection and analysis will play a very important role. And if Jack is not entirely sure about the content creation side of things, there are a variety of other websites (called "content farms") that mass-produce articles designed to generate traffic and ad revenue.[69] But his overall goal here should be to ensure the content is "sticky"—that is, the more time a user spends interacting with his content, no matter how false or toxic it is, the more opportunities there are to serve that user ads.

So, having created a "fake news" website and loaded it with whatever information he believes the targets will find appealing, Jack will now use those social media accounts to begin driving traffic to the site. This is where we encounter the term "clickbait"—digital media items (images, videos, headlines, etc.) designed to trigger an emotional response from a user that leads them to click on the item, because each person who does so generates revenue for the clickbait provider.[70] Often misleading or inaccurate, the provocative nature of the clickbait headline is typically more sensational than the content to which it directs the user.[71] A similar term is "chumming," originally a reference to the practice of luring animals (like sharks) with bait, but now also used to describe a type of Internet advertising that involves clickbait to lure visitors to a website. The goal here is to provoke a reaction—in fact, provocation is perhaps the most reliable way to attract attention to a fake news website.

Provocation

Provoking people is easier when you have the kind of information about your target that reveals the messages, images, memes, and so forth they are most likely to share, like, retweet, and respond to. And as we'll discuss in the next several chapters of this book, there are important emotional and psychological dimensions behind the success of provocation efforts, often involving fear, uncertainty, frustration, anger, and ego. For example, messages that attack our beliefs, our intellect, and our sense of self will typically trigger an ego-driven reaction. Methods of provocation can involve lies, scorn, trash talk, rumors and conspiracies, and images and videos that are either fake or real. As long as Jack knows his audience well enough, he can find ways to provoke either positive or negative emotions among them. He can use denigrating words or images to attack their treasured beliefs and opinions—a form of clickbait sometimes called "ragebait"—and provoke angry responses that are viewed by the social media platform's algorithms as merely user engagement. He can provoke outrage by playing the role of an angry, aggrieved, isolated, self-absorbed hothead constantly insulting and denigrating his perceived enemies, and if his target responds in any way, he will have succeeded in garnering their attention.

Using exclamation marks, ALL CAPS, and headline words like "unbelievable," "shocking," "leaked," "revealed," "scandal," and so forth in his digital media items will often attract the target's attention. For example, supporters of the debunked "plandemic" video (featuring a discredited former research scientist with a record of promoting scientific falsehoods and engaging in scientific misconduct) were able to attract millions of viewers by using phrases like "banned video" and "molecular biologist breaks silence" in their social media posts.[72] Shocking or graphic content, outlandish statements, and "scare stories" are just some of the many choices available to the digital influence mercenary. As we'll discuss further in the next chapter, fear is an especially powerful emotion that can be provoked in many ways. For instance, a series of messages on Twitter by IRA digital mercenaries in 2015 claimed that salmonella-contaminated turkeys were produced by Koch Foods (a U.S. poultry producer) near the Thanksgiving holiday and described the poisoning of individuals who purchased these turkeys from Walmart.[73] The whole story was false, yet provoked some people to react in ways that reflected both fear and anger.

Another prominent example of this was revealed in August 2020 through an investigation by the Alethea Group, an organization specializing in the study of disinformation.[74] They discovered a network of politically conservative websites that promoted material clearly intended to inflame the anger of their viewers, with stories of "crazed leftists" and other provocative topics. These websites—including American Pundit, Bearded Patriot, and Wolf of Washington—used similar coding and design features, and many of them shared domain registration data, IP addresses, and Google AdSense identification numbers. The true purpose of these websites, according to the investigation, was to harvest email addresses and other personal information from visitors, whose email in-boxes where then inundated by narrowly targeted advertising. The operators of the network established companies like Rightside Data and Direct Mailers Group to sell the data collected from the right-wing websites. Essentially, the report concludes, the operators of this network were using misleading political content to monetize anger for as much as $2,500 per list of contacts.[75]

Images can be particularly provocative. Consider the image of a college campus police officer casually using pepper spray in an assault on students who were sitting peacefully in a political protest. The officer is dressed in riot gear and heavily armed, and seemingly has no reservation or concern about what he is doing to the unarmed students on the ground. To some viewing this picture, it's almost as if the officer were spraying his garage to wipe out a termite infestation. Many who viewed the photo online were aghast, and in their outrage forwarded the photo to friends and family, sometimes with comments attached about police brutality. Others, however, saw no fault in the officer's actions—indeed, they even applauded the officer for doing a good job pacifying those students who were portrayed as uppity and probably obnoxious and getting what they deserved. This instance demonstrates how a single image can provoke a wide range of emotional responses.

Several of the digital influence mercenaries described in chapter 1 acknowledged having discovered how provoking anger is very good for business. So, if a target is already angry, this gives Jack an advantage, in that all he has to do is figure out the best way to amplify and exacerbate that anger. As Hany Farid notes in his June 2020 testimony before Congress, "Social media has learned that outrageous, divisive, and conspiratorial content increases engagement,"[76] and as explained earlier, engagement features centrally in the advertising profit model of social media platforms. Thus, fueling or allowing controversy is a good business plan, because it promotes engagement on the platforms, which then increases their ability to profit from serving up ads to all those highly engaged eyeballs. This, in turn, provides incentives for the digital influence mercenary to identify and then promote controversial topics, in order to increase engagement that can produce revenues.

So, Jack's goal should be to identify the most divisive, polarizing topics of contention among his target audience, as these will foster higher levels of engagement from attempts at emotional provocation.[77] Provocation can involve the dissemination of negative messages (e.g., intended to harass, discredit, suppress, dissuade, or disparage the target audience members) as well as positive messages, including those that seek to encourage action (e.g., "If you love the President, RT this!"). Posting both positive and negative information about COVID-19 vaccines, for example, can prove quite profitable. Jack should try to get the visitors to his website quarrelling among themselves about whether or not the pandemic is real, or whether or not the vaccine can be trusted. Then, as the attention given to his original message spirals and perhaps even goes viral, he can sit back and watch his website's advertising revenue soar.

It is also useful to capitalize on current events, especially when they involve violence and tragedy. Fear, anger, and many other powerful emotions are commonly higher during the aftermath of such events, which leads many people to overreact emotionally. A mercenary can also capitalize on certain annual events, like a major holiday, as long as the timing makes sense (e.g., the message "Leftist radicals want to cancel Christmas!" will have more impact in December than in June). If nothing dramatic is currently happening, another approach could be to fabricate crisis events, like the nonexistent outbreaks of Ebola in Atlanta and salmonella in New York, an explosion at the Columbian Chemicals plant in Louisiana, a phosphorus leak in Idaho, or nuclear plant accidents in Ukraine—none of which actually happened but which generated a buzz on social media nonetheless.[78]

Another prominent form of provocation is called "trolling," the act of deliberately posting offensive or inflammatory content to an online community with the intent of provoking readers or disrupting conversation.[79] Similar to trolling, the term "flaming" also refers to posting insults, often laced with profanity or other offensive language on social networking sites.[80] In both instances, the objective is to provoke a desired reaction, engage in harassment, or generate negative discourse, and is frequently done as a response to someone else's content that the "troll" disagrees with. Trolls often conceal their real identity or post anonymously and thus assume little risk for making inflammatory remarks compared to making them openly or in person.[81] Trolls usually try to deceive the target about their identity as well as the purpose of the information they are communicating. Their goals are typically focused on provocation, disruption, and distrust, but as Judith Donath described in 1998:

> Trolling is a game about identity deception, albeit one that is played without the consent of most of the players. The troll attempts to pass as a legitimate participant, sharing the group's common interests and concerns; the newsgroup members, if they are cognizant of trolls and other identity deceptions, attempt to both distinguish real from trolling postings and, upon judging a poster to be a troll, make the offending poster leave the group. Their success at the former depends on how well they—and the troll—understand identity cues; their success at the latter depends on whether the troll's enjoyment is sufficiently diminished or outweighed by the costs imposed by the group.[82]

Trolling began in the early days of the Internet—with individuals on Usenet discussion communities and email listservs—and today can be found on any social media platform and many discussion boards.[83] Rodrigo Duterte (president of the Philippines) encourages "patriotic trolling" to undermine his critics.[84] A 2017 Oxford Internet Institute report describes how "many of the so-called 'keyboard trolls' hired to spread propaganda for presidential candidate Duterte during the election continue to spread and amplify messages of his policies now that he's in power."[85] The more effective trolls are those who have a knack for offending others—and of course, people who are easily offended make excellent targets. Trolls will often use inflammatory and degrading language, images, and videos (often manipulated and fake) in order to disrupt discussions, spread fake news, provoke anger, disseminate bad advice, and damage the feeling of trust within an online community.[86] A troll may also incorporate random, off-topic messages in their provocation strategy, or even words of support for others whose provocative views and messages are aligned with those of the troll.

The term "troll farm" is used to describe a group of individuals engaged in trolling or bot-like promotion of narratives in a coordinated fashion.[87] In addition to the Internet Research Agency in Russia, there are many private-sector examples of organizations that arrange collective trolling efforts, usually supervised by someone on behalf of a client with resources (like a state sponsor). The rationale for troll farms and massive collections of automated bots is fairly straightforward: there is perceived strength in numbers. As we'll examine in later chapters of this book, the power of social validation means that people are more influenced when more than one friend endorses a topic.[88] This, in turn, is just one of several forms of what I call "engagement deception."

Engagement Deception

In the early years of the Internet, a prominent form of online engagement deception featured the so-called Google Bomb, a type of "search engine optimization" strategy (now mostly prevented) in which a group of people would make as many links as possible to one website from various other websites in order to artificially increase the Google ranking of that website among the top search-engine results for a word or phrase. Other forms soon emerged of what became known as "manufactured amplification," a term used to describe how the reach or spread of information is boosted through artificial means, including by human and automated manipulation of search engine results and trending lists, generating fake votes and signatures in online polls and petitions, and by promoting certain links or hashtags on social media. Today, digital influence mercenaries provide this type of service to their clients.[89]

On social media platforms, some of the most common tactics in this category involve manipulating perceptions of support/engagement through likes, shares, retweets, followers, and so on. Social media has shifted the terrain of influencing from mainstream media to individuals with significant numbers of followers, whose "retweets" or "shares" amplify the perception of endorsement and support that lends social proof and confirmation of a specific narrative. When these individuals are then linked in a concerted strategy to collectively amplify that narrative, the effects on the broader population of social media users can be overwhelming. This tactic is also sometimes referred to as "brigading," a coordinated effort by one online group to manipulate another—for example, through mass commenting on a certain message.[90]

A similar tactic is called "astroturfing," described as a centrally coordinated disinformation campaign in which participants pretend to be ordinary citizens acting independently.[91] Others have described it as an effort to create the image of public support or consensus where there is none.[92] Often, according to Robert Walker, manufacturing a false sense of popularity or support in this manner involves "creating buzz around a subject by posting what appear to be multiple spontaneous comments on social media, blogs, webpage comments sections, etc. The posts, while appearing random and uncoordinated, are in fact orchestrated for effect" by the digital influence mercenary, sometimes using social media "bots" in addition to real people managing fake accounts.[93]

An example of this is provided by Singer and Brooking in their book *LikeWar*. In 2010, Massachusetts held a special election to fill the seat vacated by the late Senator Ted Kennedy. Early on, it seemed unlikely that a Republican candidate would have a chance in this traditionally Democratic stronghold. But then a poll suggested Scott Brown might do well, and conservative advocacy groups launched a major social media campaign to try and swing the election his way. Thousands of fake accounts across Facebook and Twitter promoted his candidacy, while messages of support were disseminated far outside New England, expanding the Republican's donor base. When Brown became the first Republican to win a Massachusetts seat in the U.S. Senate since 1952, these efforts demonstrated how one could create the appearance of grassroots support (hence the name "astroturfing") and influence the outcome of an election.[94] More recently, as described in the previous chapter, the Arizona-based marketing firm Rally Forge was banned by Facebook after the company's investigators uncovered an astroturfing operation involving teenagers who were paid to develop fake accounts and use them to comment on news articles as well as spread pro-Trump and anti-Democrat disinformation.[95]

Another example was seen in August 2017, when National Security Advisor H. R. McMaster fired Ezra Cohen-Watnick from his position as a top intelligence official on the National Security Council (NSC). Cohen-Watnick was an extremely vocal supporter of President Trump, and his dismissal followed the departure of other Trump advocates from the NSC in previous weeks.[96] Later that evening, at least eleven different Twitter accounts posing as Americans—but operated by Russians working for the IRA in St. Petersburg—tweeted (and retweeted) a message urging that Trump fire McMaster. Among them was the Twitter account @TEN_GOP, which claimed to be the "unofficial Twitter of Tennessee Republicans." This account encouraged its followers to retweet "if you think McMaster needs to go," and many of @TEN_GOP's 140,000 followers were automated "bot" accounts, which then automatically retweeted the message.[97] The intended result of this effort was to flood the social media platform with a perception that a groundswell of support was building for the firing of the U.S. national security advisor, a former U.S. Army general who was (and remains) highly respected by both Republicans and Democrats.

Engagement deception and manipulation strategies can also utilize the hashtag, a word or phrase preceded by a hash sign (#) used on social media websites and applications (especially Twitter) to identify messages on a specific topic.[98] Using hashtags in messages allows others to access (and contribute to) a discussion addressing a common topic. Internet trolls often use multiple popular hashtags in their tweets in order to attract more visibility. For example, during the 2019 Congressional presidential impeachment hearings, the hashtag #DemocratsAreDestroyingAmerica[99] became one of the top ten hashtags used on Twitter. By adding a hashtag to a flurry of messages, typically using thousands of automated bot accounts, a troll can create the illusion of widespread support for (or against) an idea; often this tactic is used in attempts to manipulate the "what's trending" list on Twitter.

Similarly, hashtag flooding involves a coordinated effort to counter a trending hashtag with negative posts, and sometimes disinformation as well. Here, a group of accounts (humans or, more likely, bots) will incorporate a barrage of messages containing the trending hashtag along with demeaning and derogatory information, the purpose being to grab control of the narrative and manipulate perceptions in a different direction.[100] Alice Marwick and Rebecca Lewis describe this as an attempt to "hijack" the hashtag, like (for example) when right-wing extremists coordinated a huge collection of fake accounts for posting messages critical of #BlackLivesMatter, in order to diminish the ability of BLM supporters to use this hashtag to find and support each other.[101] Finally, hashtag manipulation is an effective way to grab the attention of journalists, who then publish stories about the narrative or the controversy surrounding it, and in doing so they help the digital influence mercenary achieve a central goal of promoting engagement.

Media Amplification

Attracting media coverage is another primary goal of provocation tactics used by digital influence mercenaries. Researchers Marwick and Lewis call this "attention hacking," defined as the strategic use of memes and amplifier accounts targeting journalists, bloggers, and others in order to spread messages on social media.[102] Further, they note, "for manipulators, it doesn't matter if the media is reporting on a story in order to debunk or dismiss it; the important thing is getting it covered in the first place."[103] One example of this was seen in November 2015, when Andrew Anglin (founder and editor of the right-wing outlet The Daily Stormer) directed his followers to set up fake White Student Union pages on Facebook for universities throughout the United States—and then contact local media outlets about the groups. If his goal was to provoke the media into expressing moral outrage, and simultaneously spread some racial tension throughout college campuses, he was highly successful. Local media outlets promptly reported on these Facebook pages (although some did note it was unclear whether the groups existed outside of Facebook). *USA Today* picked up the story and covered it nationwide, followed by coverage in *Gawker*, the *Daily Beast*, and the *Washington Post*—even after the whole thing was exposed online as a hoax engineered by Anglin. By then, the tactic had already worked—the media had greatly amplified his underlying message that there are legions of white people on university campuses with racial grievances, and they are seeking opportunities to unite their efforts.[104]

As veteran journalist Bruce Bartlett notes, "There are always news outlets willing to publish first and ask questions later. Sadly, this has led to a race to the bottom, in which disreputable news outlets get the clicks and make the money, while those that are responsible and perform due diligence lose out."[105] While most responsible journalists do not want to amplify disinformation like this, potentially lending credence to false narratives, they often fear missing out on an important opportunity.[106] As disinformation researcher Claire Wardle notes, "The news industry is incredibly vulnerable. There are thousands of journalists globally, many of them independently monitoring and posting on social networks every day. Convince one journalist to publish the falsehood or fabricated content, and it gets pushed almost immediately across the wider community (many newsrooms do not check reporting by other journalists or outlets with the same rigor, assuming that thorough vetting has already been completed)."[107]

Unfortunately, when mainstream media outlets amplify harmful or false information they encounter on social media, it has many impacts that benefit the digital influence mercenary, at the target's expense. For example, as Whitney Phillips notes, it makes particular stories, communities, and bad actors more visible and more influential than they would have been otherwise, and it increases the likelihood that similar disinformation and harassment tactics will be used in the future.[108] Further, even when a newsroom publishes information intended to debunk or expose falsehoods, this still benefits the digital influence mercenary by drawing attention to the original information.[109] And yet, at the same time these media outlets are also attempting to drive traffic and social engagement, which often takes priority over fact-checking to determine whether something might be disinformation.[110] As Wardle notes, "This is all happening just as newsrooms are being stripped of resources, but competition for clicks is fiercer than ever. And when many journalists haven't received the necessary training in the forensic analysis of digital sources or content, it's easier than ever to be fooled."[111]

Another way to manipulate the media into amplifying disinformation involves providing so-called "leaked documents" to journalists, in an effort to embarrass a target or undermine someone's credibility. Many news outlets have shown a preference for "leaks" (which they view as information that someone wanted to be kept secret) over press releases (which are obviously forms of information that someone wants to be made public). But real problems arise when this kind of information (or disinformation) is used to manipulate perceptions. Consider the following example:[112] on Monday, information about a government agency is "leaked" to a journalist that isn't based on any factual evidence, but it gets published (perhaps along with hedging terms like "alleged" and "reportedly," just in case it turns out to be false information). By Wednesday or Thursday, the agency in question has issued a stern denial, but by then the information has already enjoyed forty-eight hours of news cycles along with a barrage of retweets and shares on social media. As we'll discuss in later chapters, psychologists have demonstrated how difficult it can be to convince someone they have been lied to. So, regardless of the official denials, some people will still believe the information was accurate, while others won't even hear the denials anyhow. As Bruce Bartlett explains, "In the end, you have manipulated an untold number of people rather simply, exploiting the reporter's thirst for exclusive 'news' that attracts [the] attention of viewers and readers."[113]

And of course, an efficient way for digital influence mercenaries to manipulate media coverage involves simply purchasing a stake in their operations. For example, Yevgeny Prigozhin—the Russian businessman with close ties to Vladimir Putin described in chapter 1—secretly invested in a long-standing TV channel in Libya, which then began broadcasting stories with an editorial slant favorable to Russia.[114] According to the Stanford Internet Observatory, "Investigative reports have also shown Prigozhin is linked to efforts in other countries to either take over existing media outlets or . . . [launch] new ones."[115] Similarly, as Emerson Brooking and Suzanne Kianpour revealed, the Iranian government uses "independent" news outlets "to launder Iranian state media through seemingly unconnected sources."[116]

To sum up, there are multiple avenues through which digital influence mercenaries can deceive, provoke, and manipulate the perceptions of their targets. When mainstream media amplify these efforts, it proves beneficial for both the client services model and the advertising revenue generation model (described in chapter 1). And as we'll examine in later chapters, the segmented and polarized landscape of media outlets today—combined with the emergence of digital echo chambers—enables an immensely powerful (and profitable) means of influencing targets.

Targeted Attacks

Finally, digital influence mercenaries may also be contracted to attack a target directly, using what Dorothy Denning calls "virtual blockades, automated email bombs, webhacks, computer break-ins, and computer viruses and worms" against a target.[117] One well-known type of attack involves hacking a website and then changing the information it provides. For example, in October 2019 one of Norway's best-selling newspapers was forced to take its website offline after attackers inserted false stories and quotes, including a pro-pedophilia comment attributed to Norway's prime minister, Erna Solberg.[118] Similarly, in January 2020 a group calling itself "Iran Cyber Security Group Hackers" altered the website of the U.S. Federal Depository Library Program to show messages vowing revenge for the death of former Iranian military leader Qassim Suleimani (who was killed in an American drone strike), accompanied by a doctored photograph of President Trump being punched in the jaw, superimposed over a map of the Middle East.[119] And in September 2019, Chinese authorities openly instructed and encouraged independent hackers to deface websites and attack Telegram accounts of political protestors in Hong Kong.[120] In their report *Tweeting through the Great Firewall*, the Australian Strategic Policy Institute describes how Chinese-language accounts, "leveraging an influence-for-hire network," were used to target Hong Kong citizens and the global Chinese diaspora in a massive effort to discredit the pro-democracy protests.[121]

The tools of direct online attacks seem to be most frequently used for the harassment and abuse of journalists, academics, scientists, opposition politicians, activists, and celebrities. But ordinary people have also been the victims of online harassment and cyberbullying.[122] In one case, a woman in a Seattle suburb suffered a variety of attacks over several months.[123] Images and videos were posted to a fake Facebook page, and she received a barrage of phone calls and email messages. Even her mother and coworkers received calls. Police were sent to her home numerous times after receiving "tips" about nonexistent child abuse. At least fifteen of her neighbors received a "community alert" in the mail warning them that they were living near a dangerous abuser. She and her husband eventually won a lawsuit against her cyberattacker, and yet the abusive emails continued.

Other direct attacks used in digital influence efforts may involve hacking into servers and accounts in order to steal compromising information or gain access to key networks, and then expose a target's secrets, leaking documents and images that were not meant for public consumption. As noted earlier, an influence mercenary can capture attention when they "leak" official-looking documents, or "secretly recorded" audio or video, because it adds perceived value to the material. And a similar type of cyberattack is called doxing (or doxxing), defined by Claire Wardle as "the act of publishing private or identifying information about an individual online, without his or her permission, information that can include full names, addresses, phone numbers, photos, and more."[124] An example of this was seen in 2019 when the website "HK Leaks" (hosted on Russian servers) posted personal details—names, home addresses, personal telephone numbers—of hundreds of Hong Kong pro-democracy protestors.[125]

Unfortunately, the ability to mask your identity online has prompted a toxic lack of accountability and enabled a proliferation of cyberbullies, harassers, and trolls.[126] Individuals feel emboldened to say and do things online that they would never say or do in the physical world. Researchers have described several dimensions of this so-called "online disinhibition," including the ability to manufacture an online "presence" that is separate from reality—like being able to schedule messages to be sent at a time that we're not actually online, or using different accounts under fake identities. Individuals may consider themselves "invisible" when online, scrolling through websites and social media feeds without overtly revealing the fact to others that they are online. Another dimension is treating our online activity as a game or fantasy ("it's just online, it's not the real world, so whatever I do here doesn't really matter").[127] Similarly, many people believe that different rules and laws apply when they're online. There is no central control, no overarching authority policing your behavior or the things you say. My ideas, beliefs, and opinions are just as valuable as those of any other user (or at least that's what certain individuals may tell themselves when firing off a barrage of angry tweets early in the morning).[128]

Some attacks may involve shutting down a target's web server or email service using tools that are widely available today, particularly via the Dark Web. The "denial-of-service" (DoS) attack, and the related "distributed denial-of-service" (DDoS) attack, both use similar methods to overload a server's capacity, causing it to malfunction. Sometimes the purpose of a cyberattack may be to intimidate or frustrate the target, or to provoke an individual into saying or behaving in some kind of self-sabotaging way—for example, continually prodding them until they lose their cool and irrationally lash out at others, showcasing their temper in front of all who might be watching. Or the mercenary can use the tools of deception to trick the target into saying controversial or embarrassing things on an audio or video recording that undermines their own credibility. There have also been efforts to try and mute opposing messages and accounts. As Samantha Bradshaw and Philip N. Howard describe, one social media takedown strategy involves "mustering an array of human and automated accounts to falsely mass-report legitimate content or users in an attempt to have the social media platform to suspend the accounts of those with whom they disagree. Even a temporary suspension of an account could affect the spread of information promoted by that opposing viewpoint," thus tipping the digital influence scales in favor of the attacker.[129] The overall goal here would be to drown out or silence the opinions of the target. As a 2018 NATO report observed, "It is difficult to mount a successful DDoS attack on Facebook or Google because of the sheer volume of ordinary traffic. . . . [However,] this new form of directed attack achieves much the same purpose as traditional DDoS attacks once did."[130] This tactic, sometimes called a "coordinated DDoS attack," will no doubt be a prominent feature of digital influence warfare efforts in the future.

Finally, as you might imagine, there is a large and likely growing hackers-for-hire industry, as exemplified by the uncovering of the "Dark Basin" network in June 2020. According to a report published by Citizen Lab (part of the University of Toronto's Munk School), 28,000 webpages were created by the hackers for personalized "spear phishing" attacks designed to steal passwords, and the network targeted thousands of individuals and hundreds of institutions around the world, including advocacy groups, journalists, elected officials, lawyers, hedge funds, and companies.[131] Several of the firms described in chapter 1 have their own in-house teams of competent computer hackers, or they can subcontract freelance hackers when needed to support their digital influence efforts.

Conclusion

To wrap up this brief exploration of methods and tactics employed by digital influence mercenaries, it should be noted that this is only a representative sampling—to cover the entire spectrum of such things would require a book several times larger than this. But by addressing the basic themes of deception (e.g., false identities, information sources, engagement indicators, etc.), provocation, and target manipulation, my hope is that readers will be inspired to explore this terrain further, as more books and reports are being published on these topics each year.

Unfortunately, we now inhabit an information ecosystem in which digital influence mercenaries can exploit any of us. Both the client services and the online advertising profit models described in the previous chapter are highly dependent on the quality of information available about the intended target. This is where the social media environment has proven especially unique compared to earlier forms of influence efforts. Our daily online activity generates a tremendous amount of data that can be recorded, analyzed, and then used to influence us. From Facebook profiles and comments to the photos and videos we post online, all of our online activities leave digital trails that reveal much about us. Underground forums provide an astonishing array of service offers including clickbait headlines, coordinated social media engagement (with both humans and bots) to amplify influence efforts, original content creation (including deepfake videos), and much more. Digital influence firms and freelancers can also be paid to attack websites or accounts, delete content, silence dissenters, or increase the approval ratings of a product or service on a shopping website.[132] They can also utilize profit-driven mainstream media outlets as a means of amplifying disinformation, and of course the engagement algorithms of the social media platforms provide other avenues for generating revenue.

But amid all these technical capabilities, it is important to recognize that the real success of these efforts involves exploiting a broad range of emotional and psychological vulnerabilities, as we will examine in the next several chapters of this book. First, in chapter 3, we'll explore the central role of uncertainty—a powerful force in cognitive and emotional reasoning that can be manipulated in order to undermine scientific facts. Efforts to intentionally create uncertainty (like the "tobacco strategy" of the 1960s) have contributed to the age of "post-truth,"[133] in which corporate and political leaders can spread lies and fabricate "alternate facts" with impunity. Then chapter 4 will discuss why "alternate facts" and conspiracy theories appeal to so many people as a means for reducing their uncertainty. In chapter 5, we'll explore how cognitive biases (particularly confirmation bias) shape our willingness to embrace disinformation. Chapter 6 will describe how group identities and conformity can amplify uncertainty, fear, conspiracy theories, and confirmation bias. And chapter 7 delves into the research on how digital echo chambers and filter bubbles impact an individual's information processing choices.

Together, these psychological, emotional and social dimensions create myriad opportunities for digital influence mercenaries to deceive, provoke, and manipulate the perceptions of targets like you and me. This underscores why confronting digital influence efforts in the future will require much more than a technical response by social media platforms and government agencies. As we'll discuss in the concluding chapter, a wholesale shift in society is needed, not only in terms of widespread media literacy and education, but also in reevaluating our own responsibilities as participants in the spread of online disinformation.

3

FEAR AND UNCERTAINTY

The next several chapters of this book will explore how digital influence mercenaries exploit a range of emotional, psychological, and behavioral attributes of their targets. In most cases, the influence efforts described in the previous chapter are considered successful when the targets do something that benefits their (or their clients') goals, like click, vote, buy, forward, like, share, comment, protest, and so forth. A wide variety of strategies and tactics can be used to try and provoke the target to do these kinds of things, but beyond the technological dimensions it is important to recognize the underlying human traits that prime targets to react in these ways.

We'll begin in this chapter by looking at the central role that uncertainty and fear play in a person's susceptibility to influence efforts, as well as why increasing uncertainty can be a beneficial strategy for digital influence mercenaries, and some tactics they use to do this. Then we'll proceed in the following chapter with a discussion on why falsehoods and conspiracy theories appear attractive to those seeking to remedy their feelings of uncertainty. Strategies that increase uncertainty provide particular advantages to the deceiver, because the target begins to consider that disinformation could be true, and this primes a target's receptivity to conspiracy theories and outright falsehoods. Later chapters will examine why too much certainty is just as harmful as too much uncertainty, particularly when overconfidence and cognitive biases lead a target to instinctively defend that which is patently untrue. Essentially, weak convictions can be called into question, manipulated, and altered, while strong convictions can be strengthened despite evidence that contradicts those convictions. So, examining these human traits provides insights into how and why digital influence mercenaries can succeed in provoking emotional and behavioral responses from the target that will achieve their strategic objectives.

Trust, Uncertainty, and Fear

Being uncertain about something implies some amount of risk is possible, and we are surrounded by uncertainty every day. Beyond philosophizing about the existential nature of uncertainty and mortality, just a few moments of self-reflection on the ordinary things we have thought about or done just this week will reveal a wide variety of decisions we have made punctuated by uncertainty. Throughout our lives, we are plagued by millions of questions, and at some stage in life (usually as a child, but not always), a rational human being learns that the future is unknowable, and no matter what we do today, there can never be absolute certainty about what will happen tomorrow. In the United States, a common anecdote is that the only things we can all be truly certain about are death and taxes. Through our experiences we learn about cause and effect, yet we also learn about the many exceptions that question the certainty of a causal relationship. And we also learn that some things are simply uncontrollable—the daily weather, for example, or natural disasters like earthquakes and hurricanes. Being confronted with the reality of what we cannot control, or what we can't be certain about, is often a humbling and inherently uncomfortable part of life.

Our uncertainty can also increase and decrease periodically. Researchers have found that some of the most impactful sources of uncertainty include changes to the status quo, such as the loss of a job or economic security, the loss of a loved one, the onset of a significant illness, and relocation (especially if involuntary, e.g., refugees fleeing a conflict in their home country). Other important sources of uncertainty include rapidly changing demographics (e.g., a huge influx of immigrants), sudden changes in policies and laws, and of course dramatic events like war, insurgency, and terrorism. A recent example is how the COVID-19 pandemic of 2020 generated massive uncertainty and insecurity for many people around the world. Not only did the crisis result in widespread loss of life, but it also had a dramatic impact on our social and family lives, and caused millions of people to lose their jobs or close their small businesses, creating another major source of uncertainty.

Further, the widespread anxiety provoked by this event was often made much worse by a central question about what information should be believed, which in turn led some people toward extreme and sometimes violent behavior. While many online sources of information were providing true scientific facts about the disease, others were providing politically or ideologically infused narratives that were not based at all on factual evidence. A worldwide health issue became an intensely political, polarized issue. Individuals of one political orientation took overt and very public safety precautions (like wearing a mask and avoiding crowds), as advised by public health officials. Meanwhile, their political opponents refused to adopt those safety measures, gathered in (sometimes armed) protests, and threatened health workers, government officials, law enforcement, and even ordinary citizens who had decided to follow those safety measures. By late 2020, the disease was hitting hardest the populations of states that had earlier refused to impose the kinds of public safety precautions that had been advised by the scientific community.

The uncertainty, fear, and insecurity witnessed in this instance can be linked to a much broader struggle over trust and scientific facts that has been ongoing for well over a half century. One dimension of this war was launched by the tobacco industry, seeking to undermine the acceptance of scientific evidence linking cigarette smoking with various illnesses. We'll examine those strategies to increase uncertainty—and their impacts—in considerable detail later in this chapter. But as Michiko Kakutani describes in her book *The Death of Truth*, left-leaning academics in the humanities departments of universities launched another dimension of this war in the 1960s, when they began viewing science as "the province of a hawkish, pro-business, right-wing power structure . . . that cared little for the spiritual or holistic wellness of our souls, our bodies, or our Mother Earth."[1] This in turn led to the rise of what became known as "postmodernism." As Lee McIntyre explains, postmodernists argue that "everything" could be interpreted as a "text" that was open to multiple interpretations, indicating that there may never be a right or wrong answer to any question, nor is there any kind of unchallengeable truth: "The postmodernist approach is one in which everything is questioned and little is taken at face value. There is no right answer, only narrative."[2]

For centuries, scientific research has established various facts and truths that enlighten and empower people. For example, we know with certainty that if we stand in a field and throw a rock up in the air, it will always come back down. It is also a scientific fact that neither you nor I can hold our breath underwater for ten minutes. This is not a narrative. If you don't believe this is a scientific fact, go ahead and give it a try. Let us know how it turns out for you. Many scientific facts—like the importance of air and drinkable water for our survival—are accepted to such a degree that we often take them for granted. Everybody knows them, period. And then there are many things that we believe with high levels of probability, which we use as a substitute for certainty. For example, we believe that there will be a tomorrow, and that we will be alive to see it. Without such basic beliefs, many people wouldn't be able to function.

Our systems of education and scientific research teach us that truth comes from facts that lead to coherent theories. But truths can be challenged by further research and evidence—for example, centuries ago it was considered common knowledge that the world was flat, and positioned at the center of the universe, with a benevolent sun circling us. Scientists like Copernicus and Galileo were skeptical, and through their efforts our understanding of truth evolved. Similarly, for hundreds of years the medical community (such as it was back then) did not know or understand about germs, or the benefits of sanitizing hands and instruments before and after performing surgery. As a consequence, many people unnecessarily died in hospitals and clinics from infections. But then during the nineteenth century, new scientific facts were produced through research and experiments, resulting in a much-improved likelihood today that you or I will avoid a life-threatening infection at our local hospital.

As former CIA director Michael Hayden observed, "A healthy skepticism teaches that theories (i.e., current truths) are only temporary tolls, subject to inquiry and observation, but this is the only path to knowledge, which is—in the Nobel tradition—the only course to betterment."[3] However, postmodernists argued that since there is no such thing as objective "truth," anyone claiming to "know" something to be true is really just expressing a political ideology and trying to oppress us. In their view, "having power allows us to control what is true, not the other way around. If there are many perspectives, then insisting that we accept any particular one is a form of fascism."[4]

This postmodernist discourse eventually contributed to what Tom Nichols describes as a willful hostility toward established knowledge on both the left and right wings of the American political spectrum, with people aggressively arguing that "every opinion on any matter is as good as every other."[5] In his book *The*

Death of Expertise, Nichols explains how debates over what constitutes "knowledge" have led American society to abandon previously accepted notions of expertise. Now everyone believes they are experts because they saw something on the Internet. Colleges and universities have become viewed as businesses that only serve a credentialing function. No longer needed as producers or conveyers of knowledge, they provide athletic entertainment, and comfortable "safe spaces" to exchange opinions, and then bestow degrees upon graduates who haven't really earned them but feel entitled to receive them nonetheless.[6]

Further, the decline in deference to experts that Nichols describes appears to be just one symptom of a much larger phenomenon. Rohit Bhargava, who teaches economics at Georgetown University, has described a "modern believability crisis" in which a trust gap is expanding "between people and the organizations that they interact with."[7] According to annual surveys conducted by several organizations, trust in businesses and the financial sector, politicians, and the legal profession is particularly low among a majority of Americans. Distrust is even a global problem—for example, according to a 2011 *Reader's Digest* survey of 33,000 people across sixteen European countries, three out of four people did not trust their government, and in Romania trust was as low as 6 percent.[8] No doubt some of the decline in trust toward governmental and societal institutions in the United States is a direct result of events over the past few decades—including the housing mortgage crisis and the huge bailout package for major banks, scandals in the White House and Congress, and a significant number of convicted felons being exonerated by DNA evidence. And recently, confidence in American police forces has been damaged by a number of events and videos depicting overt brutality (particularly against minorities).

Similarly, as Marwick and Lewis recently noted, trust in the mainstream media is also at an all-time low. A Gallup poll released in September 2016 found that Americans' trust in the mass media "to report the news fully, accurately, and fairly" was (at 32 percent) the lowest in the organization's polling history.[9] Another report, published by *Data & Society*, found that most teens surveyed expressed distrust of the news and assumed much of it was biased.[10] And yet, perhaps ironically, the decline in trust toward the media has occurred alongside the rapid expansion of new (and often politically oriented) media outlets and the emergence of twenty-four-hour news cycles. Some media outlets provide a constant stream of "breaking news" and developing stories, frequently dramatic and repetitive, while others broadcast blatant falsehoods and opinions thinly veiled as "news" that their audience responds to favorably. This proliferation of media has perhaps reached a point of oversaturation, overwhelming a society that is already struggling to separate fact from fiction. Information overwhelm is exacerbating the trust gap indicated in public surveys. As Bhargava explains, most consumers are bombarded with so many messages each day, "we are all conditioned to automatically distrust everything as a defense mechanism."[11]

Distrust and uncertainty make it possible for people to embrace a wide range of disinformation and conspiracy theories. A half century ago, publishing disinformation became a lucrative business model, as illustrated by popular magazines displayed in racks at your local grocery store checkout counter that contained predictions by psychics, salacious (but unfounded) rumors about celebrities, conspiracy theories, fake exposés, and much more. Fake photos and deception became commonplace in these rags, and some publishers were sued for libel or defamation by the victims of their so-called reporting. But then along came the Internet, arguably the largest source of disinformation, information overload, and uncertainty humankind has ever experienced. Today there is no need to purchase a gossip magazine when you can surf the Web for hours on end and read all kinds of gossip about virtually anyone of interest. Further, you can even post your own gossip to various blogs and websites, or via your own social media accounts.

Naturally, just like those trashy magazines, what you say online does not have to be true to be believed. Soon, websites full of conspiracy theories and disinformation ("The Holocaust never happened!" "The 9/11 terrorist attacks were an inside job!") began proliferating worldwide, in multiple languages. Thus, the globally interconnected information ecosystem increased our exposure to increasing amounts of complicated (and often conflicting) information, creating higher levels of uncertainty, anxiety, and fear. And as we all know, fear leads to hate, and hate leads to the dark side of the force. The changes in the media landscape combined with the Internet have led to what Jennifer Kavanagh and Michael Rich describe as an erosion of trust in and reliance on objective facts in political debate and civil discourse about public policy. Further, "a sharp rise in political partisanship and polarization" has been nurtured by "a seeming explosion of misinformation and disinformation . . . [that] proliferates through conventional and social media channels."[12] Many observers today agree that what Michiko Kakutani saliently calls "the death of truth" has terrible consequences for our future.[13]

A similar tone is set by a recent RAND Corporation report that defines "truth decay" as a set of four related trends: (1) increasing disagreement about facts and analytical interpretations of facts and data (e.g., efforts to fabricate debate about the effects of tobacco, acid rain, climate change, vaccines, and other topics that we'll examine later in this chapter); (2) a blurring of the line between opinion and fact; (3) the increasing relative volume, and resulting influence, of opinion and personal experience over fact (e.g., speculation, opinion, and falsehoods disseminated in traditional media along with social media channels that drown out verifiable data); and (4) declining trust in formerly respected sources of factual information.[14] These trends have produced a "growing imbalance in political and civil discourse between, on the one hand, trust and reliance on facts and analytical interpretations of facts and data and, on the other, opinions and personal attitudes—a balance that seems to be increasingly shifting in favor of the latter."[15] And when opinions and attitudes carry more weight than facts and data, this creates a wealth of opportunities for digital influence mercenaries to exploit.

Uncertainty as an Exploitable Vulnerability

As former vice president Al Gore notes in his book *The Assault on Reason*, the culmination of the contexts and trends described above is an ill-informed electorate, campaigns dominated by money, media manipulation, and "the persistent and sustained reliance on falsehoods as the basis of policy, even in the face of massive and well-understood evidence to the contrary."[16] Similarly, as Jennifer Kavanagh and Michael Rich explain, a "gap between the challenges of the information system and the training provided to students drives and perpetuates truth decay by contributing to the creation of an electorate that is susceptible to consuming and disseminating disinformation, misinformation, and information that blur the line between fact and opinion. In this context, truth decay flourishes."[17]

Certainly there are many reasons why it seems to be increasingly difficult for us to effectively manage uncertainty in the modern information era. And yet, how we respond to uncertainty is really what makes us vulnerable to influence. In fact, our happiness (and sometimes even our very survival) often depends on our ability to process information quickly while navigating various kinds of uncertainty. We are natural seekers of information—it is our universal strategy for managing and trying to reduce uncertainty—and digital influence mercenaries can take advantage of our information-seeking efforts. We seek information that will help us make decisions about whom to vote for in an election, where to eat, what to order on the menu once we get there, what movie to watch, which route will be the fastest way to our destination, what clothes we look the best in, which car, computer or smartphone to buy, and so forth. We seek information about laws and policies on issues that we care about: for some, this could be zoning requirements to meet before establishing a day care center, while others may want information about tax relief policies related to conservation land.

Uncertainty creates questions, and we want answers to those questions. We often look for information to help us reduce our uncertainty about possibly making a bad decision. But we also respond to uncertainty about the future with speculation, and perhaps some measure of hope. Many of us are deficient in probabilistic reasoning, while overly optimistic, which is why national lottery tickets are such a hot selling item, especially when the jackpot amount climbs into the range of hundreds of millions of dollars. As Aubrey De Grey notes, "We respond to inherent uncertainty with varying mixtures of faith and scientific fact." And yet, "both are increasingly called into question, leaving us in a very uncomfortable place," shaky ground upon which our feelings of insecurity about what we know, and who we are, become inevitable.[18]

While we seek to orient ourselves to our physical environment, we also have a deep need to orient ourselves to the ever-expanding information landscape. The Internet provides an array of tools we can use to search for an understanding of what matters most to us on a given day: who is this, what is that, where is this, and so forth. In turn, our daily searches for information—both online and in the physical world—meet a fundamental objective in our lives: managing uncertainty. Some information sources have carved out a reputation as credible and useful for helping us make decisions about our purchases. For example, *Consumer Reports* is a particularly popular source of information that tests products and ranks them according to various scales of quality and reliability. To reduce our uncertainty about which product to buy, many of us will consult such a resource. The myriad "customer reviews" on Amazon, TripAdvisor, and other websites have also become a popular go-to source of information for the same reason. However, as described in chapter 2, online resources like those can be manipulated, even converted into forms of disinformation, all too easily. People who have never purchased a certain product or service can still provide a review about it on many websites, influencing your perceptions with false information. Some companies may even pay individuals just to post favorable reviews about them on different websites, in order to manufacture the illusion of high customer satisfaction, as described in chapter 1.

And yet, while we seek information in our quest to manage uncertainty, knowledge itself can also increase our uncertainty—as suggested by the well-known adage "the more we learn, the more we realize we do not know."[19] So, in order to navigate an excruciatingly complex and uncertain world, we typically impose a kind of order and regularity, what some researchers refer to as our "assumptive world." As psychologist Denise Winn explains, "From personal experiences, everyone learns to make a set of assumptions that enable him or her to predict how others will behave or what to expect from their environment. At the most basic level, we all start from the assumption that there will be a tomorrow, that we will wake up from sleep to a new day, and plan our lives accordingly. It is a practical and necessary assumption."[20] The assumptions we make, combined with the questions we seek to answer, impact the kinds of information sources we tend to rely upon. When an influencer understands the assumptions and beliefs held by the target, they can craft messages that are more likely to effectively influence the target.

To alleviate the discomfort of uncertainty, we naturally seek various forms of certainty in our lives, and when external sources of information offer some support for what we already believe (or want to believe), that form of comforting certainty can be quite welcome indeed. We often rely on our preferences—the way we want things to be—and look for information that can confirm those preferences, even in the face of factual evidence that contradicts those information sources. Essentially, as we'll examine more fully in later chapters, we may actively seek out sources of disinformation, just as long as those sources provide a comforting level of certainty about what we want to believe is real. Further, a common response to uncertainty is to retreat into the solace of what we believe we know, and when people have surrounded themselves with information sources that reinforce that self-perception, they find comfort. And we now have the ability to wrap ourselves within the cocoon of an echo chamber, virtually assuring that the only information we receive is that which reinforces our certainty about what we want to believe. But first, in this chapter we'll focus our attention on influence strategies used to manipulate our uncertainty.

To sum up, research shows how uncertainty is a powerful force that leads people to behave in a variety of ways. It is an inherent and inescapable reality in our lives, but it can be radically uneven in how it is perceived, how it is understood, and how each of us responds to it.[21] Our uncertainty generally makes us uncomfortable, and as a result we seek ways to remedy it. The more uncertain someone is about something they feel is relevant, the more they will turn to information sources like the news media, or increasingly, social media. This, in turn, provides numerous opportunities for the influence campaign to shape your perceptions through disinformation, provocation, and other tactics described in previous chapters of this book.

At the risk of oversimplifying a complicated topic, the remainder of this chapter will describe strategies for increasing uncertainty and anxiety, while chapter 4 will discuss influence efforts meant to provide remedies for the discomfort of uncertainty. Some digital influence efforts may seek to increase our uncertainty and decrease our trust in what we think we know, while other efforts seek to do the reverse—decrease our uncertainty by convincing us to trust whatever the influencer wants us to believe, even if it's a baseless conspiracy theory. Then chapters 5 through 7 will examine the other side of the rhetorical coin, where overconfidence, confirmation bias, collective identity, and echo chambers create opportunities for digital influence mercenaries to capitalize on a manufactured sense of certainty, even in the face of contradictory evidence.

Influence Strategies That Manufacture and Enhance Uncertainty

According to Facebook's Nathan Gleicher, "Information operations are fundamentally about weaponizing uncertainty; they're not about achieving a measurable, clear goal so much as they are about increasing distrust."[22] Today's digital influence efforts purposefully try to elevate uncertainty about a range of topics, because the more we begin to question ourselves and our beliefs, the more likely we are to accept so-called "alternate facts," conspiracies, and outright falsehoods. According to Alex Romero, "Disinformation works effectively in vulnerable contexts, and if individuals lose trust in content on the Internet then one of the key goals of disinformation warfare has been achieved."[23] Further, we must keep in mind that trust is much easier to destroy than to build. So, a digital influence strategic goal is to diminish the target's trust in what they think they know, as well as the sources of that knowledge.

Manipulation of uncertainty has been a cornerstone of interrogations and brainwashing, while defense lawyers and prosecutors do their own kind of doubt-raising all the time in order to manipulate the perceptions of juries. Similarly, by raising the level of uncertainty, influencers can sow confusion, provoke anger and outrage, create disunity in a society, and distract people from what they don't want them to see. As Richard Stengel noted in his recent book *Information Wars*, "You succeed if you simply muddy the waters. It's far easier to create confusion than clarity."[24] The strategy involves raising the level of doubt about the target's beliefs, because making them uncertain about what they know is an important preliminary step toward making them more receptive to subsequent persuasion. According to Charlie Sykes, "The essence of propaganda is . . . to overwhelm your critical sensibilities. It's to make you doubt the existence of a knowable truth."[25]

There is also a powerful emotional component to this. Uncertainty can lead to insecurity, which can lead to suspicion and fear. So, increasing confusion and uncertainty can amplify fear and anxiety, powerful feelings that can stimulate emotional arousal in the target. Further, as a *New York Times* editorial once noted, "A simple truth of human existence is that it is vastly easier to amplify fear than to assuage it."[26] This is especially the case when the uncertainty pertains to something that the target is already anxious about (e.g., economic changes, crime, security, etc.). This is why politicians who amplify and play on our worst fears get our attention, much the same as horror films tend to do fairly well at the box office. Research in the field of psychology has found a positive relationship between the intensity of fear arousal and the amount of influence the source of that arousal will have.[27] Thus it makes sense that the psychology of fear plays a central role in effective digital influence campaigns.

In fact, this is one way in which Russia's attempts to interfere in recent U.S. elections have paid such dividends. In late 2019, the United States announced a new process for notifying the public about foreign election interference.[28] But the very fact that this is deemed necessary can itself raise uncertainty and fear about the integrity of election processes in the United States. Even if Russia fails to do anything significant in future elections, the perceived threat that they *could* or *might* (and further, that we might not even know until it's too late) gives Russia's disinformation warfare strategy a clear win. Similarly, Russia can take advantage of mass voter fraud conspiracies, encouraging voters to believe in possible irregularities where none exist in order to undermine confidence in democratic elections.

The digital influence mercenaries employed by Russia (like the IRA, described in chapter 1) sought to increase uncertainty in order to prime their targets for influence and persuasion. Among the tactics they pursued for this purpose, gaslighting (described below) is perhaps the most well known. Similarly, the motto of the Russian-based media outlet RT (described in chapter 1) is literally "Question More," which—as explained by Matt Armstrong, a former member of the U.S. Broadcasting Board of Governors—"is not about finding answers, but fomenting confusion, chaos, and distrust. They spin up their audience to chase myths, believe in fantasies, listen to faux... 'experts' until the audience simply tunes out."[29] Essentially, tactics for increasing uncertainty are used to attack the very notion that an objective truth exists. And when effective, these tactics make the target susceptible to a range of other influences and narratives.

GASLIGHTING AND SALAMI SLICING

The most common description of gaslighting involves an influencer trying to deceive the target into believing things that aren't true, while also showing concern about the fact that others are questioning or attacking the target because of those false beliefs. The perpetrator orchestrates deceptions and inaccurately narrates events to the extent that their victim stops trusting their own judgments and perceptions.[30] The term derives from the 1938 play (and subsequent film in 1944) *Gas Light*, featuring a woman whose husband slowly manipulates her into believing that she is going insane. He secretly orchestrates a variety of mysterious experiences (including remotely raising and lowering the lights), and then eventually convinces her to voluntarily check into an asylum.

Gaslighting is one of several digital influence tactics that involve both deception and provocation. It typically often involves a relationship initially based on trust or respect, which devolves into a series of increasingly damaging exchanges between deceiver and victim. The deceiver will typically try to convince the victim that everyone else is lying to them, and cause them to question their own beliefs or decisions. Meanwhile, the deceiver is also repeatedly lying to the victim and will criticize the victim for raising any questions about those lies, using derogatory terms like "hysterical" or "insane" (gaslighters are often patronizing and downright ruthless). Then they may suddenly switch from criticizing the victim to supporting and praising the victim, in order to provoke confusion and uncertainty about what the victim should believe. The deceiver may say something or promise to do something, and then later deny they ever said that or made that promise. In addition to arousing powerful emotions of confusion, fear, and distress, another goal of gaslighting could be to provoke anger at those who (according to the influencer) have deceived the victim.

The most effective gaslighting is done slowly over an extended period of time. According to Robert Walker, this will "keep the victims unaware of the process [and] ... convince [them] ... that false information is factual, which then slowly erodes the [victims'] grip on reality and thus builds reliance on the purveyors of the false information."[31] In the end, the influencer wants the victim to distrust their own memory or perceptions, and to doubt their own judgment or understanding of reality, which will then lead them to make a choice or behave in some way that will benefit the deceiver's strategic objectives. Sometimes, individuals engage in trolling or gaslighting solely for their own perverse amusement or thrills, gaining some sort of enjoyment from harassing or bullying specific people, causing grief and stress. Gaslighting is considered a particularly nasty form of aggression and is a common weapon of domestic abusers and narcissistic individuals in positions of power over others. However, an increasingly significant body of research has emerged clearly describing how these efforts are also intended to achieve specific political, social, economic, and psychological goals.

Authoritarian figures (like cult leaders and dictators) use the tactic of gaslighting to raise the target's level of confusion and uncertainty, and then provide the illusion that they have access to privileged information ("what's really going on") due to a position of relative authority. Based on this perceived authority, they can then blatantly lie to their target with impunity. They will lie to their target repeatedly, and then also deny having said anything at all—even when there is clear evidence *that the person did indeed say it*. Eventually, gaslighting will result in the victim questioning his or her own sense of reality. Due to the powerful urge to avoid cognitive dissonance, the victim will simply convince themselves that someone they respect and trust would not behave in any sort of unhinged manner, and thus will turn their focus on internal doubts about whether they misunderstood or heard something incorrectly. It also encourages an increased attention to social proof—looking to others for confirmation of what is true and what is not, as we'll discuss more thoroughly later in chapter 6. However, as chapter 7 will explain, when the only other individuals you turn to for social proof are secluded within the same echo chamber that you have embraced, the result is often a sense of reality that has been skewed, manipulated, and misleading.

Similar to gaslighting is the so-called "salami slice tactic"—comparable to slicing a salami into multiple pieces, this term is used to describe efforts to slowly diminish a person's belief in a perceived reality, a slow reduction in what they were previously convinced they knew: "Wait a moment, wasn't that salami stick larger a moment ago?" The key here is to move slowly and gradually, mostly because moving too quickly would risk being detected and countered. In this context, the influence aggressor is able to advance toward their goal very gradually, one thin slice at a time, in such a manner that no one notices until suddenly they have what they want. This is one of the things they teach you to look out for and avoid in negotiations: by getting you to concede to a minor thing, then another, then another, the other party can dramatically compromise your original position. This strategy is meant to foster a creeping change, small piece by small piece—similar to the urban legend (or yucky metaphor) of boiling a frog, which suggests that the frog would try to escape if you dropped it directly into the boiling water, but if you put the poor creature into room temperature water and then turn the stove on to heat up, the frog would not discover the danger until it's too late.

For both the gaslighting and salami slice tactics, the core objective is to slowly break down the target's sense of reality and eventually replace it with increased self-doubt. These tactics are often used by deceptive authoritarians as a way to divide and conquer, where members of the target population increasingly fight among themselves about perceived reality instead of looking more closely at what the deceiver is really doing. People in a state of heightened uncertainty are easier to influence about a broad range of things. As strategies for increasing uncertainty, a primary objective of both gaslighting and salami tactics is to undermine the target's faith in what kinds of information can or cannot be trusted. This was also the driving rationale behind efforts throughout the last half of the twentieth century to question scientific facts, or even deny the existence of factual evidence supporting an inconvenient truth.

MANUFACTURING UNCERTAINTY BY REPLICATING THE TOBACCO STRATEGY

During the 1960s, a mountain of scientific evidence had emerged that linked smoking with various illnesses, including cancer.[32] The tobacco industry responded with a long-term, well-resourced effort to confuse the public about the dangers of smoking. "Doubt is our product," proclaimed a 1969 memo written by a tobacco industry executive, "since it is the best means of competing with the 'body of fact' that exists in the minds of the general public."[33] Essentially, their strategy involved identifying a handful of seemingly reputable professionals who were willing (and paid handsomely) to refute established science, or argue that more research is needed, and then publish their arguments as broadly as possible.

The tobacco industry was facing quite a challenge during this time period. In 1957, the U.S. Public Health Service had concluded that smoking was "the principal etiological factor in the increased incidence of lung cancer."[34] In 1959, leading researchers had declared in the peer-reviewed scientific literature that the evidence linking cigarettes and cancer was "beyond dispute."[35] That same year, the

American Cancer Society had issued a formal statement declaring that "cigarette smoking is the major causative factor in lung cancer."[36] By 1967, the U.S. surgeon general had reviewed more than two thousand scientific studies that all supported three conclusions: "One, smokers lived sicker and died sooner than their non-smoking counterparts. Two, a substantial portion of these early deaths would not have occurred if these people had never smoked. Three, were it not for smoking, 'practically none' of the early deaths from lung cancer would have occurred. Smoking killed people. It was as simple as that."[37]

As Naomi Oreskes and Erik Conway explain in their groundbreaking book *Merchants of Doubt*, the tobacco industry responded to these reports by spending billions of dollars on fabricating the impression of uncertainty about the scientific evidence that linked smoking and illnesses. Their strategy involved attacking the legitimacy of scientists and institutions behind the research that produced these inconvenient facts. During the 1950s, they created the Tobacco Industry Research Council (TIRC) in order to "cast doubt on scientific consensus that smoking cigarettes causes cancer, to convince the media that there were two sides to the story about the risks of tobacco and that each side should be considered with equal weight."[38] They paid for massive public relations campaigns to shape public opinion, hiring famous athletes and Hollywood celebrities to endorse their message, and sponsoring full-page newspaper ads across the country claiming that "no conclusive link" between cigarettes and cancer had been found.[39] They also funded biased research projects and pro-smoking scientists. When Congress held hearings in 1965 on bills to require health warnings on tobacco packaging and advertisements, the tobacco industry responded with "a parade of dissenting doctors" and a "cancer specialist [who warned] against going off 'half-cocked' in the controversy."[40]

As a RAND Corporation report explains, "The goal was to frame the issue and shape the narrative, controlling how at least a significant minority of the population understood the issue."[41] Even if most people hearing the tobacco industry's counternarrative rejected their argument (or rather, their lie) that the scientific evidence against smoking was inconclusive, some individuals are willing to believe anything. The goal, therefore, in pursuing the strategy of "doubt is our product" was to convince just enough people that there might be something to reconsider, there might be an alternative view of the scientific evidence. Just because something is not true does not mean it can't be believed, as we know.

For nearly fifty years, the tobacco industry sought to have scientists raise questions about whether we could (or should) be certain about the research findings demonstrating the links between smoking and illness. They realized "that you could use *normal* scientific uncertainty to undermine the status of actual scientific knowledge."[42] They consistently repeated the mantra "no proof" for decades, including during the 1990s when attention turned to the impact of secondhand smoke on public health. As Oreskes and Conway explain, this massive industry campaign was designed to confuse the public in order for the industry to "defend itself when the vast majority of independent experts agreed that tobacco was harmful, and their own documents showed that they knew this"[43]—in fact, "it was part of a criminal conspiracy to commit fraud."[44]

In 1998, the tobacco companies closed down these efforts as part of a $200 billion settlement that shielded them from future lawsuits.[45] And in 2006, the tobacco industry was found guilty under the Racketeer Influenced and Corrupt Organizations (RICO) Act, the same laws used to take down mafias and organized crime networks. U.S. district judge Gladys Kessler found that the tobacco industry had "devised and executed a scheme to defraud consumers and potential consumers" about the hazards of cigarettes, hazards that their own internal company documents proved they had known about since the 1950s.[46]

Despite the eventual failure of this strategy for the tobacco industry, it has been adopted by many other science-denial efforts. In fact, manufacturing doubt and uncertainty has been the strategy of choice on several occasions when the factual evidence seems to weigh very heavily toward one conclusion. During the Cold War, scientists showed that a nuclear exchange between the Soviets and Americans would destroy the planet, and therefore a nuclear war could not be won. Nonetheless, some politicians were adamant that the United States could win a nuclear war against the Soviets (and argued that our arsenal of nuclear weapons must be increased), so they enlisted the aid of scientists sympathetic to their political agenda to raise questions and doubts about the certainty of the scientific evidence.[47]

Similarly, many scientific studies during the 1960s and 1970s began to show alarming increases in the acidity of rain and snow, ostensibly linked to industrial chemicals polluting water sources and air quality. Industry leaders responded with the same kind of "manufacturing doubt" strategy, first raising questions about whether acid rain was real, and then raising questions about the nature of its causes and potential impacts. In the 1980s they were aided by conservative politicians in Congress and the White House who favored a pro-business agenda over what they characterized as environmentalist activism.[48] They argued that industrial pollution control measures are costly, and those costs would likely be passed along to consumers. Further, as Oreskes and Conway note, the costs and the economic impacts of pollution mitigation efforts could be calculated—while in contrast, it was impossible to place monetary values on clean air and water, species conservation, beautiful views, pristine land, a clear blue sky.[49] In truth, as a recent U.S. president has illustrated, raising doubts and uncertainty is far easier than actually producing real evidence to support your assertions and claims. Opponents of environmental regulation continued to do so, well beyond the Reagan years. In 2007, the George C. Marshall Institute insisted that the damages associated with acid rain were always "largely hypothetical" and that "further scientific investigation revealed that most of them were not in fact occurring." However, the institute provided no evidence or studies to support this extraordinary claim.[50]

A similar sequence of events took place when scientists began to focus attention on the impact of chlorofluorocarbons (CFCs) on the Earth's ozone layer. During the 1970s, billions of pounds of CFCs were being produced for use in spray cans, air conditioners, and refrigerators. Scientific studies found that when these chemicals were released into the air, the decomposition process caused ozone depletion. The aerosol industry tried the same kind of public relations "raising doubts" strategy that was described in the previous examples. As Oreskes and Conway explain, "Scientific claims were being published in scientific journals, where only scientists would read them, but unscientific claims were being published in the mass media. The public was left with the impression that the ozone layer was fine, and that the 'alarmists' had got it wrong."[51]

Industry representatives and other skeptics doubted that ozone depletion was real, or argued that if it was real, it was inconsequential, or caused by volcanoes. Conservative think tanks—often anti-environmentalist and pro-business interests and free market economic policies—amplified the message that people were overreacting to the threat of ozone layer depletion. One of the most prominent voices was Fred Singer, a fellow at the Heritage Foundation with an extensive history of helping industry try to undermine the credibility of damaging scientific evidence. He put forward three interrelated arguments, as Oreskes and Conway explain: "The science is incomplete and uncertain; replacing CFCs will be difficult, dangerous, and expensive; and the scientific community is corrupt and motivated by self-interest and political ideology."[52] In one instance, he published a scathing critique of the scientific community in general, accusing it of being motivated by self-interest. "It's not difficult to understand some of the motivations behind the drive to regulate CFCs out of existence," he wrote in 1989. "For scientists, prestige, more grants for research, press conferences, and newspaper stories."[53]

Of course, in all three of these cases—smoking, acid rain, and CFCs—the scientific evidence was upheld despite rigorous scrutiny and attempts to delegitimize it. Industry leaders, politicians, and even a few scientists consistently rejected the weight of the scientific evidence and repeated arguments that were thoroughly debunked and rebutted by the scientific community. They successfully manufactured doubts about scientific research that have persisted to this very day, and importantly, the Internet has now made this much easier and more effective. Whereas scientific evidence is published in peer-reviewed scientific journals that few people outside of science professions read or understand, the politically motivated arguments about the uncertainty of science are typically communicated in a variety of mainstream media and other venues, particularly via the Internet and social media, where most Americans now get their news. This gives a considerable advantage to those seeking to provoke uncertainty and doubt. No matter who you are, the ability to challenge reality is now squarely in your hands via your laptop or smartphone, with no factual evidence required.

Doubts about scientific evidence also fuel the modern anti-vaccine movement in the United States and elsewhere. In 1998, a team of scientists led by Andrew Wakefield published an article with falsified data in the premier medical journal *The Lancet*. The argument made in this article was that the measles, mumps, and rubella (MMR) vaccine causes autism. Twelve years later, after it had been thoroughly proven fraudulent, this article was retracted.[54] However, by then it had already influenced the perceptions and beliefs of millions of people who wanted something easy and simple to blame for autism. Wakefield and his colleagues had manipulated the data gathering and analysis for their article in a way that seemed to provide support for his argument. Research findings that did not confirm their argument had been altered or deleted. This sort of scientific misconduct is roundly (and rightly) condemned. Because of his fraud, Wakefield's medical license was eventually revoked. And yet, this one article has been (and continues to be) used to support the central narrative of an anti-vaccination movement in the United States and elsewhere.

The anti-science discourse has obvious relevance for the recent COVID-19 pandemic. Trump's denigration of medical experts like Dr. Anthony Fauci, along with his promotion of dubious medical remedies (e.g., drinking bleach), emboldened those who felt that cautionary public health measures like wearing a mask were infringing on their civil liberties. Even while people were dying by the thousands each day all across the country, Trump and his supporters continued to reject medical and scientific expertise. The "decay of truth" and the "death of expertise" described earlier in this chapter now contributed to the United States having (by a huge margin) the world's highest numbers of COVID-19 infections and deaths.

And a final "increasing uncertainty" example worth noting is the debate over climate change. As Lee McIntyre notes, "In 2004, researchers published a literature review of the then-current 928 scientific papers on climate change and found that exactly zero of them disputed the idea that anthropogenic climate change was real. In a 2012 update to these findings, other researchers found that the number of dissenters was 0.17 percent out of 13,950 papers."[55] According to a 2019 BBC report, drawing on studies based on forty years of data on a range of measures, more than 11,000 scientists from 153 countries concluded "clearly and unequivocally that planet Earth is facing a climate emergency."[56]

Just like the tobacco industry's response to scientific evidence about smoking, the fossil fuel industry has responded by promoting skepticism about climate change, because it is in their best interests to do so. For example, in 1998, the American Petroleum Institute (API) convened a series of meetings in Washington, D.C., to discuss potential industry responses to a major treaty (the Kyoto Protocol) being negotiated to reduce global emissions of greenhouse gases. A variety of formal recommendations and conclusions were produced by these meetings, explaining that the objectives the API wanted to achieve would be deemed successful when: average citizens "understand" (recognize) uncertainties in climate science; recognition of uncertainties becomes part of the "conventional wisdom"; media coverage reflects balance on climate science and recognition of the validity of viewpoints that challenge the current "conventional wisdom"; and industry senior leadership understands uncertainties in climate science, making them stronger ambassadors to those who shape climate policy.[57]

In addition to API, as McIntyre notes, "the George C. Marshall Institute also played a prominent role in generating skepticism about climate change (as well as secondhand tobacco smoke, acid rain, and the ozone hole) until it closed in 2015."[58] And similarly, the Heartland Institute adopted as its mission, according to a *New York Times* report, "to undermine the teaching of global warming in public schools [and] promote a curriculum that would cast doubt on the scientific finding that fossil fuel emissions endanger the long-term welfare of the planet."[59] Their website even declared themselves to be "the world's most prominent think tank promoting skepticism about man-made climate change."[60] As Ari Rabin-Havt notes, "Paid experts produced fake research that was converted into talking points and memes, then repeated on television by paid shills and spread through social media and, when necessary, hammered into the public consciousness through paid advertising."[61]

The strategy of manufacturing doubt and uncertainty has now been adopted by politicians, right-wing think tanks, the fossil fuel industry, and other corporate interests who are intent on discrediting science about the reality of climate change, the hazards of asbestos, the impacts of secondhand smoke or acid rain, and even the scientific recommendations for wearing protective masks during a global pandemic. In particular, as Judith Warner notes, "questioning accepted fact, revealing the myths and politics behind established certainties . . . [and] attacking science became a sport of the radical right."[62] The strategy involves enlisting a number of individuals with adequately impressive credentials who will try to refute (or at least question) whatever facts or truths people have come to accept.[63] It does not matter if their scientific expertise is in a different field, as long as they have impressive enough credentials.

As a result, family doctors with no immunology expertise have been enlisted by the anti-vaccination movement. Retired nuclear engineers were enlisted by the tobacco industry to question the scientific evidence showing the links between smoking and cancer or other illnesses. All that matters is their willingness to articulate false arguments in their talking points and repeat them to whoever will listen, with themes that include arguing that more research is needed and attacking the reputations or integrity of scientists and researchers whose facts they disagree with.[64] Again, the goal of this strategy is not to prove "Hey, we have the truth, we have more evidence than the other guys' argument"; rather it is always "Hey, they are claiming they have the truth but their evidence is inconclusive." It is not necessary—nor even part of the strategy—to prove something isn't true. The effort simply involves continually raising questions about it, in order to increase the level of doubt.

THE "BOTH SIDES" STRATEGY

Drawing lessons from the corporate-driven examples described above, today's digital influence mercenaries seek to convince the target that there is no objective truth at all. Because, as Lee McIntyre notes in his book *Post-truth*, "if there is no truth, how can we ever really know anything? Why not doubt the mainstream news or embrace a conspiracy theory? Indeed, if news is just political expression, why not make it up? Whose facts should be dominant? Whose perspective is the right one?"[65] This is essentially what Hannah Arendt observed when writing about the role that propaganda played in Nazi Germany and Soviet Russia: "In an ever-changing, incomprehensible world the masses had reached the point where they would, at the same time, believe everything and nothing; they would think that everything was possible and nothing was true."[66] If there is no longer any ability or will for members of a society to determine truth from lies, it creates an information environment in which anything—even the most outlandish conspiracy theories—may be believed, as we'll discuss further in chapter 4.

Unfortunately, postmodernism introduced a way to argue for "both sides" of various scientific explanations that had until recently been incontrovertible. Creationists, for example, call for teaching "intelligent design" alongside evolution in schools. And over the past several decades, mainstream media have fallen into a sort of "both sides" trap. In response to the massive growth of audiences for politically oriented cable networks (like Fox News and MSNBC), traditional news broadcast programs began to focus on providing both liberal and conservative views on topics, which in many cases meant providing equal airtime to opposite sides of a debate. The phenomenon of "split screen" television debates emerged, with two "expert" guests sharing opposing viewpoints, the host giving them fairly equal amounts of time, and declaring the issue "controversial." As McIntyre points out, this created a "false equivalence" between two sides of an issue "even when there are not really two credible sides."[67] It also amplified the opportunities for perception manipulation by science deniers, who could then give the public an impression (though based on no evidence at all) that there were controversies about the scientific facts on climate change, vaccines, tobacco, acid rain, COVID-19, and other topics. In essence, by trying to demonstrate that they were not biased (or at least not as biased as cable news channels), the traditional news broadcast programs "played right into the hands of those who were seeking to create confusion on factual matters through nothing more than bogus skepticism."[68]

As a result, uncertainty is increased by critically important sources of information that are trying to portray themselves as objective and neutral by presenting opposing sides of a debate—regardless of the fact that in many cases, one side of the argument is supported by facts and evidence, and the other side is supported only by strong opinion and no facts. And this is not just something we see on television—print media has also seen the pressure for "balanced reporting" and the same kind of outcome. As McIntyre notes, "Including information by partisans who have a stake in pushing the reporter toward something other than the truth creates a 'denial discourse' that can give undue credibility to fringe opinions."[69]

A variation of the "both sides" argument was employed by Trump when he tried to equate people demonstrating against white supremacy with the neo-Nazis who had marched on Charlottesville, Virginia, in August 2017. During a press conference, after one of the neo-Nazis had intentionally rammed his car into a crowd, killing a young woman and injuring several other people, Trump stated that there were "some very fine people on both sides. . . . We condemn in the strongest possible terms this egregious display of hatred, bigotry, and violence on many sides, on many sides."[70] The inconvenient fact remains that only one side throughout this event represented hatred, bigotry, and violence.

This sort of rhetorical false balancing produces a perception of credibility where it does not belong. It creates a false equivalence; the narrative that competing explanations or interpretations of something are equally valid. The liar can simply combine this false equivalence with the narrative that each of us is entitled to his or her own opinion regardless of what the facts and evidence point to, and then the lies are more likely to be believed by the target audience. This is essentially the worst impact of postmodernism. As Michiko Kakutani explains, "The postmodernist argument that all truths are partial (and a function of one's perspective) led to the related argument that there are many legitimate ways to understand or represent an event."[71] For the influence strategies involving disinformation, a key tactic now is to use relativistic arguments and promote different interpretations and narratives, arguing that there are no more objective truths anymore, just different perceptions and competing facts. As Lee McIntyre notes, "Post-truth is in part a strategy for the political subordination of reality."[72] And few things benefit the liar more than being able to subordinate reality.

Conclusion

These and other strategies for increasing uncertainty have direct benefits for digital influence mercenaries. When people deny the existence of an objective truth, this makes it easier for liars to convince them to believe in things that can be factually disproven. So, the kind of environment that benefits the mercenaries most is one in which truth is consistently attacked, denigrated, and undermined by those who feel most threatened by truth. Further, increased insecurity and distrust can lead to anger, frustration, and even a refusal to validate other perspectives, creating opportunities for mercenaries to employ various strategies (described in chapter 2) for provoking engagement. Our information ecosystem provides a wealth of opportunities for what Michiko Kakutani describes as a "firehose of falsehoods," an effort "to overwhelm and numb people while simultaneously defining deviancy down and normalizing the unacceptable. Outrage gives way to outrage fatigue, which gives way to the sort of cynicism and weariness that empowers those disseminating the lies."[73] If the influence efforts can get people to the point where it seems like they can't believe anything, then the influencer can get away with everything.

Most of us find discomfort in uncertainty and fear. Today's digital influence mercenaries can exploit this discomfort in order to pursue their strategic objectives. Because of the overwhelmingly busy and complex modern information ecosystem, people have less confidence in what is true or not, leading some to embrace fake news and disinformation. At the same time, the proliferation of fake news and disinformation makes people even less confident about what is true and what is not. This creates a mutually reinforcing spiral of increasing uncertainty that can be exploited by using strategies like gaslighting, salami slicing, questioning scientific facts, attacking the integrity of those who disagree with a certain point of view, and trying to undermine the notion that an objective, fact-based truth even exists. As a result of these strategies for increasing uncertainty and doubt, some people will simply believe that if there are questions to be raised, there must be either an effort to hide the truth, or the truth is just unknown—a core tenet of conspiracy theories, as we'll explore in the next chapter.

When we begin to reflexively question every headline, every piece of information we see online, it becomes increasingly difficult to decide what is true and what is not. This is the state of mind that influence mercenaries want the target to be in, for the same reasons that these kinds of strategies have been deployed by authoritarian political leaders around the world. As McKay Coppins explains, "Rather than shutting down dissenting voices, these leaders have learned to harness the democratizing power of social media for their own purposes—jamming the signals, sowing confusion. They no longer need to silence the dissident shouting in the streets; they can use a megaphone to drown him out. Scholars have a name for this: censorship through noise."[74] And there is no better producer of noise today than our social media platforms.

As Lee McIntyre notes, "The rise of social media has facilitated an informational free-for-all. With fact and opinion now presented side by side on the Internet, who knows what to believe anymore?"[75] This, in turn, creates an information environment in which public audiences are more accepting of alternate narratives, including simplistic demagoguery and conspiracy theories, which we'll examine in the next chapter. In this complex and uncertain world, those who appear to have strong convictions can influence others with the appearance of certainty, even when ample evidence refutes, undermines, and contradicts those convictions. Because we so desperately want to do away with uncertainty, we are willing to accept remedies, particularly if offered in convincing ways, by convincing sources. Higher levels of uncertainty then allow the influencer to present the "alternative facts" they want the target to believe, leading people to accept baseless factoids and conspiracy theories—the topic of the next chapter.

4

COMFORTING FALSEHOODS AND CONSPIRACIES

Disinformation researcher Claire Wardle recently observed how "we have an emotional relationship to information. It is not rational," but is instead deeply tied to feelings and the way we express our identity.[1] Our emotional state in any given moment impacts how we search for information. At the same time, our emotional state both impacts and is impacted by how we process the information we find. For example, we have already discussed how uncertainty and fear can drive our information-seeking behavior, and how they are exacerbated by information overload. Because uncertainty creates such discomfort for most people, many kinds of influence efforts can exploit our emotions by increasing uncertainty.

Digital influence mercenaries rarely find profit by disseminating truth—rather, it is disinformation that most often provokes the kind of engagement that generates revenue. And as explained earlier, fake news becomes a much more profitable endeavor when the target audience no longer believes in an objective truth. Meanwhile, we respond to insecurity and distrust by looking for information that reduces uncertainty, and often prefer to see information that reinforces our conviction in what we want to believe (regardless of the facts). This in turn also creates opportunities for digital influence mercenaries; just like they can get paid to fabricate uncertainty, they can also get paid to provide false remedies for it. For example, a profitable strategy for digital influence mercenaries involves choosing a popular lie, finding people who believe that lie, targeting them with clickbait, and bringing them to a fake news website where they will see advertisements and perhaps even buy something or donate to a cause they believe in.

So, while the previous chapter examined strategies for manufacturing and increasing uncertainty as a means of making the target more susceptible to disinformation, we now turn to look at another collection of powerful strategies that involve providing alternate narratives—even conspiracy theories—as potentially attractive means for the target to remedy their uncomfortable uncertainty. Further, there are obvious benefits to be derived from pursuing both types of uncertainty manipulation strategies in tandem. The more uncertain we become, the more receptive we may be to an alternate narrative—that is, the influencer's preferred interpretation of events. And the more we become uncertain about whether there is actually a truthful answer to our questions, the more likely we are to accept a variety of information, even if the source is of questionable credibility. Thus, disinformation can be seen as a means of both increasing and decreasing uncertainty, and both approaches create opportunities for digital influence mercenaries to provoke the kinds of engagement that generate revenue.

How We Process Information

Research by Richard E. Petty and John T. Cacioppo identified two primary ways in which we process information—central and peripheral.[2] The former involves a careful and rational assessment of the information, perhaps leading the person to ask clarifying questions and search for additional information. As Manheim explains, "The persuasiveness of the narrative is determined by how well it can stand up to this scrutiny."[3] In contrast, when we process information in a more peripheral way, our acceptance of it relies less on the objective quality of the information and more on packaging—for example, the attractiveness of the message or the medium, the ability to entertain and stimulate a type of arousal, whether or not the people around you agree with the information presented, and so forth.

All human beings have limits to their ability to process information. Further, researchers like Manheim have noted how "we often adopt the strategies of the peripheral route for simplifying complex problems," mainly because we "tend to be cognitive misers, forever trying to conserve our cognitive energy."[4] This becomes especially problematic in an industrialized, information-rich society like ours, because many people have developed a type of laziness that diminishes any interest in seeking out new sources of information in order to verify (or reject) the information that has been so conveniently provided to us with little or no effort on our part. Understanding this peripheral information processing tendency helps us understand how some people will mindlessly accept a conclusion or a proposition (like "Build a wall," "Lock her up," "Send them back") for no good reason other than because it is accompanied by a simplistic device. As Anthony R. Pratkanis and Elliot Aronson explain, modern propaganda promotes the use of the peripheral route to persuasion and is designed to take advantage of the limited processing capabilities of the cognitive miser (the target). "The characteristics of modern persuasion—the message-dense environment, the thirty-second ad, the immediacy of persuasion—make it increasingly more difficult to think deeply about important issues and decisions."[5] Thus, our uncertainty about all this complexity around us can be alleviated more easily by relying on our peripheral mode of information processing.

A similar approach to manipulating uncertainty involves a two-part process that takes advantage of our sensitivity to stress. As psychologist Kathleen Taylor explains, the influencer will begin by "arousing some kind of negative feeling in the target—guilt, fear, cognitive dissonance of some kind—and then present the behavior they want to evoke as the way to get rid of all this emotional pressure."[6] Similarly, an influence method that some have called "the rationalization trap" begins by arousing a sense of dissonance, particularly focused on fear of the present or future, issues of perceived inadequacy, hypocrisy or shame among the target audience, and then offering this audience one specific solution as the way to reduce this uncomfortable dissonance. For example, a political candidate could greatly exaggerate the level of perceived threat about foreigners invading the homeland, portray their political opponents as too weak or unwilling to confront that threat, and conclude with the obvious exhortation to "vote for me, I will make us all more secure."[7] In these instances, a solution is processed (in a peripheral way) by the target as a means of alleviating their uncertainty. If I can give you a sense of certainty about something you value, thereby reducing the risks and discomfort that accompany uncertainty, the chances are good that you will like that and want more of it.

These and other methods of exploiting the target's uncertainty can sometimes result in troubling—even violent—behavior. According to Pratkanis and Aronson, "When a propagandist unscrupulously plays on our feelings of insecurity, or exploits our darkest fears, or offers fake hope, exploration and inquiry stop. . . . Our emotions overwhelm our critical abilities. And we take actions that we might not otherwise consider wise to take."[8] Authoritarians instinctively use these strategies in their efforts to influence a perception of the unquestionable and all-knowing leader, deriving power simply by being impervious to anyone else's opinions or views. Similarly, as Pankaj Mishra writes in *Age of Anger*, "The appeal of demagogues lies in their ability to take a generalized discontent, the mood of drift, resentment, disillusionment, and economic shakiness, and transform it into a plan for *doing* something. They make inaction seem morally degrading. And many young men and women become eager to transform their powerlessness into an irrepressible rage to hurt or destroy."[9]

In sum, because uncertainty is a fact of life, influence mercenaries can use various strategies and tactics to question what we believe or think we know, and then manipulate us into embracing the possibility of alternative perspectives and false narratives. As a recent UNESCO (United Nations Educational, Scientific, and Cultural Organization) report notes, "The forces behind disinformation do not necessarily expect to persuade journalists or broader audiences about the truth of false claims, as much as cast doubt on the status of verifiable information produced by professional news producers. This confusion means that many news consumers feel increasingly entitled to choose or create their own 'facts.'"[10] Increasing uncertainty allows the influencer to introduce new questions and ideas that have no basis in fact—and yet (the central argument is) "they could be true, we just don't know for sure one way or another." Further, any facts that challenge your beliefs can simply be ignored or rejected as invalid.

In fact, the decline of faith in experts, factual evidence, and objective reality has also been combined with "othering" to denigrate anyone who argues for fact-checking a story or narrative. Standing up for factual accuracy now makes you a target for those who don't want any facts that contradict or question what they want to believe. There is no need ever again to face the cognitive dissonance that comes with admitting you were wrong. You don't ever have to be wrong anymore. Unfortunately, as myriad lessons of history (and likely our own personal experiences) have shown, considering oneself infallible is a precondition for making bad mistakes. In such instances, we run the risk of pushing the pendulum too far away from the hell of uncertainties, and into the hell of too much uncontested certainty.

Power and Profit from Attacking Truth

As described earlier in this book, a prominent goal of digital influence mercenaries is acquiring the power to shape the perceptions and behaviors of their target. One form of power is derived from lying with impunity, when no one will (or can) hold you accountable, much less punish you for your lies. Once you begin to get away with lying, you gain the power to do it more and more. The key is to convince your audience from the start that facts and reality can be interpreted in different ways; by fabricating uncertainty, and then lying and gaslighting, you undermine the audience's confidence in their ability to confront you, to call you out on your lies. Once they have entered that state of cognition, you can lie more frequently, and the audience will face an uncomfortable choice: (1) admit they were wrong to accept your earlier lies, and then face the cognitive dissonance and humiliation that comes with acknowledging that mistake; or (2) accept the new streams of lies uncontested. The liar who understands egocentric human behavior can now benefit from the natural inclination of many people to avoid cognitive dissonance.

In order to convince the audience to believe in something for which there is no evidence or factual basis, the liar will use phrases like "people are telling me" or "people are saying" to preface a statement that is then delivered as if it were unquestionably true. If the audience presses with, "Which people, precisely?" or "On what evidence do they base these opinions?" the liar will simply provide more of the unverified, unfounded, unverifiable phrases like "people are saying." Anyone can easily make up a statement and preface it by "people are saying," and some members of the audience will believe the statement as fact—because they want to believe it, particularly when it confirms what they already believe. Some will even repeat it as fact to their friends, neighbors, and family members, citing the liar as the original source of the information.

Think about this for a moment. No factual evidence supports your opinion, and yet by stating "everybody's talking about it," "people are saying," "many people feel the same way," and "millions of people agree with me," your viewers, readers, and listeners—people who are already predisposed to like what you say—accept that as your proof. Then, because you now have people who embrace your lies, you can use their acceptance of lying as a source of proof when you continue spreading your lie. As a result, truth no longer matters, all that matters is the ability to influence what people believe to be true. As Lee McIntyre explains, "In its purest form, post-truth is when one thinks that the crowd's reaction actually does change the facts about a lie."[11]

As mentioned earlier, digital influence mercenaries rarely find profit by disseminating truth—rather, it is disinformation that most often provokes the kind of engagement that generates revenue. And as explained in previous chapters, when people deny the existence of an objective truth, this makes it easier for liars to convince them to believe in things that can be factually disproven. So, the kind of environment that benefits the mercenaries most is one in which truth is consistently attacked, denigrated, and undermined by those who feel most threatened by truth. Fortunately for malicious influencers (but not for the rest of us), various efforts have succeeded in convincing at least some people that there is no objective truth at all. Prominent examples include the 1970s postmodernist movement, and the mainstream media's attempts to present "both sides" of an argument where only one side actually is supported by factual evidence. In a report published by the RAND Corporation, Mazarr et al. describe how "many people now view the very idea of objective knowledge as elitist. Increasingly, the idea of 'expertise' has given way to a perception that 'everyone has their viewpoint,' the Nietzschean idea that perspective is everything."[12] The decline of faith in expertise means nobody knows for sure, so nothing is true and everything is possible. This is actually a cornerstone of Russia's digital influence warfare program (and the title of a terrific book by Peter Pomerantsev).[13]

In George Orwell's famous book *1984*, about a fictional society of the future, the narrator explains that there is no word for "science" in that society because "the empirical method of thought, on which all the scientific achievements of the past were founded, represents an objective reality that threatens the power of Big Brother to determine what truth is."[14] If a majority of your target audience believes in the existence of an objective truth, you will have a more difficult time convincing them of lies and disinformation. In contrast, if you can convince your audience that truth itself is merely a matter of interpretation, you have created the conditions that will allow you to lie at will. Further, not only does lying produce the power to lie more, in some ways lying with impunity is also a demonstration of the liar's power, a type of power that under certain circumstances can inspire fear and awe among a target audience.

In 2016, during the Republican National Convention, the following exchange took place in an on-camera interview of Newt Gingrich, a prominent Republican and former member of Congress from Georgia, by CNN anchor Alisyn Camerota:[15]

CNN: Trump's speech inaccurately depicted America as a country inundated by violence and crime, and yet the statistics don't support that view.

Gingrich: The current view is that liberals have a whole set of statistics which theoretically may be right, but it's not where human beings are. People are frightened. People feel that their government has abandoned them.

CNN: Wait a moment, these crime statistics are not liberal numbers, they came from the FBI.

Gingrich: No, but what I said is equally true. People feel it.

CNN: They feel it, yes, but the facts don't support it.

Gingrich: As a political candidate, I'll go with how people feel and I'll let you go with the theoreticians.

This is a great example of how an influencer—in this case, a prominent politician—attempts to reject inconvenient facts and truth in order to support a political narrative that some people will believe. When facts threaten to undermine those political beliefs, the liar simply encourages people to ignore or reject those facts as invalid. This is particularly effective in an information ecosystem in which countless influencers have already raised the level of uncertainty about the very existence of an objective truth. This makes it easy for digital influence mercenaries to frame the disinformation as a reinterpreted form of reality that their audience is entitled to have.

In other words, similar to con artists and conspiracy theories, the main purpose of disinformation and fake news is to get people to believe something that is not true. The strategy here is to replace inconvenient truths with "alternative facts." In doing so, "fake news" and "alternative facts" provide the illusion that facts can be contextual—you can have your facts, but I'll have my own facts. Alternatively, the deceiver can simply claim there is no such thing as an objective fact anymore. Unfortunately, the denial of objective facts has been a core strategy of a recent U.S. president and his political supporters, and this in turn has emboldened a broad range of new media outlets who now thrive in disseminating wholesale fabrications to an audience that has proven all too eager to consume a narrative that has no basis in factual evidence. When no one is holding a liar accountable, they can (and usually will) continue to lie about anything and everything they can get away with, and this enables the proliferation of conspiracy theories that can be uniquely profitable for digital influence mercenaries.

Factoids and Conspiracy Theories

The novelist Norman Mailer coined the term "factoid," which he described as "facts which have no existence before appearing in a magazine or newspaper."[16] Pratkanis and Aronson define a factoid as an "assertion of fact that is not backed up by evidence, usually because the fact is false or because evidence in support of the assertion cannot be obtained." A factoid is a common tool used by all kinds of influence warfare campaigns, where rumors, gossip, and urban legends are presented in such a manner that they become widely treated as true, although in a court of law factoids are called hearsay and are inadmissible as evidence.[17] Factoids can meet some of our psychological needs; they may be stimulating and entertaining; they may help us rationalize something we are worried, concerned, or confused about. Similarly, believing a factoid suggesting that immigrants are responsible for rampant crime in our neighborhoods reinforces an individual's prejudices about immigrants, and gives them a comforting sort of confirmation that those prejudices are based in fact—even when they are completely false.

The barrage of factoids we now see each day—in person and online—threatens to wear us down. Some lead us to question what we think we know, while others seek to alter our views and behaviors in ways the influencer intended. As described in the previous chapter, a digital influence mercenary can score a victory if they can get us to question our stance, increase our uncertainty, and consider that something else might be possible. Eventually, rather than spending time and energy critically analyzing the merits of all the information flowing at us, we may opt to take the easier route of accepting the factoids presented to us, particularly when they are presented to us by some of our friends or the social media accounts we follow. Similarly, conspiracy theories thrive on how we manage our uncertainty. The purveyors of rumors and conspiracies naturally claim to base their knowledge on "secret information" that inherently cannot be verified nor factually discredited, so all that's needed is a target willing to accept that the falsehood or conspiracy is something that might be possible.

Further, spreading these kinds of rumors, conspiracies, and factoids to others can give some people a false sense of superiority, a feeling that they "know" some kind of secret information that others are currently "in the dark" about, producing an ego-driven rush of adrenaline that serves our psychological need to feel "right."[18] And most critically—as Pratkanis and Aronson explain—factoids, rumors, and conspiracies swirl around us in a form of pre-persuasion; they influence "social reality . . . as bits and pieces that are used to construct our picture of the world."[19] When we don't know the answers to important, contextually relevant questions, it is human nature to search for those answers. We are frequently seeking a form of reassurance in order to reduce the terribly uncomfortable uncertainty in our lives. But this in turn provides an advantage to information aggressors, who may be able to convince us of many kinds of disinformation.

A core purpose of conspiracy theorists is to manipulate uncertainty about something by encouraging alternate—and often wildly controversial—narratives. Examples include: "Vaccines are bad for you!" "The CIA created the crack epidemic, and is covering up the fact that the Earth is actually flat!" "Aliens built the pyramids; the CIA is covering that up, too!" "NASA is a tool of U.S. imperialism!" A common tactic in promoting "alternative facts" is to claim various conspiracies have suppressed the truth of the matter. For example, during a discussion with a caller to *The Rush Limbaugh Show* in April 2015, Limbaugh denied that secondhand smoke was a danger. "That is a myth. That has been disproven at the World Health Organization and the report was suppressed . . . it will not make you sick, and it will not kill you," he claimed.[20] Using a classic conspiracy theory model, his claim to the truth was supported by an additional claim that it can't be proven because the evidence for the truth is being suppressed by some entity. Meanwhile, according to the Centers for Disease Control and Prevention, approximately 2.5 million nonsmokers have died from health problems caused by exposure to secondhand smoke since 1964.[21]

Research in psychology suggests that people can be drawn to conspiracy theories for a variety of cognitive, psychological, and social reasons. According to Karen Douglas et al., "Deficiencies in available information, cognitive ability, and motivation to think critically may contribute to conspiracy belief . . . [which is also] associated with narcissism—an inflated view of oneself that requires external validation and is linked to paranoid ideation."[22] Researchers have also found that belief in conspiracy theories appears to be stronger when people experience distress as a result of feeling uncertain; when events are especially large in scale or significant and leave people dissatisfied with mundane, small-scale explanations; and among people who habitually seek meaning and patterns in the environment, including believers in paranormal phenomena.[23] And research also indicates that a lack of trust in authority is a common attribute among people who believe in conspiracies, and this appears to be consistent regardless of what the conspiracy is about.[24]

Many of the things we know to be true are actually based on tons of evidence, some of it personally witnessed, but much of it tested or witnessed by others who documented what they observed. And yet there may also be a few holes in a theory or account of events, perhaps even information that is believed but unconfirmed (or cannot be confirmed). In such cases these holes are filled by probability, estimates that lead us to conclude what is most likely based on whatever evidence is available. This juncture is where we typically find the core roots of conspiracy theories. When you or I have not personally witnessed something, others have an opportunity to manipulate our level of uncertainty about what we know or don't know. Often, a conspiracy monger will argue, "That's just your version of the truth" and, without being able to offer evidence or facts to support an alternative version, they will still call yours into question.

Additionally, from early childhood our values and behaviors are influenced by perceived linkages between cause and effect. Do something bad, there are consequences; do something good, there are rewards. One event happens and influences a subsequent event. Thus, we as human beings draw lessons from the past in order to understand the present and possible future, which allows our brains to process complex information in an energy-efficient manner. However, this information processing habit also develops expectations that events must have some kind of causality, whether or not we know and understand what that might be. From this core tendency comes the incentive to believe in a conspiracy theory: an event happened, but I don't understand (or like, or believe in) what I'm being told about why it happened, so there must be some concerted effort to keep the true reasons hidden from me. As Peter Pomerantsev explains, "If all the world is a conspiracy, then your own failures are no longer all your fault. The fact that you achieved less than you hoped for, that your life is a mess—it's all the fault of the conspiracy."[25]

Unfortunately, researchers suggest conspiracy theories are spreading more easily in today's information universe, with the Internet functioning as a superconductor.[26] Through our social media accounts, we can validate conspiracy claims extremely easily just by the simple act of liking, sharing, or retweeting. This generates a form of social proof-driven authority for that information (or disinformation), and when repeated by others to whom you are connected, it fuels broader and stronger belief in that conspiracy.[27] Conspiracy theories provide an alternative narrative, one that suggests evil forces are aligned against you, withholding the truth from you, trying to harm you in some way. This helps explain why experts in psychology have noted that people who feel powerless and have higher levels of anxiety are more likely to believe in conspiracy theories.[28] Other risk factors include low levels of education and critical thinking abilities, extreme political convictions, and feelings of superiority (national, racial, ethnic, etc.), while the best predictor of believing in one conspiracy is that you already believe in another.[29] Conspiracies can be particularly harmful when their underlying purpose is to tear apart social trust, make people angry at those perceived forces of evil, and act out in ways that reflect our worst human attributes. As a *Washington Post* report notes, "They often transmit racist, anti-Semitic, Islamophobic beliefs. In their most toxic form, these theories have led to violence, including mass shootings. Behind many conspiracy theories lurks a pervasive rage. Many researchers and communicators who deal with fringe conspiracy theories endure venomous and misogynistic threats and harassment."[30]

Encouraging belief in conspiracy theories is thus a unique kind of disinformation because it promotes the idea that there is a "hidden truth" that is being purposefully withheld from you, even though you have a right to know. It capitalizes on uncertainty in multiple ways. If you are already inclined to believe (a) that there is no such thing as facts or objective truth, and (b) that a sinister group of "others" are responsible for what's gone wrong in your world, a conspiracy theory adds fuel to that fire. Further, research shows that people who believe in one conspiracy theory are more likely than others to believe in additional conspiracies. And according to social psychologist Karen Douglas, "once ideas become fixed, they are difficult to shake off. So, once a person believes in a conspiracy theory it is difficult to convince them otherwise."[31] This is why digital influence efforts of both foreign and domestic origin have incorporated the spread of conspiracy theories in order to achieve specific strategic objectives.

Profiting from Conspiracy Theories

A uniquely beneficial form of lying involves convincing people they have been deceived by what's actually true, or at the very least cannot be proven true. And unfortunately, as we have become increasingly aware of how easily we can be deceived online, this has created the context in which it becomes easier for the deceiver to convince an audience not to believe what they see or hear. Robert Chesney and Danielle Keats Citron coined the term "liar's dividend" to describe the problem that arises when a public becomes aware of deepfake technologies and other means by which they can be deceived, and as a result they begin to have increasing skepticism about the authenticity of everything, even real audio and video evidence that is wholly true.[32] This gives enormous power to the deceiver. As the researchers explain, individuals caught doing or saying something horrible in authentic audio or video recordings can simply exploit that skepticism in an effort to "try and escape accountability for their actions by denouncing authentic video and audio as deep fakes."[33]

The logical conclusion from this is that virtually anything and everything could potentially be false. It is no coincidence that, as discussed in the previous chapter, the motto of the Russian-based media outlet RT is literally "Question More," an overt effort to foment confusion, chaos, and distrust.[34] Here, convincing the target of the mere possibility that they might be deceived becomes the primary goal and the source of uncertainty, which the liar can then capitalize upon when conditioning the target audience to believe only the sources of information that the liar can influence. All other information sources are to be deemed illegitimate. Further, a fake website, image, or video doesn't have to actually exist—the target audience merely needs to be made uncertain and fearful that it may exist.

Raising the level of the target's uncertainty about what is real and what is not then leads them to conclude that nothing may be real and anything may be possible. This, in turn, provides opportunities for the digital influence mercenaries to deceive, provoke, and manipulate their perceptions at will.[35] As part of this quest for information dominance, the liar will call other sources "fake news," use derogatory and demeaning language toward the individuals producing and disseminating that information (like journalists, fact checkers, academics, think tanks, etc.), and perhaps even label them "enemies of the people." Overall, the liar wants the target audience to distrust any information source that the liar cannot control, and will incorporate useful conspiracy theories into their attempts to shape the perceptions of their target audiences. Amazingly, there's even a website that will try to convince you of a "conspiracy against tobacco," one in which the "anti-smoking lobby" (the ones advocating for a ban on smoking in clubs and other public spaces) is actually part of "a vast racketeering empire of institutionalized lies and social control."[36] The website roundly criticizes "the cowards of Congress" for giving in to "the anti-smoker vermin" who are "committing scientific fraud and corrupting the EPA."[37] Conspiracy websites like these often seek to rake in cash donations from true believers who feel compelled to support what they believe is a "fight for truth" (even though in reality, they're being scammed).

Sadly, the chances are good that each of us knows at least some people today who rely on gossip magazines and low-quality Internet resources to reinforce their conviction (and try to convince others) that the earth is flat, that UFOs are visiting our planet with regularity, that the Holocaust never happened, or that climate change is a hoax perpetrated by environmental extremists (or by the Chinese). A 2014 study by two professors at the University of Chicago found that half of Americans believed in a conspiracy theory. Further, 24 percent of Americans (at the time of the study) believed former president Barack Obama was not born in the United States, and 19 percent of Americans believed the U.S. government was responsible for 9/11.[38] Other researchers found that "nearly 30% of Americans think that 'a secretive elite with a globalist agenda is conspiring to eventually rule the world,' and 15% think media or government add secret 'mind controlling' technology to TV broadcasts."[39] And another public poll found that 51 percent of American voters believe there was a larger conspiracy at work in the JFK assassination; 44 percent believe the Bush administration intentionally misled the public about weapons of mass destruction in order to promote the Iraq War; 21 percent believe a UFO crashed at Roswell in 1947; 5 percent of respondents believe that Paul McCartney died and was secretly replaced in the Beatles in 1966; 7 percent think that the 1969 moon landing was staged in a television studio; and 4 percent believe that shape-shifting reptilian people control our world by taking on human form and gaining power.[40] These are of course just a small sampling of a much larger terrain of conspiracies, but you get the point.

In 2016, a particular conspiracy known as #Pizzagate went viral online, alleging that the Clintons and other high-profile Democrats and celebrities ran a child trafficking ring out of the basement of a Washington, D.C., pizza restaurant—one that actually does not even have a basement.[41] On December 4, 2016, Edgar Maddison Welch—a twenty-eight-year-old man from North Carolina—left his wife and child at home and drove to Washington with his AR-15 assault-style rifle. Motivated by his belief in this unsubstantiated conspiracy, he then walked in the front door of the Comet Ping Pong restaurant and pointed a firearm in the direction of a restaurant employee. The employee was able to flee and notify police. Police later said Welch proceeded to discharge the rifle inside the restaurant.[42] He was quickly arrested, and the following year pleaded guilty and was sentenced to four years in prison.

The fact that Fox News, Breitbart, and other conservative media sources were the main (if not exclusive) source of this narrative is very telling. In fact, there were no stories at all supporting this conspiracy in any other prominent news outlet. The *New York Times*, *Washington Post*, *Boston Globe*, *Chicago Tribune*, CNN, ABC, CBS, NBC—basically all reputable news media—recognized this as the bogus, fake conspiracy that it was and declined to give it any attention whatsoever. And yet it received enough repetition inside the conservative media ecosystem that Mr. Welch felt compelled to act upon what he believed was fact. Digital influence mercenaries were behind a significant amount of that repetition, using "bots" (computerized accounts engineered to like, share, and retweet whatever they are programmed to endorse) to drive traffic toward advertisement-heavy fake news websites promoting this and other conspiracies. This resulted in a sort of computer-manipulated social confirmation bias combined with "news" sources deemed credible solely for their political orientation, not for any fact-based objectivity. The appearance that large numbers of individuals believed in this conspiracy helped convince Mr. Welch that it was true.

Falsehoods and conspiracy theories are also frequently used in attempts to undermine the perceived credibility of a political candidate. For example, consider what happened during Canada's presidential election in October 2019, when a flurry of rumors were spread online about an alleged sex scandal involving Prime Minister Justin Trudeau. Political opponents even issued a news release that fueled conspiracy theories about a possible government cover-up—all of which was completely false and forcefully denied by Trudeau.[43] But rumors like this have a significant impact on Canadian voters with already heightened levels of uncertainty or a previous inclination to believe in some kind of conspiracy, along with a potential distrust of politicians in general. They are likely to view these kinds of allegations as verifiable facts, rather than acknowledging that there may actually be no factual evidence to support these conspiracy theories in the first place. As with the #Pizzagate incident, here too we saw examples of digital influence mercenaries profiting by putting together ad-heavy fake news websites and driving traffic to them, sometimes by claiming to have exclusive lurid details about the sex scandal. Meanwhile, certain political marketing agencies were also paid to disseminate the rumors and falsehoods, contributing to the impact that repetition has on convincing people that a conspiracy theory might have some validity.

Unfortunately, ideas—including conspiracy theories—do not have to be true to be believed, and this belief can have very real impacts on society. This is particularly the case regarding the anti-vaccination conspiracy theories emboldened by the now-disgraced physician Andrew Wakefield (described in chapter 3), whose fraudulent research article convinced millions that vaccination causes autism. Even though the research article and its author have been completely discredited, people still believe—*they want to believe*—that vaccination causes autism. As a result, millions of children are no longer being vaccinated—and consequently, rates of childhood diseases that should have been prevented (like mumps and measles) are on the rise.

Most recently, this same community of anti-vaccination conspiracy believers threatened America's ability to effectively confront the COVID-19 pandemic that has killed more than 800,000 of our citizens (and millions more globally). Many bizarre claims were made by these people about the origins of the virus—even that the virus itself was a complete hoax. As Joel Mathis explains, the so-called "coronavirus deniers have offered up questionable research and conspiracy theories to contest expert-driven guidelines on social distancing—and to outright deny that the coronavirus is a threat. Sometimes they even throw multiple, contrasting arguments out to the public. The point is not to inform or be consistent, but to generate noise and skepticism among the wider citizenry."[44] One of the most prominent disinformation videos, called *Plandemic*, featured the discredited medical researcher Judy Mikovitz (who is largely known as an anti-vaccine activist). In the video, Mikovitz promotes a (widely debunked) conspiracy theory that Dr. Fauci and Bill Gates are leveraging the coronavirus pandemic for monetary and political gain.[45] Despite efforts by major social media platforms to limit its dissemination, copies of the video were spread largely through niche online conspiracy communities, as a report by the Atlantic Council's Digital Forensics Research Lab explained. "Once Facebook, Twitter, and YouTube began proactively removing the video, users from groups like QAnon [discussed below] promoted it, hosting the video on 'alt-tech' platforms that cast themselves as 'pro-free speech' options, while continuing to share links to the video on Facebook and Twitter at a rapid rate."[46]

Disinformation about the virus was also complemented by disinformation about the cure. For example: In December 2020, a video circulating on YouTube and Twitter claimed to show a nurse registered in Nashville, Tennessee, talking about getting Bell's palsy due to the recently-approved COVID-19 vaccine, but according to the Tennessee Department of Health there was no nurse registered under that name in the state. Here, too, digital influence mercenaries can profit by launching fake news websites proclaiming various "dangerous side effects" or other kinds of falsehoods about the COVID-19 vaccine. In addition to profiting from ads viewed by visitors to these websites, the mercenaries can also earn commissions on "alternative medicines" or other fake remedies that are promoted and purchased through their website. This accounts for a large portion of the anti-vaccination clickbait that emerged in late 2020 (like the fake video from Tennessee), the central purpose of which is to drive traffic to such websites, while also diminishing trust in government public health experts and exacerbating fear and anxiety.

These disinformation efforts by COVID-related conspiracy adherents provide opportunities for digital influence mercenaries (foreign and domestic) to pursue their overall strategic goals of encouraging confusion, frustration, and animosity in an increasingly polarized society. For example, a study in April 2020 found "multiple networks of fake accounts that use conversations about coronavirus as a tool for political attacks. To right-leaning Americans, these trolls criticize the response from liberals, suggest the coronavirus is being used to take away their freedoms, and point the finger of blame at China. To left-wing Americans, they suggest the administration's response is immoral and inadequate and point the finger of blame at Trump."[47] As with many other controversial topics and events discussed in this book, digital mercenaries have been able to generate significant amounts of profitable social media engagement by capitalizing on this public health crisis.

Meanwhile, one of the most prominent examples of the conspiracy theory phenomenon in recent years is known as QAnon, a bizarre collection of claims by an anonymous individual (using the name "Q") who in late 2017 began posting ominous predictions, cryptic riddles, and often provocative messages on Internet forums 4Chan and 8Chan.[48] As a conspiracy theory, QAnon is complex and confusing, but essentially "Q" claimed to have uncovered evidence that corrupt world leaders are secretly torturing children all over the world, that high-profile Democrats are pedophiles, that President Donald Trump is leading the fight against the group, and that so-called "deep state" malicious government actors are obstructing his efforts.[49] QAnon messages contain code words and phrases such as "the calm before the storm," and "nothing can stop what is coming." A post like "Find the reflection inside the castle" leads to open discussions on message boards through which adherents conclude that the "castle" is the White House, and "crumbs" are clues.[50]

Belief in QAnon is propelled by paranoia, populism, and sometimes the language of evangelical Christianity (Q occasionally quotes from scripture). Adherents reject mainstream institutions, including government officials, and particularly despise the media. According to Adrienne LaFrance, "Q followers agree that a Great Awakening lies ahead, and will bring salvation. . . . The eventual destruction of the global cabal is imminent, . . . but can be accomplished only with the support of patriots who search for meaning in Q's clues."[51] One message "alleged a coordinated propaganda effort by Democrats, Hollywood, and the media, while another accused Democrats of promoting 'mass hysteria' about the coronavirus for political gain."[52] Finally, QAnon adherents see Q's anonymity as proof of Q's credibility, although the individual behind these messages appears to want followers to believe he (or she) is an intelligence officer or military official with Q clearance, a level of access to classified information that includes nuclear-weapons design and other highly sensitive material. A promise of foreknowledge is part of this conspiracy's appeal, as is the feeling of being part of a secret community—one that was even praised by Trump.[53]

While websites and social media engagement have helped fuel the rise of QAnon and other conspiracy believer movements, it's also important to note that major e-commerce platforms like Amazon have played a large role. An investigation in December 2020 found hundreds of books associated with both QAnon and COVID-19 conspiracies, with titles like *Scamdemic: The COVID-19 Agenda*, *QAnon: The Awakening Begins*, *Vaccines Are Dangerous—and Don't Work*, and *QAnon: An Invitation to the Great Awakening* (a "field guide" to the movement).[54] These books (most of which are either self-published or promoted by small publishing houses) have often garnered thousands of positive reviews in which customers (and trolls posing as customers) endorse the wild conspiratorial claims within. Clearly, there is a demand for this kind of literature—as well as for QAnon-branded merchandise. Similar to the anti-vaccination websites selling fake remedies among their fake news, dozens of QAnon-supporting websites and Facebook group pages have generated income not only from ad revenues but also from the sale of hats, T-shirts, bumper stickers, and other merchandise that these individuals are buying. And while a number of social media platforms like Facebook, Twitter, and YouTube have now banned QAnon content from their networks, in part because of its connections to real-world violence, there is no clear effort to constrain the many e-commerce possibilities associated with these conspiracy theory movements.

After several acts of violence by members of the QAnon-supporting movement, the FBI classified QAnon as a domestic terrorism threat in 2019.[55] Examples of these acts include a man accused of murdering his brother with a sword, a man who reportedly threatened to kill YouTube employees, and even a man who threatened to assassinate Trump.[56] The aforementioned Edgar Welch (and the "Pizzagate" conspiracy) is perhaps the most well known among violent perpetrators linked to QAnon, but there have been several others who received considerable news coverage as well. In June 2018, Matthew Philip Wright used his armored truck to block the southbound lanes of a bridge near the Hoover Dam, and during a ninety-minute standoff with police he demanded the government release a report that QAnon followers believed would support their allegations. Upon his arrest, authorities found two assault-style rifles, handguns, and nine hundred rounds of ammunition in his vehicle.[57] When Anthony Comello murdered Frank Cali (a senior member of the Gambino crime family) on the front steps of his home in March 2019, he claimed that Cali was part of a purported deep state and announced at his first court hearing that he was "Trump's chosen vigilante."[58]

A year later, Eduardo Moreno allegedly derailed a train in San Pedro, California, in order to "wake people up," and Jessica Prim drove from Illinois to New York City livestreaming her threats to murder Joe Biden because of his supposed involvement in a "deep state" sex-trafficking ring.[59] Prim had also previously broadcast her QAnon support in a closed Facebook group named Pizzagate Investigations Worldwide, including sharing a link to the QAnon "documentary" *Out of the Shadows*. In June 2020, Alpalus Slyman was arrested after he took his five children hostage on a high-speed police-car chase while livestreaming QAnon theories, including that COVID-19 was manmade and that Donald Trump would save him.[60] According to Alex Kaplan, supporters of QAnon have even targeted a charter school and forced it to cancel an annual fundraiser, "and the conspiracy theory has become increasingly popular among border militias and anti-government groups."[61]

These incidents illustrate that there are very real—and sometimes potentially deadly—implications from believing in conspiracy theories. Anti-vaccination conspiracy believers (some of whom are also linked to QAnon communities) have threatened the lives of well-respected public health officials, like Dr. Anthony Fauci, who was forced to hire security to protect his daughters.[62] More worrisome yet, in late December 2020 a pharmacist in Wisconsin purposefully sabotaged more than five hundred doses of COVID-19 vaccines.[63] In this instance, Steven Brandenburg (an admitted conspiracy theorist) believed the vaccine would harm people and "change their DNA."[64] After his arrest he acknowledged to authorities that he was aware "that people who received the vaccinations would think they had been vaccinated against the virus when in fact they were not."[65] Imagine what could have happened if one or more individuals who had received the ruined vaccines became ill, or even died, from COVID-19 (or unknowingly infected others who then died) as a result of this criminal act. Additionally, a report published by the Global Health Security Network describes how motivated conspiracy theorists like these "could seek to disrupt vaccination efforts through attacks on critical infrastructure and transportation routes, storage or school delivery mechanisms" and recommends that "additional security measures may be required to guard stocks and supplies, as well as drivers, doctors, researchers" and others.[66] The December 2020 bombing attack in Nashville, which injured three people and damaged more than forty buildings, is likely an example of this threat.[67] Anthony Quinn Warner, the bomber identified by authorities, sent packages containing writings and videos promoting conspiracy theories to multiple people just days prior to the blast.[68]

In late 2019, after the Internet forums 4Chan and 8Chan were closed down by their respective hosts, the community of QAnon supporters migrated to other forums like Endchan and 8kun, where they tried to muster support for Trump's presidential reelection campaign in 2020.[69] But following Trump's loss that year, this community became part of another source of profits for digital influence mercenaries. Millions of Americans supported various claims (all proven false) that the election had somehow been rigged and began donating hundreds of millions of dollars to help fund legal challenges to the election results. For months, a broad range of angry, aggrieved Trump supporters appeared all too willing to part with their money in order to support one "election fraud investigation" scam after another. Of course, amid the several phony "fight for Trump" and "stop the steal" efforts, it should be noted that the Trump campaign also did this as well, sending a flood of messages to supporters containing a tiny disclaimer noting that donations under $8,000 would be put toward paying off Trump's campaign debt, not for supporting the ongoing court challenges.[70]

Meanwhile, a network of YouTube channels was launched shortly after the election, connected to the pro-Trump media outlet Epoch Times. As Craig Silverman reported, by January 2021 these channels had more than 1 million subscribers and tens of millions of views. Despite names like "Eye Opener," "Sound of Hope News," and "Facts Matter," these channels carried tons of obvious disinformation and conspiracy theories about the 2020 election, spreading lies about voting technology companies, votes being flipped from Trump to Biden, disappearing USB drives, suspicious servers in Germany, and other topics.[71] YouTube eventually removed several videos from the channels because they violated the site's Presidential Election Integrity policy,[72] according to Farshad Shadloo (the site's head of policy communications); but this amount of traffic—driven by an eager audience angry and frustrated by Trump's electoral loss—generated a considerable amount of advertising revenue for the channels' owners.

To sum up, digital influence mercenaries can profit in various ways from conspiracy theories. The idea that a truth is being suppressed provides the illusion of logical reasons for uncertainty, which can be appealing. Not only do we want to reduce our uncertainty, we also want to know why this uncertainty is there in the first place. And in many cases, the conspiracy theory places the blame on someone or something that an individual is already prone to dislike, reflecting a type of in-group/out-group divisiveness that we'll explore in chapter 6. As J. M. Berger explains, conspiracies are used "to explain real or perceived problems afflicting the in-group, attributing them to secret machinations by a powerful cabal of elite out-group members."[73] As we'll see in the next chapter, a conceptual framework that blames your problems on others is attractive to many people, and reinforces one's certainty about themselves and their beliefs, particularly in terms of being "better than others." Adherents of conspiracy theories absorb a belief in the falsehood as part of their identity, which helps explain why they will then instinctively reject reasonably sound, evidence-based arguments that threaten to undermine the certainty about their world that they have worked so hard to acquire.

Conclusion

The psychology of uncertainty (and how we manage it) now combines with an information ecosystem of digital overload in which general "trust" devolves into "who you want to trust" based on whatever makes you feel most comfortable. This is how even the most ridiculous lies have given solace to people for whom certain facts and truths have been uncomfortable and inconvenient. And because so many people are willing (even eager) to accept lies, and are often actively seeking out certain kinds of disinformation, a great deal of power and profit can be derived from the kinds of disinformation and provocation efforts described in this book. Digital influence mercenaries can be paid by those who want to disseminate lies to a target audience, and they can also draw traffic to deceitful ad-heavy websites that promote pleasing lies and conspiracy theories. And in a democratic society that values the freedom of speech, there seems to be no viable option through which we might curb these activities and rebuild a shared commitment to objective facts.

The year 2020 may be remembered by many Americans as a whirlwind of assaults on our collective sense of reality. Between the massive amounts of disinformation surrounding the presidential election and the political polarization surrounding the COVID-19 pandemic, attacks against objective truth seemed to skyrocket out of control. Much of this was fueled, tragically, by four years of wild fabrications by the occupant of the White House. And according to a team of fact checkers at the *Washington Post*, the longer he was president, the more frequently he made false or misleading claims. "Trump made about six false or misleading claims a day in his first year, 16 a day in his second year, 22 a day in his third year, and 39 a day in his final year," culminating in a final tally of 30,573 untruths.[74] Throughout his tenure in office, Trump's overt hostility toward truth or reality—combined with his penchant for popularizing disinformation—placed millions of Americans in jeopardy, most visibly reflected in the January 2021 violent insurrection at the U.S. Capitol.

The future will surely bring more attempts to increase uncertainty about what we think we know, to raise fear about what we don't know or understand, and to reinforce people's beliefs in things that may have no grounding in truth or factual evidence. Groups and individuals who have no factual evidence to support their views will nonetheless find the means of empowerment on social media, where they will question scientific evidence and established truth. Instead of arguing the facts, they will play the "what about" game, and argue that "alternate facts" should be given as much consideration. The sense of entitlement to an opinion—regardless of any evidence to support that opinion—gives these people confidence to wrongly declare their opinion as equal to (or more valid than) other opinions.

Meanwhile, these trends threaten to undermine the broader population's relationship with truth, which is under siege by a combination of self-absorbed "Me" and "selfie" generations, isolating themselves into ideological echo chambers, as we'll discuss in chapter 7. In describing the use of bots in manipulating public opinion, Kakutani explains how "social media tends to undermine trust in institutions and makes it more difficult to have the sorts of fact-based debates and discussions that are essential to democracy. The microtargeted ads on social media and the algorithms designed to customize people's news feeds blur the distinctions between what is popular and what is verifiable, and diminish the ability of people to take part in a shared conversation."[75] When truth is treated as an interpretive commodity—one that can be bought or sold, rather than something that exists in nature—this enables the many perceptions manipulation strategies and tactics described in chapter 2.

While digital influence mercenaries are disseminating the kinds of lies and conspiracy theories that provoke engagement and generate revenue on social media platforms, they will also continue to turn the communities of a democratic society against each other. They will continue to fan the flames of mutual hostility as long as doing so results in profits. Further, the economic incentives that stem from the increasing demand for disinformation and conspiracy theories will drive an expansion of the online influence industry and will also encourage greater peer competition among digital influence mercenaries, leading to new (and likely successful) tactical innovations in their tradecraft. And unless American society finds a way to build a new respect for truth and factual evidence, we will remain a profitable target for digital influence mercenaries, both foreign and domestic.

5

OVERCONFIDENCE AND CONFIRMATION BIAS

In his book *Weaponized Lies*, Daniel Levitin explains the concept of belief perseverance: "An odd feature of human cognition is that once we form a belief or accept a claim, it's very hard for us to let go, even in the face of overwhelming evidence and scientific proof to the contrary."[1] This gives power to those who lie to us. If the liar can forge a connection between what they want you to believe and what you already believe (or want to believe), the lack of any factual evidence goes unnoticed. Further, in a climate of increased uncertainty, the liar can disseminate their disinformation with impunity, even when there is an overwhelming amount of evidence that they are indeed lying. This makes it exceedingly difficult to dissuade people from believing in lies and conspiracy theories that they find attractive. In fact, it is virtually impossible to reason someone out of a belief that they were not reasoned into.

As explained in the previous chapter, people have an emotional relationship with information. Knowing this, digital influence mercenaries can manipulate emotions by providing fabricated "proof" of something that the target wants to believe, even when it's completely untrue. Meanwhile, few kinds of information are more attractive to human beings than that which comforts our ego. As the old adage goes, "Telling people what they want to hear rather than what you may want to say can be far more persuasive." This observation governed the influence efforts of the California-based influence mercenary Cyrus Massoumi (described in chapter 1), who noted, "I think that people like what they like. And my goal at one point was to deliver to them what they like."² Further, an effective type of digital influence involves provoking defensive reactions, especially about something we hold dear. For example, messages can be geared toward attacking our credibility or identity, and questioning the validity of things we believe. When confronted with this kind of discomforting information, we often respond by doubling down on our initial position, even in the face of overwhelming proof that we may be wrong.

The previous chapters have examined a handful of influence strategies for manipulating the target's uncertainty, and explained how gaslighting, the so-called "tobacco strategy," and other approaches focus on raising levels of uncertainty about what people think they know. Our inevitable yet discomforting uncertainty is amplified by news media that try to offer perspectives of an issue from "both sides" (even when only one "side" is supported, or even supportable, by factual evidence), by the overall decline in people trusting experts, and by the rise of Internet platforms that allow anyone to publish virtually any kind of information. And yet, because people want to remedy the discomfort of uncertainty, they can easily fall prey to disinformation, including a variety of falsehoods and conspiracy theories.

Meanwhile, influence mercenaries can also deploy strategies to reinforce the target's confidence in something that they already believe (or want to believe). In "The Science of Fake News," David Lazer and his colleagues explain that individuals tend to accept information uncritically and not question the credibility of information unless it violates their preconceived notions, or if they are incentivized in some other way to challenge it. According to research published in the highly respected *Science* magazine, "people tend to align their beliefs with the values of their community. . . . [They] prefer information that confirms their preexisting attitudes, view information consistent with their preexisting beliefs as more persuasive than dissonant information, and are inclined to accept information that pleases them. Prior ideological beliefs might prevent acceptance of fact checking of a given fake news story, [and people] are more likely to accept familiar information as true."³ As a result, "facts" can be packaged and provided in many different forms and sold to those who desperately want specific "facts" to support their predetermined beliefs.

Because of their prior beliefs, the target audience will choose to embrace these "facts" regardless of the inherent deficiencies, and will even spread them and defend them if necessary. As Joseph Goebbels—Hitler's propaganda minister—once said, "propaganda works best when those who are being manipulated are confident they are acting on their own free will."⁴ Some people actively want to be lied to and are seeking out their own sources of disinformation—just as Goebbels would have wanted. And these people seeking their own sources of disinformation are a prime target for the digital influence mercenaries described in this book, who can profit at their expense. The target of an influence strategy may have particularly strong convictions, but these can be influenced either by messages that challenge the merits of those convictions (often provoking an emotional response), or by messages that praise and reinforce those convictions (provoking a favorable in-group affiliation response). The latter approach, reinforcing a sense of certainty, is the main topic addressed in this chapter. Further, reinforcing certainty is a particularly powerful technique when we can identify—and amplify—the target's preexisting biases and prejudices, something that social media allows us to do with increasing regularity and sophistication.

So, while we previously examined how the amount of information (too little or too much) often leads to heightened uncertainty, in this chapter we discover the power of a limited, narrow orientation of available information—particularly when it provides some level of comforting affirmation of what we want to believe. This, as described below, offers an entirely different and equally powerful vector for influence efforts. Specifically, disinformation campaigns of this type are more geared toward reinforcing beliefs in the untrue than convincing people to change their minds about something. And unfortunately, human history is replete with examples of people believing in something that was proven untrue. Even when confronted with factual evidence that undermines their belief, some people still choose to believe in the lie.

Years ago, people believed the Earth was flat—amazingly, there are still some who claim this today. A belief in the unbelievable—like conspiracy theories—is more than a psychological curiosity. When a group of people express their belief in a conspiracy, repeating and reinforcing the spread of it through a sort of self-perpetuating influence feedback loop, it becomes virtually impossible for any rational, evidence-based arguments to diminish their belief. As described in the previous chapter, a conspiracy theory offers an explanation for complicated phenomena and frightening events, and that explanation (as far-fetched as it may be) provides a sense of certainty. And once we have arrived at this certainty, we will defend it with increasing ferocity. We have made a personal investment in this belief, so any challenges to it are seen as a personal attack. Admitting that you have made a mistake, that you have been fooled or deceived, is not easy for many people, especially those with fragile egos. In a sense, our own psychological makeup explains why there are a surprising number of people who adamantly believe in conspiracy theories. Even more surprising, there are some Americans who have convinced themselves that a certain political leader is blessed by God, despite a mountain of evidence revealing the absolute moral bankruptcy of that politician. In truth, many kinds of beliefs are quite troublesome, but as the writer C. S. Lewis once noted, "A belief in invisible cats cannot be logically disproved."[5]

This propensity to believe is being used against us in many ways, much to our disadvantage. Whether the influencer is pursuing economic, social, religious, political, or other strategic goals, they can rely on at least some percentage of their target to be rather deficient in how they cope with uncertainty. Each of us wants to have at least some sense of certainty about ourselves, about the course of actions we choose, and about many other things. As the strong, constant winds of time blow us through the foggy forest of uncertainty, we grasp at branches hoping to find some source of stability, some grounding to help us navigate the terrain. Some of us find certainty in faith and organized religions, or political parties, or some other collective entity. We tend to like virtually anything that can give us a sense of certainty about something (thereby reducing the risks and discomfort that accompany uncertainty), and we want more of that. Our desire to reduce uncertainty about our future drives the high levels of applications for admissions to places like Stanford, Oxford, Princeton, Harvard, and other top-tier universities, because the perception is that "a degree from a place like X will ensure your success" (despite plenty of examples to the contrary).

In the previous chapter we examined how our deep desire to reduce uncertainty makes us vulnerable to the power of lies and the liar. But clinging to certainty and beliefs also makes us vulnerable. In both of these human dimensions, disinformation and conspiracy theories find a great deal of psychological traction. And as described earlier, there has been a tremendous shift in America's relationship with the truth over the past half century. While manipulating a narrative (via persuasion and social influence) has been an eternal part of human interactions, the decline in deference toward the presentation of facts is a fairly recent development. Not long ago, it was assumed by most that in order to be viewed as credible, a public figure needed to be able to substantiate their claims with some amount of evidence. Broadly speaking, this was an accepted professional norm among scientists, lawyers, engineers, business leaders, academic researchers, and many others. If you were proven wrong by others with more convincing evidence, you could lose credibility, although acknowledging a mistake in research or interpretation of facts could salvage the damage to your reputation moving forward. But this is clearly no longer the case.

It remains true that if people don't believe you, the level of power and influence you might have will decline. But as prolific liars like Rush Limbaugh, Alex Jones, and Donald Trump have shown us, you no longer need to be right or even credible to still be believed. Some of Trump's supporters may not entirely buy into everything he is saying, but it is the way in which he is saying it that influences their belief in Trump. More importantly, truth has come to matter less than beliefs. And for many of us, our beliefs are sacred, things to be defended at all costs. As Cailin O'Connor and James Owen Weatherall observed in *The Misinformation Age*, "We generally expect our beliefs to conform with and be supported by the available evidence."[6] However, when evidence is unavailable, or when the available evidence points in a different direction, we have a tendency to ignore the evidence and continue to believe what we want to believe. Further, as Denise Winn explains in *The Manipulated Mind*, "the framework of assumptions we each construct around our world is very precious—it acts as a kind of road map. If it is found that a particular set of assumptions does not correspond to reality, a disabling emotional upheaval is experienced."[7] And of course, what we believe—and more pointedly, what we want to believe—can be influenced and manipulated in many ways. Most critically, our pride in what we think we know and what we believe to be true is a form of hubris that makes us especially vulnerable to influence.

Pride, Prejudice, and Confirmation Bias

In *The Social Animal*, psychologist Elliot Aronson explains that often "beliefs we hold are never called into question; when they are not, it is relatively easy for us to lose sight of why we hold them."[8] When we view something as highly relevant, and we feel we have a high level of certainty in what we know (or think we know) about it, we tend to seek (or require) much less information about it. For example, individuals may have all the information that they desire about an issue or a political candidate. This low degree of uncertainty makes them fairly confident in the decisions they make as a result. In fact, we may be so confident in our convictions that we ignore new information and reject any alternative or competing interpretations of information altogether. As discussed in previous chapters, the implications of this for effective influence operations are fairly clear.

When processing new information, our brain often looks for connections with what we already know as a way of simplifying the navigation of our complex neural pathways. As described in the previous chapter, researchers have shown that people "tend to be cognitive misers, forever trying to conserve our cognitive energy," which frequently leads us "to adopt strategies that simplify complex problems and make information processing easier."[9] However, this introduces a variety of tendencies called "cognitive biases"—mental shortcuts that influence our decision-making.[10] Some of these biases may lead us to make assumptions based on stereotypes or personal memories. Other biases may help us see patterns in data, or notice things that we have seen before, or identify particular flaws in other people more easily than we recognize the same flaws in ourselves. Cognitive biases can lead us to misinterpret information, or even draw the wrong conclusions about a situation. A particularly powerful form of cognitive bias is called "confirmation bias," which happens when you interpret new evidence as confirmation of your existing beliefs or theories. When we have an idea about something, or especially a strongly held belief about it, we tend to look for confirmation, some kind of supporting evidence to help us feel validated in our belief. We certainly won't be looking for information that seems contrary or contradictory, and if we see such information, we may choose to ignore it or dismiss it as invalid.

The scientific method requires objective, neutral gathering and analysis of all available data, which is then used to confirm or reject a hypothesis. Thousands of important scientific discoveries would never have happened if the researchers had not held true to the basic tenets of the scientific method. Looking for data to help us validate a belief (or in some cases just making it up, as in the case of Andrew Wakefield and the anti-vaccination conspiracy theorists described previously) can have very negative consequences. Among academic scholars and scientists, there is a term for this kind of tendency: "cherry picking." This term refers to the scientifically (and morally) unacceptable practice of looking for data that support your hypothesis, and disregarding data that do not support it. As Philip Howard notes, this kind of behavior is also seen beyond the scientific realm, in terms of how many people selectively expose themselves to only news and information that fits an ideology they subscribe to, is consistent with things they already know, or helps them avoid the work of rethinking their assumptions.[11]

According to Elizabeth Kolbert, "Assorted theories have been advanced to explain confirmation bias—why people rush to embrace information that supports their beliefs while rejecting information that disputes them; that first impressions are difficult to dislodge, that there's a primitive instinct to defend one's turf, that people tend to have emotional rather than intellectual responses to being challenged and are loath to carefully examine evidence."[12] Confirmation bias also holds a huge amount of appeal for many people. Having confidence in what you believe is far more appealing than confronting the fear and ignorance imposed by the unknown or the uncertain.[13]

However, confirmation bias can also lead to the problem of overconfidence, a dangerous hubris that often blinds us to reality. In fact, some people have way, way too much certainty in their own convictions and instincts. As psychologist Bert Hodges explains, "There are clear cases where people trust themselves too much, and others far too little."[14] For example, one person who has demonstrated minimal (if any) uncertainty or doubt is Donald Trump, who famously declared on the campaign trail in 2016, "My primary consultant is myself and I have a good instinct for this stuff, I'm speaking with myself, number one, because I have a very good brain."[15] Similarly, when asked in the summer of 2016 whether he read much, he replied, "I never have. I'm always busy doing a lot."[16] The obvious problems associated with overconfidence in one's own knowledge and abilities have been well documented throughout human history, even dramatized in ancient Greek tragedies. This overconfidence also plays a prominent role in the spread and acceptance of disinformation.

Each of us has specific attributes that impact how we receive and examine information. We depend on our grasp of what we think we know, and the less knowledge and information we have about something, the more likely we are to rely on belief than on factual evidence. Further, the more ignorant we are in general, the more likely we are to arrogantly defend that which we believe. This is particularly true with regard to our beliefs about other people. Ignorance and prejudice go hand in hand. Centuries of mankind's darker history reveal myriad examples, from inquisitions and witch burnings to pogroms and genocide—all of which were based on beliefs and prejudices (not facts) about other people.

In addition to ignorance and arrogance, confirmation bias can also lead to a dangerous form of self-deception. According to Lee McIntyre, "The Dunning-Kruger effect (sometimes called the 'too stupid to know they're stupid' effect) is a cognitive bias that concerns how low-ability subjects are often unable to recognize their own ineptitude. This 'overconfidence bias' has serious consequences; 'I am an excellent driver, at any speed and in any weather conditions' is a bias that can frequently get people hurt or even killed."[17] Further, as Dunning and Kruger put it, "incompetence robs [people] of their ability to realize it; the greatest inflation in one's assessment of one's own ability comes from the lowest performers.... What seems to be going on here is self-deception. We love ourselves so much that we cannot see our own weaknesses."[18]

As Lee McIntyre explains, "Our inherent cognitive biases make us ripe for manipulation and exploitation by those who have an agenda to push, especially if they can discredit all other sources of information."[19] If you are predisposed to be against certain government policies, watching a news program in which convincing or compelling arguments are made in support of those policies begins to make you uncomfortable. As you become slightly less confident in your opposition to those policies, you begin to question your judgment, and uncertainty rises. At this point, it is most likely that you will simply change the station and watch something else. A study by Lance Canon found that when people lose confidence in themselves, they become less willing to listen to arguments that challenge what they believe. As a result, "the very people you most want to convince and whose opinions might be the most susceptible to being changed are the ones least likely to continue to expose themselves to a communication designed for that purpose."[20]

This resistance to factual evidence that might challenge our beliefs is frequently rooted in our physical makeup. When the chemical neurotransmitter dopamine is released in large amounts, it creates feelings of pleasure and reward, which motivates us to repeat the specific behavior that resulted in those feelings. The term "dopamine hit" is frequently used to describe a type of consistent social media use that feeds an individual's biases and ego in this way. As Elizabeth Kolbert notes, "People experience genuine pleasure—a rush of dopamine—when processing information that supports their beliefs."[21] This is a big reason why, as the RAND report on "truth decay" explains, "the ways in which human beings process information and make decisions cause people to look for opinions and analysis that confirm preexisting beliefs, more heavily weight personal experience over data and facts, and rely on mental shortcuts and the opinions of others in the same social networks. These tendencies contribute to the blurring of the line between opinion and fact and, in some cases, allow opinion to subsume fact."[22] People desperately want to be right (in order to navigate the inherent uncertainty of our daily world). They hate to be proven wrong and will frequently fight against any effort to undermine the "certainty" they have worked so hard to acquire and that they feel others share.

Many people do not want to be humbled by the recognition of all that they don't know or understand, and so they adopt personal strategies to deflect that kind of information. This is why, even in the face of insurmountable evidence, confirmation bias often prevents people from acknowledging any validity in a competing narrative. Confirmation bias provides a comfort blanket when confronting uncertainty about the many complexities in life. Influence efforts that exploit overconfidence and confirmation bias are not trying to convince a large group of people about something they didn't already believe. Instead of increasing or decreasing uncertainty, the goal here is to make people defend what they already believe. Once the influencer understands the beliefs and values of a particular target, they can provoke emotional responses (including fear and anger about a perceived threat to those beliefs), in order to achieve the strategic goal of increasing divisions within the society.

Exploiting Overconfidence and Confirmation Bias

Generally speaking, there is a broad range of influence strategies that exploit the ego and defensive mechanisms of an individual target. The goal in many of these instances is to reinforce the target's conviction about false information, a basic "You're right!" narrative that the target's ego will find highly attractive. In truth, we frequently seek out this kind of narrative, even in the face of ample evidence that contradicts that belief, because it diminishes uncertainty and provides a source of self-esteem. Further, as we'll explore in chapter 6, social groups and collective identity can provide an attractive and powerful narrative of "You're right, because you're one of us and they're wrong!" But before we address those topics, in the remainder of this chapter we'll focus on individual-level dimensions of exploiting our overconfidence in what we think we know. At the risk of oversimplifying a complex terrain of digital influence strategies that can be employed for this purpose, I've organized this discussion around the following themes: avoiding cognitive dissonance, motivated reasoning, lazy reasoning, and the strategy of escalating commitment.

Exploiting the Target's Desire to Avoid Cognitive Dissonance

In his 1957 book *A Theory of Cognitive Dissonance*, psychologist Leon Festinger explains that people want to maintain internal consistency among their beliefs, attitudes, and behaviors, and experience mental distress when there is inconsistency.[23] As noted earlier, our cognitive biases stem from this aspect of human nature, whereby we choose to reject information that contradicts something we believe. According to Lee McIntyre, "A central concept of human psychology is that we strive to avoid psychic discomfort. It is not a pleasant thing to think badly of oneself. Some psychologists call this 'ego defense,'" but the basic fact is that "it just feels better for us to think that we are smart, well-informed, capable people than that we are not."[24] As a result, when we are confronted with factual evidence that something we believe may not be true, it creates a form of psychological tension, which typically provokes a variety of attempts to remedy that tension. Some will be persuaded to accept that they made a mistake and embrace the fact-based narrative, but others will find this produces an internal inconsistency about their self-image and thus will argue against—and even reject—what the factual evidence shows.[25]

We frequently do not want our beliefs questioned or challenged, for that leads to greater uncertainty, fear, and cognitive dissonance. The receipt of new information that significantly challenges what we think we know can create considerable discomfort, increasing uncertainty to a level where we suddenly feel the need for additional information that either confirms or rejects the newly offered narrative. The desire to avoid and resolve this discomfort leads people to rationalize, ignore, and even deny things that are inconsistent with their core beliefs. According to psychological research, when we are directly confronted with information that contradicts deeply held beliefs, a common response is to become emotionally upset and openly hostile, and often we simply reaffirm our certainty in what we want to believe is true.[26] Refusing to acknowledge any contrary information about oneself or one's views is called being "anti-intraceptive."[27]

Our desperate desire to avoid the discomfort of uncertainty and cognitive dissonance may even compel us to defend the indefensible. In some cases, a person who has latched onto views that appear to be reinforced by other people (as we'll discuss in chapters 6 and 7) will vigorously defend those views even in the face of overwhelming evidence that they are wrong. Social media has come to play a prominent role in this kind of behavioral influencing. Further, some people cannot tolerate inconsistencies between their own worldview and that of others whom they trust and admire. This discrepancy can cause an uncomfortable tension that people naturally try to reduce or eliminate.[28] As Pratkanis and Aronson explain, cognitive dissonance emerges when we discover something that conflicts with our beliefs or a choice we have made—for example, when the policies of a president you voted for are proven to be responsible for increased racism and poverty. "To reduce our dissonance, we label the disconcerting information 'propaganda' and deny the validity of the claim. Thus discredited, the fact no longer needs to be considered in our decision making."[29]

Further, we actively seek confirmation of what we believe, which provides numerous opportunities for the purveyors of fake news to influence us.[30] Because we want to avoid cognitive dissonance, we will embrace as strongly as we can any messages that align with our predispositions. Thus, one goal of influence efforts will be to amplify the target's biases and prejudices, reinforcing their certainty about a belief in something that in reality is patently false. Several of the examples provided in chapter 1 demonstrate the effectiveness of this approach, where digital influence mercenaries like Jestin Coler and Cameron Harris made significant profits in ad revenues by spreading fake news that supported a pro-Trump narrative among Trump supporters.[31]

Once you have taken ownership of a particular narrative, you instinctively feel the need to defend it against competing narratives. Voting and purchasing decisions are even more so. We make claims like "I support [candidate X] because what he says makes sense to me" (despite the fact that it's completely false), or "I bought this brand of truck instead of that other brand of truck because it's clearly the best choice." Our ego drives us to defend our decisions, because our self-image becomes associated with those decisions. We feel compelled to convince others that our decisions were sound, logical, right, and just. When presented with information that calls these decisions into question, we can choose to humbly acknowledge we were mistaken—but that is a mainly unattractive choice, one that brings a wave of uncomfortable uncertainty crashing down upon us. No, we prefer instead to protect our self-image and defend our decision-making. Digital influence mercenaries can exploit this tendency by manufacturing or increasing cognitive dissonance (e.g., "things are not as you had believed they were") and then providing the target with a proposed remedy, a way to resolve that dissonance. As Manheim explains, "Because the individuals being subjected to persuasion will generally seek out the path of least resistance that leads toward cognitive dissonance reduction, the persuader will want insofar as possible to foreclose all options that lead to dissonance reduction except the one (attitude change, behavior change, etc.) that serves the needs of the [influence] campaign."[32] By providing a clear path to a more comforting certainty, you can provoke the target to defend their belief in something that is untrue, as a means of ensuring they reject more forcefully what you don't want them to believe.

Exploiting Motivated Reasoning and Lazy Reasoning

Our deep desire to avoid cognitive dissonance leads us to what researchers have described as "motivated reasoning."[33] As Lee McIntyre explains in his book *Post-truth*, when we are motivated to defend an idea or belief, we look for evidence to confirm it. "Motivated reasoning is a state of mind in which we find ourselves willing (perhaps at an unconscious level) to shade our beliefs in light of our opinions; confirmation bias is the mechanism by which we may try to accomplish this, by interpreting information so that it confirms our preexisting beliefs."[34] Further, according to a recent report by the National Endowment for Democracy, many people actively seek out disinformation—they are eagerly looking for lies that confirm what they already believe in, while rejecting other information sources.[35] The researchers identified psychological drivers behind this "demand for disinformation" and described how "across geographic contexts, deeply polarized societies with low trust in the media appear more susceptible to these drivers." Further, they note, "fact-checkers face challenges in confronting demand for disinformation: news consumers who are invested in a particular political narrative may be more likely to reject corrective information and rationalize their preexisting beliefs."[36] This is a key facet of human psychology that digital influence mercenaries are exploiting with considerable success.

Psychologist Denise Winn explains that "an unwitting emotional investment in believing certain 'facts' may impair one's intellectual detachment."[37] If there is higher uncertainty, as explained earlier, we tend to lean toward sources of information that we are likely to agree with, and avoid (or even condemn outright) those sources we disagree with. And as Lee McIntyre observes, motivated reasoning leads us to "color our perception of what actually is true" in terms of what we hope to be true. "When we feel psychic discomfort we are motivated to find a non-ego-threatening way to reduce it, which can lead to the irrational tendency to accommodate our beliefs to our feelings, rather than the other way around."[38]

The implications of this research are fairly clear. As psychologists Gordon Pennycook and David Rand explain, people succumb to the effects of digital influence efforts—including information that is wholly false—because they are predisposed to certain biases and prejudices that filter how they perceive what they see and hear.[39] Because of our tendency for motivated reasoning, we embrace information that provides confirmation of those biases and prejudices, while instinctively doubting or rejecting information that contradicts them. As a result, our analytical reasoning is rarely (if ever) purely objective, but instead has an inherent subjective quality that can lead to virtually any of us being duped from time to time by fake news.[40] And further, some people will actively seek out disinformation that reinforces their incorrect interpretation of events, policies, people, and so forth. Researchers have even found that being confronted with evidence undoubtedly proving a belief to be wrong can sometimes provoke a "backfire effect," through which the individual will simply reject the evidence and "double down" on their mistaken belief.[41] For example, a study by Brendan Nyhan and Jason Reifler found that providing evidence not only failed to reduce misperceptions among the targeted ideological group, this evidence actually increased misperceptions among the group in question.[42] "It seemed as if people ideologically inclined to believe a given falsehood worked so hard to come up with reasons that the correction was wrong that they came to believe the falsehood even more strongly."[43]

The "tobacco strategy" described in chapter 3 has relevance here: A person who *wants* to believe that smoking is not as harmful as the scientific evidence indicates will be more likely to disagree with, ignore, or challenge those individuals and studies linking cancer and illnesses with tobacco use. Further, they can be emboldened to do so by various websites, blogs, and social media accounts that tell them what they want to hear. In fact, people searching for sources of confirming disinformation on any number of topics can now readily find it on InfoWars, Breitbart, Daily Caller, Newsmax, and other media outlets. And as explained in chapter 2, there are many social media tools and tactics that are being used to deceive us into thinking we have reason to be certain about things that are not supported by any factual evidence. Using various kinds of data and algorithms, digital influence mercenaries can now identify and target Internet users (and their social media accounts) that have demonstrated support for conspiracy theories and frequently visited the aforementioned media outlets. And they can also target political propaganda and disinformation toward the mostly likely receptive audiences using search engine optimization strategies that recommend specific sources of information over others to the target audience.[44]

Studies have also suggested that "political misconceptions are resistant to explicit corrections," and that individuals may be susceptible to fake news stories that are amenable to their political ideology.[45] As Pennycook and Rand observe, a person will support political candidates who appear aligned with their own values and beliefs and will "passively and uncritically accept arguments that support their political ideology."[46] This is why millions of Americans came to believe in Trump:

because they wanted to. Like Trump, many of them reject the inconvenient scientific facts behind climate change and other such realities, and they hate the so-called "politically correct" movement, in which certain kinds of speech are considered socially unacceptable. As Francis Fukuyama noted, "At a time when many Americans believe that public speech is excessively policed, Trump's supporters like that he is not intimidated by the pressure to avoid giving offense. In an era shaped by political correctness, Trump represents a kind of authenticity that many Americans admire: he may be malicious, bigoted, and unpresidential, but at least he says what he thinks."[47] What his supporters wanted is someone who confirms their worst fears about immigration, gun control, Muslims, China, Democrats, and other topics. They found this confirmation in Trump.

But while so many researchers have identified "motivated reasoning" as having a significant effect on various forms of decision-making, there is also a certain passive laziness in our information processing that can be exploited by digital influence efforts as well. As Pennycook and Rand note, "People who think more analytically (those who are more likely to exercise their analytic skills and not just trust their 'gut' response) are less superstitious, less likely to believe in conspiracy theories, and less receptive to seemingly profound but actually empty assertions." But unfortunately, they conclude, "people often just don't think critically enough about the information they encounter."[48]

As explained earlier in this chapter, our tendency to find ways to help conserve our cognitive energy leads us to adopt information processing strategies that simplify complex problems and make information processing easier.[49] For example, in the previous chapter we discussed how people often use peripheral information processing in order to simplify complex problems. Researchers have described how we rely on "heuristics"—generally defined as assumptions or artificial constructs—when we make quick judgments using the peripheral route of information processing.[50] Further, the Dunning-Kruger effect described earlier often links a certain kind of ignorance with pure laziness. Confronting and reducing our own ignorance takes time and effort, so choosing not to do so represents a form of laziness. In one study on "the cognitive mechanisms that explain why patently false (and often quite implausible) news stories have been able to gain traction on social media," the researchers determined that "more analytic individuals were better able to differentiate between fake and real news."[51] Essentially, those of us who choose to apply greater cognitive energy in our analytical reasoning tend to be less vulnerable to disinformation.

Influence efforts can exploit lazy reasoning through what Robert Lifton calls "loading the language"—compressing complex ideas into brief, highly reductive, definitive-sounding phrases easily memorized and easily expressed (e.g., "Make America Great Again"), whose aim is to shut down independent thinking.[52] Corporate marketers and politicians have long recognized the power of slogans that imply group unity, particularly regarding beliefs that the target audience shares, and the importance of making the audience feel good, valid, and justified in believing certain things. This is an important predicate to making them more receptive to subsequent influence efforts, including those that seek to capitalize on their desire for certainty with claims like "We are the only news station that tells you the truth," and "I am the only politician telling you the truth."

Trump's political success in this regard came from targeting millions of racist, bigoted Americans and making them feel good about being racist and bigoted. People's egos are extremely powerful influencers of their behavior. If attending a Trump rally makes you feel good about all the things you feel and say about nonwhites, you will want to attend more Trump rallies or share, like, and retweet messages posted online by Trump and his supporters. The combination of motivated reasoning, cognitive laziness, and our desire for certainty helps explain how people could self-identify as patriotic Americans while contradicting themselves by cheering for someone who routinely insulted and denigrated military heroes (like then-senator John McCain or retired admiral William McRaven) as well as families whose loved ones had died serving their country, while defending statues and flags representing the Confederate rebellion against the United States.[53] Essentially, the problem is that many people are willing to be lied to—and apparently even *want* to be lied to, some more eagerly than others—in order to confirm what they believe. As a result, attacking truths and factual evidence that threaten to contradict those lies becomes a useful strategy to be pursued in digital influence operations.

It is in this kind of information ecosystem that the digital influence mercenary flourishes, as illustrated by the examples discussed in chapter 1. This is particularly the case when the lies being proliferated reinforce the beliefs, hopes, hatreds, and prejudices of the recipients. In other words, pleasing lies will always do better than uncomfortable truths. "Only to a limited extent does man want truth," Friedrich Nietzsche argued. "He desires the pleasant, life-preserving consequences of truth; to pure knowledge without consequences he is indifferent, to potentially harmful and destructive truths he is even hostile."[54] As a result of this human tendency, news media and the entertainment industry have increasingly chosen to focus on giving people what they want (in order to generate the most revenues). In many cases, as Mazarr et al. observe, they have determined that what people want is information that is "sensational, extreme, and targeted against some sort of out-group that allows the audience to deepen its sense of social membership."[55]

Overall, because people accept being deceived and want to be deceived (in order to get that "dopamine rush"), the digital influence mercenaries have a clear advantage in shaping a target's beliefs and behaviors in ways that help achieve their strategic objectives. For example, they may provoke the target to share and endorse a lie, or to defend their belief in a lie. They may lure the target into visiting an advertisement-heavy "news" website full of disinformation that supports their prejudices. Using the emotion manipulation tactics described earlier, they can influence the target to vote a certain way, or to buy something, because of a perceived alignment with the target's beliefs. Once a target's preferences and biases are understood, they can potentially be manipulated into doing all these things and more.

Escalating the Target's Commitment

Another individual ego-driven influence strategy involves what Robert Cialdini refers to as "commitment and consistency traps."[56] Basically, if we have agreed to do something small, and can be persuaded to at least consider doing something greater that is consistent with the previous action, our internal drive combined with social pressures will often compel us to follow through with that greater commitment. As Pratkanis and Aronson explain, "Commitment can be self-perpetuating, resulting in an escalating commitment to an often failing course of action. Once a small commitment is made, it sets the stage for ever-increasing commitments. The original behavior needs to be justified . . . [resulting in] a seemingly irrational commitment to a poor business plan, a purchase that makes no sense, a war that has no realistic objectives, or an arms race gone out of control."[57]

The underlying influence strategy here involves encouraging the kinds of peripheral information processing described in the previous chapter, and rejecting any consideration of competing or contradictory narratives. According to Philip Howard, "People pay attention to political content that fits the ideological package they already subscribe to. If they've already expressed a preference for a particular candidate, they will select messages that strengthen, not weaken, that preference."[58] This, in turn, directly relates to how certainty impacts our decision-making. As noted earlier, humans seek a type of internal consistency. So, once you have determined you are certain about something (by making a small public commitment), it becomes increasingly difficult to resist making a larger public commitment based on that initial certainty, because doing so would feel internally inconsistent. Once we have been convinced of a particular direction, even just a little, our self-image often requires us to do whatever it takes to justify continuing in that direction. As Pratkanis and Aronson explain, "Having done a small favor creates internal pressure to agree to do a larger favor; in effect, we comply with the large request to be consistent with our earlier commitment."[59] Further, for those who care deeply about how others feel about them, the external pressures to appear consistent and reliable also make it very likely you will agree to the larger public commitment once you have previously made the smaller one. To do otherwise would reintroduce that nasty uncertainty that we so desperately wanted to eradicate in the first place.

For example, when attending a political rally the speaker first convinces the audience of a crisis brewing. Your initial commitment indicator could be simply agreeing with phrases used by the speaker that convey a sense of certainty (even if there is no evidence to support it), like "No one could disagree with the statement...," or "You must acknowledge that...," or "Everybody is convinced...," and so forth. As natural seekers of certainty, we look for these kinds of markers as indicators of what we can have some certainty about. Our initial agreement thus signals to the influencer that they can influence other related beliefs and behaviors. For example, the speaker could then convince the audience that their favored political candidate is the only one capable of resolving that crisis. The audience members' commitment shifts from agreeing that a crisis exists to supporting that candidate's recommended solution to that crisis. Or, as Manheim notes, commitment and participation can be generated and escalated through participation in protests, public demonstrations, attendance at rallies, or other events; through grassroots lobbying activities; or through invitations to help shape the influence campaign itself—for example, by developing your own blog or creating and sharing campaign-related videos and other materials.[60]

Translating this into the world of digital influence warfare is fairly straightforward. By tracking your online behavior—the digital evidence of your likes and dislikes, personal values, in-group identity, and so forth—the influencer can generate a profile of the little commitments you have already made, and then identify what sorts of larger commitments you would be ready to make in order to be consistent with your earlier ones. Think of the many "like and retweet" or "please comment" appeals you see on social media, seeking to provoke our engagement and solicit our commitment to a position on something. You can "like" or "share" or "retweet" something quite easily, and in doing so have made a small commitment, a small indication of support for that which you recommended or passed along to others. This small commitment, in turn, is recorded by a website or social media platform, becoming part of the vast data resources that can inform effective influence efforts. Your indications of an initial commitment to a position on something are recorded and added to an algorithm to determine what other kinds of commitment you might be willing to make. The influencer can then more easily convince you to make future commitments, manipulating your internal drive to remain consistent. For example, if you have at one point expressed support for the statement, opinion, or platform of a political candidate, you should expect to receive further information about how to support that candidate by purchasing a bumper sticker or T-shirt, and attending meetings or campaign rallies planned for your region. Because you made the earlier commitment, the assumption is that you are more likely to be persuaded by a request to make a more significant commitment in the future.

In a similar way, think of the significant challenge that emerges for the individual who has publicly committed to a position (e.g., pro-life, pro-NRA), but then privately has a change of heart due to some tragic incident (e.g., an abortion clinic bombing or a mass shooting at a local school). This creates an uncomfortable cognitive dissonance that must be reconciled in some way. The individual can choose to alter their public position in a different direction, or they can choose to bury deep down inside those private doubts and reservations they may have. When surrounded by others whose public commitment mirrors their own, and who remain consistent to their initial position on the issue, it becomes very difficult not to remain consistent as well. They come to view the alternative course of action (recognizing they were wrong and changing their public position) as the least desirable option. Further, as noted earlier, our motivated reasoning and drive for internal consistency frequently mean that being confronted with evidence undoubtedly proving a belief to be wrong can sometimes provoke a "backfire effect," through which the individual will simply reject the evidence and "double down" on their mistaken belief.[61]

This is where disinformation becomes particularly effective. Once the target has convinced themselves to a level of certainty about one false narrative, it becomes easier to increase their certainty by providing similar messages that amplify that false narrative in various ways. As a result, the individual's commitment escalates from "embracing the narrative" to "defending the narrative" even in the face of significant evidence that it is indeed false. The effective influencer is one who conveys messages that the target accepts and then adopts as their own, willing to defend against competing arguments or counternarratives. If you can enlist the target's ego to defend their decision to accept the message as credible, your influence campaign will likely succeed. And when the influencer can incorporate indicators of social proof—for example, a flurry of social media accounts embracing that false narrative—the target's certainty in their position becomes further solidified. This emphasizes the importance of group identity and collective-oriented strategies to reinforce certainty, as we'll explore in chapter 6.

Conclusion

To sum up, research on several aspects of human nature—including cognitive dissonance, motivated reasoning, and confirmation bias—helps us understand why, as Lee McIntyre notes, "so many people seem prone to form their beliefs outside the norms of reason and good standards of evidence, in favor of accommodating their own intuitions or those of their peers."[62] An effective digital influence mercenary knows that rationalizations for falsehoods don't have to be rational statements. Pseudoscientific arguments have been used for centuries to support prejudice and bigotry toward others. Racism, anti-Semitism, misogyny, anti-immigrant sentiment, and so forth have all incorporated rational-sounding arguments (darker skinned people are less intelligent; women are too emotional to be trusted with the right to vote; Mexicans are lazy, etc.) that have no basis in fact, and yet were accepted as truth by millions of people who took comfort in such things as evidential support for their opinions. Confirmation bias and motivated reasoning help them reinforce their biases and prejudices, fueling a type of analytical reasoning that can exacerbate political differences and increase polarization.[63]

Influence efforts that exploit these aspects of human nature are not trying to convince a large group of people about something they didn't already believe. Rather, their goal is to make people defend what they already believe. Once the influencer understands the beliefs and values of a particular target, they can provoke emotional responses (including fear and anger about a perceived threat to those beliefs) in order to achieve the strategic goal of increasing divisions within the society. Further, reflecting the previous chapter's discussion on the impact of postmodernism, if anything and everything is open to interpretation, confirmation bias allows you—even encourages you—to interpret facts (or lack thereof) any way you like. When truth is seen only as an interpretive commodity, this allows the strategies and tactics of digital influence warfare to become especially powerful.[64] The influencer can obfuscate and distort facts that aren't aligned with their strategic goals, and shape the target audience's perceptions at will—and the audience will embrace those facts just as long as they conform to their predetermined values and beliefs.

Finally, efforts to bolster our confidence in beliefs or a particular narrative are strengthened considerably when embedded within our daily social interactions. Because we are social creatures, human beings generally desire social contact and validation—one of the core attractions of social media. But as we'll see in the next chapter, digital influence efforts can take advantage of collective identity and other aspects of social groups (like the pressures of conformity) to deceive, provoke, and manipulate the perceptions of target audiences.

6

COLLECTIVE IDENTITY AND CONFORMITY

The influence strategies described in the previous chapters are especially effective when reinforced by a community of like-minded people. The psychology of persuasion and influence is directly tied to our search for what and whom to trust. Our uncertainty can lead to a range of behaviors, including conformity and obedience to authority. When making choices, many of us—in order to overcome the discomfort of uncertainty—cope by accepting unquestioned the advice of others about whom or what to trust. For example, researchers like Elihu Katz and Paul Lazarsfeld have found that "people listen to what their neighbors, family, and community members have to say about politics, and that personal influence is a pivotal aspect of persuasion—perhaps even more important than mass media messages."[1] Thus, information of any kind (including a social media post) received from someone we know and trust will likely have more impact on our perceptions and behavior than that which is received from a government agency or other formal source.

According to psychological research, information shared socially is treated as reliable by most people.[2] Successful digital influence mercenaries understand the importance of the trusted source—the close friend, family member, colleague, and so forth, to whom we turn when seeking answers to our questions. In essence, we allow these people—invite them, even—to influence our decisions. As young children we learn whom we can trust (and unfortunately, whom we can't) as we develop our personal strategies for reducing uncertainty and insecurity. For most of us, a parent or guardian earns our trust naturally by providing food, water, shelter, protection from others, and so forth. In turn, this trust helps us reduce uncertainty about the chances of our survival and comfort from day to day. As a result, those in whom we have the most trust are usually those who can influence us the most. As social psychologists Amber Gaffney and Michael Hogg explain, "People are motivated to understand themselves and the world around them. When they cannot adequately assess the veracity of their own opinions and the extent of their own abilities through objective means, they turn to similar others. The actions and opinions of others are informative because they often tell us the correct path to take or they outline where our abilities stand in relation to others."[3] Arie Kruglanski and Edward Orehek agree, noting that "[a] major aspect of people's social nature is their reliance on the opinions of valued others, members of significant groups of which they are members."[4]

An individual's group affiliations are thus a critical dimension to how their views of the world are influenced. Uncertainty-identity theory, also from the field of psychology, explains how an individual will adopt a group identity in order to diminish the discomfort and anxiety produced by uncertainty. This in turn influences the behavior of that individual, particularly regarding members of an "in-group" or "out-group."[5] The in-group is a term used to describe how a person's identity is often closely linked to others with shared interests and mutual affinity. The out-group is generally considered to be all people outside the particular in-group. Often, the out-group is seen as inferior compared to the revered in-group members because of key differences like race, gender, religion, nationality, sexual orientation, and other attributes. According to J. M. Berger, efforts to promote greater cohesion among the in-group members can lead to increasingly hostile attitudes toward others (the "out-group").[6] Additionally, research by Kruglanski and Orehek points to "greater preference for in-groups over out-groups because the in-group provides the shared reality that group members are seeking, while the out-group suggests a potentially threatening alternative."[7]

Social identity and group membership can become a very powerful motivator of individual behavior, as Anthony Pratkanis and Elliot Aronson describe in their book *Age of Propaganda*. Research in this field has uncovered "two basic psychological processes, one cognitive and one motivational. First, the knowledge that 'I am in this group' is used to divide up and make sense of the world. . . . Differences between groups are exaggerated, whereas similarities among members [of the in-group] are emphasized in the secure knowledge that 'this is what our type does.'"[8] Further, according to researchers in social psychology, the desire for acceptance by others in the in-group drives decisions, some of which may not have been even considered prior to group membership.[9] For example, some in-groups may have certain logos, mottos, and other visible attributes that demonstrate a shared identity and can promote a type of self-esteem derived from group membership. Whether it's a political candidate, a social movement, a sports team, or a racial supremacy movement, there are hats, T-shirts, bumper stickers, and other branded items that you can purchase in order to proudly display your in-group identity. And simultaneously, you are able to establish a comforting certainty about something simply from the fact that your in-group has embraced it, and the out-group has not. In other words, you are right simply because "they" are wrong.

Humans tend to form "in-groups" and "out-groups" in virtually all types of countries and cultures. You, the reader, are a part of several in-groups (the schools you attended, your workplace, your church, your political affiliation, etc.) that inherently define specific out-groups (people who attended other schools, work elsewhere, attend different churches, etc.). You may not be conscious of some of the in-groups you belong to—for example, since you are reading this book, you are now part of the in-group of people who have read this book, while members of the "out-group," loosely defined, are those who have not read this book, or who likely will never read a book like this. This binary in-group/out-group arrangement also means that most people are far more likely to pay attention to (and believe) what is said by a member of their in-group. Further, if a particular in-group is perceived as potentially attractive (e.g., a throng of boisterous supporters at a political rally), individuals will want to become part of that in-group, and to do so requires them to pay closer attention to what is said by members of that in-group. At the same time, "othering" also works to diminish the resonance of outside (i.e., not part of the in-group) sources of information. These and other aspects of our relationships with others in a social setting—including social media—can be exploited by digital influence mercenaries to manipulate our perceptions and behaviors.

Exploiting Collective Identity

While the influence strategies described in the previous chapter are focused on exploiting aspects of an individual's ego, as well as their desire for confirmation of their beliefs, prejudices, and sense of self, there are also several group-oriented strategies that can be used by digital influencers to reinforce certainty in false information. It begins with our drive to be not only internally consistent but to also be seen by others as conforming with socially acceptable norms and behaviors. Humans beings are social creatures who thrive on a sense of "belonging," and this compels us to align our beliefs to conform with those around us whom we trust. Typically, those whom we trust most contribute to the formation of our values, beliefs, and convictions. These trusted bonds incentivize us to conform to the norms and behavior deemed acceptable by our family upbringing, the friends and associates with whom we form trusted bonds, our spouses, coworkers, neighbors, and others. This, in turn, impacts our choice of religion, political party, professional occupation, and so forth. Conformity is essential to relationships, groups, and culture.[10] As psychologist Bert Hodges notes, "Humans have a natural affinity for conformity. Using others to guide or modify one's own actions is a crucial feature of human existence, as is coordinating the direction and pace of one's movements to align with others with whom one is interacting. Without this conformity and coordination, human culture and its many forms of learning and sharing would not be possible."[11]

In 1974, the German political scientist Elisabeth Noelle-Neumann demonstrated how people will go along with the majority opinion to fit in. The need to belong is one of the deepest human inclinations, she argued, and people are motivated by fear of isolation. That is why exile, expulsion from the group, is one of the oldest forms of punishment.[12] It is human nature to crave social contact and approval. We divide ourselves up according to identity affiliations (tribes, clans, national patriotism, favorite sports teams, educational and economic status, etc.) and then gravitate toward others who share our attributes, our likes and dislikes. We give natural preference to those who are like us. How does this lead to conformity, behavior that those around us will approve of, rather than individually independent expressions of choice and preference? If we want to dress a certain way, but we know that our friends, family, neighbors, and coworkers will frown upon it, deeming it inappropriate, the chances are high we will not dress that way. This is particularly true for certain kinds of social events—if it's a formal affair, showing up in a T-shirt and cargo shorts will earn you swift rebuke, while showing up to an informal pool party in coat and tie would mark you as socially inept, or worse, an outcast, someone who doesn't "fit in," doesn't conform with the expectations of that social setting and is therefore in the wrong.

Conformity is thus part of the human developmental process that begins during our childhood years. As psychologist Denise Winn explains, we learn at a very early stage what our parents or guardians consider to be "right" or "wrong," and we quickly realize that choosing one over the other has consequences. As a child seeks love, affection, and approval, "the child will learn that his needs are more likely to be met if he conforms to what is expected of him."[13] As we grow older, our relationship to conformity becomes much more complicated. We may rebel against our parents and others who want to impose various rules and discipline on us, while simultaneously conforming to peer group members of our age who are also rebelling against their parents.

One way that conformity facilitates the influence of our thoughts and actions is through our tendency to look closely at the behavior of others when determining the appropriate response to a given situation—a type of information often called social validation or social proof.[14] Social validation provides a form of contextual relevance about the information we are viewing at any given time. It becomes a form of influential authority that creates and reinforces certainty in a particular course of action. According to Robert Cialdini, the power of social proof to influence our behavior transcends the physical and online world. When we see crowds of social media users endorsing a narrative in some way or another, it becomes more difficult to reject it or resist it. "We assume that if a lot of people are doing the same thing, they must know something we don't. Especially when we are uncertain, we are willing to place an enormous amount of trust in the collective knowledge of the crowd."[15] And further, the tendency to look for social validation is enhanced when people are uncertain about the appropriate guidelines for behavior. Because of uncertainty, the perception of like-minded fellow travelers choosing a certain path gives us some comfort that choosing the same path as they did will be best, or at least will carry less risk than other paths we might choose.

A large body of research in psychology explains how we want social affirmation of our beliefs, and why we seek social proof for clues about what to do, what and whom to believe, what is meaningful and relevant, and so forth. But how can this social proof be manufactured by an influence strategy? Consider for a moment the typical political campaign rally, where supporters of a particular candidate are the only ones allowed to attend (as protestors are quickly ushered out and sometimes even physically attacked by the candidate's supporters). These are staged events in which the candidate is speaking to an audience of individuals who have already made an initial commitment (of their time and presence) to the candidate (see the "tactic of escalating commitment" described in chapter 5). This in turn gives the impression to others beyond the event that "all these people support the candidate, so maybe I should as well; I mean, could all these people be wrong?

Could this many people have been misled or deceived?" This is what Pratkanis and Aronson refer to as creating a bandwagon effect—the impression that many people support the candidate. Further, they note, "success in the polls (an indication of popular support) is essential if the candidate hopes to secure campaign contributions."[16] So, manufacturing the appearance of support is just as important as having real support.

The same kind of bandwagon social proof influence is seen online as well. For example, the number of followers on a person's social media account serves as an indicator of someone whom others are listening to, which suggests perhaps you should listen to them as well. However, as explained in chapter 2, the number of followers attached to a person's social media account may not in fact be people; instead they can be fake accounts, automated bots made to look and act like real user accounts. This is also the case with sharing, liking, and retweeting a message, where digital influence tactics of deception can be used to manipulate the target's perception about what other people are certain about. When a flood of social media accounts are all saying and reinforcing the same narrative, it can convince you to embrace it as well. Using social proof in this manner to represent (or misrepresent) the so-called "wisdom of the crowd" becomes a means for influencing the target's beliefs and behaviors in the direction of conformity. In these instances, the target has been duped by the façade of credibility.

A paradox of social proof is that we want our own virtual tip of the iceberg to be seen by others, particularly if we are looking for confirmation that our beliefs are shared by others or just validation in our lives more generally, some sort of external reinforcement that we do matter. Our ego defenses drive us to establish an identity that is approved by others and conforms (at least to some degree) to social expectations. Our personal websites and social media accounts provide us with the means to post virtually any kind of information, and our incentives for doing so are usually personal and individually specific in nature. To mediate our individual insecurities about self-worth, we may find ourselves posting an endless stream of photos, videos, personal opinions, and so forth online as a form of seeking validation and recognition from others. When we receive positive feedback, it reinforces our certainty in our beliefs and our self-worth. As a RAND Corporation report concludes, "By allowing people to seek out similar individuals, social media platforms and other forms of engagement offer an important psychological reassurance."[17]

Yet this is another way that certainty, conformity, and social validity can be used against us. We want others to know who we are, where we are, and what we are doing. But all of this revealing information is then taken advantage of by Internet companies, marketers, and malicious actors (including terrorists and Russian trolls) who can tailor specific messages targeting us in ways that are likely to resonate with us and influence our beliefs and behavior. As Kathleen Taylor observes, unless the influencer knows their target well, "they are working in the dark to some extent. Their aim is to get their preferred beliefs accepted by the target, a task which is much easier if those beliefs are not inconsistent with that the target already believes."[18] This is why data mining and analysis become such an essential part of effective digital influence operations, as discussed in first two chapters of this book.

Social validity can be an especially powerful vector of influence when connected to group identity. The study of how people influence one another requires taking into account a diverse landscape of group memberships, political affiliations, and social contacts (attributes that also become part of the targeting profile about us generated by the influencer). Research in social psychology suggests that adoption of a group identity may be intended to reduce feelings of uncertainty about one's self and identity.[19] Identity politics—social identity, group identity, national identity—give a person some sense of certainty, a perceived "solid ground" to stand upon. Who we think we are in this huge, complex world shapes a ton of decisions we make every week. As explained earlier, if we are uncertain about our identity, or if what we believe to be true about ourselves gets called into question, this creates a very uncomfortable cognitive dissonance that we are anxious to navigate and then replace with some form of certainty.

So, we are drawn toward groups that we believe are worth belonging to, based on our perceptions of shared identity, values, concerns, and so forth. Then, once we have established our membership within the group, we begin to embrace the values and narratives of this group. Often, these values are framed as being in stark contrast with the values of others outside the group, with the "in-group" being inherently better than the "out-group." Delineating in-group and out-group membership in this way provides a comforting sense of certainty and superiority, strengthening the individual's commitment to the group. For example, prejudiced attitudes may serve an ego-defensive function, whereby a person's perceived certainty about the world and their place within it is only sustainable when referencing a comparison group of individuals to whom they feel superior.[20]

Exploiting In-Group Conformity

As Gaffney and Hogg explain, "People who identify strongly with their in-group accept group norms and personal standards, because norms provide invaluable information about the in-group and thus the self."[21] This is how in-group identity encourages a form of individual conformity to the group's most commonly accepted position. By embracing a perceived "shared reality" you become "one of us." Then, once you have been convinced you are "one of us" the next step is to convince you that "this is what we do" and why it's important. An example of collective identity formation and reinforcement was witnessed when right-wing extremists built a collective identity among the like-minded visitors of the popular social news aggregation site Reddit, where visitors can "upvote" content that they like. By using the site's voting algorithm (especially within the notoriously hateful subreddit community, r/The_Donald), users were able to promote extremist content and foster a "sense of community," creating an information environment wherein extreme right-wing perspectives were continuously validated.[22]

Social groups are a source of self-esteem and pride for many people. But in order to secure the kinds of self-esteem the group can provide, members need to defend the group and adopt its symbols, rituals, and beliefs, and embrace the view that the group is (at least in some ways) superior to others. Digital influence mercenaries can then use this in-group identity—and all the attributes and responsibilities that come with it—to their advantage by proudly amplifying the customs of the group in order to create the appearance that "I am one of you, you can trust me, now here's what we all are going to do . . ." The con artist makes himself more believable to his audience by demonstrating, "Hey, we're all part of this same in-group, so you can trust me, and do what I say."[23]

We see more extreme examples of this behavior among members of charismatic cults or terrorist groups. Once you have bought into the ideology of the group or movement, one of the first and most common demands made of you will be to ignore all other sources of information not approved by the group. You will also frequently be forced to sever ties with your former friends and family members, virtually anyone who is not (or would not consider becoming) a true believer. It is true that some people treat political parties with a similar kind of unalterable devotion; a pro-Trump cult, for example, members of which will fiercely defend against any criticism of their beliefs, even when that criticism is supported by overwhelming evidence and facts that prove their position is wrong. And as described in the next chapter, digital echo chambers can sequester us to a large degree from others, while providing interactions with fellow "true believers" who offer comforting social confirmation of our beliefs and values.[24]

The in-group/out-group framing of a complex world is appealing to many people because it simplifies things and gives them a target to focus their blame on. For example, something bad is happening (or perceived to be happening) about which facts and evidence are being contested, but we can explain it by blaming an identified villain (the out-group). An aggrieved in-group could even be a community of conspiracy theory adherents, like the QAnon followers described in chapter 4. Adrienne LaFrance recently explained how "these kinds of conspiracy theories are generally characterized by acceptance of the following propositions: Our lives are controlled by plots hatched in secret places. Although we ostensibly live in a democracy, a small group of people run everything, but we don't know who they are. When big events occur—pandemics, recessions, wars, terrorist attacks—it is because that secretive group is working against the rest of us."[25]

As J. M. Berger explains, there are a wide variety of political, social, religious, racial, and other narratives that attribute the grievances of an in-group to members of the out-group.[26] Many conspiracy theories are used "to explain real or perceived problems afflicting the in-group, attributing them to secret machinations by a powerful cabal of elite out-group members . . . [and] argue that out-groups directly control, through secretive means, the success or survival of the in-group."[27] Further, being part of a community of "true believers" in a conspiracy (or a charismatic cult leader, a terrorist group's ideology, or many other things) helps a person feel special, one of "the enlightened few" or "the chosen ones." They are "in the know," as opposed to the ignorant majority, and uniquely equipped to battle the insidious out-group (e.g., anyone who opposes Trump). In fact, conspiracy theories often become popular because of the lure of collective identity, and particularly the role of in-group/out-group membership that identifies a villain who is responsible for something bad happening. And crucially, this conceptual framework provides the true believers with a potential solution to the crisis: because this awful thing is the fault of the out-group, we must exclude them, fight them, and crush them in order to make things right again.[28] As discussed in chapter 2, a variety of deception and provocation strategies can amplify these types of narratives very well.

A core reason why a conspiracy like QAnon has become popular among Trump supporters is an egocentric belief in their own superiority. In their view, the world is not treating them nearly as well as they believe they deserve. Conspiracies that provide some explanation for this reinforce their false sense of superiority through a conviction that they "know" some kind of secret information that others are currently "in the dark" about, producing an ego-driven rush of adrenaline that serves their psychological need to feel "right."[29] Additionally, this egocentrism and collective identity also fuel demand for QAnon-branded merchandise, which provides unique opportunities for digital influence mercenaries to derive profits from the sale of hats, T-shirts, bumper stickers, and other merchandise that these individuals are buying as a means of proclaiming that collective identity.

A community of conspiracy theory adherents is also where we find a key intersection of confirmation bias and fear (which is directly related to the acceptance and spread of both disinformation and conspiracy theories). Some aspects of group identity can fuel a fear of the "others," a fear of the threat that outsiders pose to the revered in-group, its way of life, its very identity. According to "attribution theory," as Taylor explains, "our tendency to attribute responsibility (in a case where no obvious reason for action is apparent) depends on the person and the action involved. Someone we like will be judged more responsible if the action is praiseworthy, and less responsible if the action deserves blame. For someone we don't like, the reverse is the case."[30] This reflects an inherent bias in the social judgments used to assign responsibility. And when your in-group has already prejudged the out-group as inherently inferior, it does not take much to convince some members of the in-group that "others" are a potential threat. Once "others" have been portrayed as being responsible for all that is wrong with the world, it takes little to view them as an existential threat to all that the in-group holds dear. Having certainty about the threat posed by "others" brings a certain level of cognitive comfort to some people. As David Bodanis notes, "With a good enemy to hate, atomized individuals get a warm sense of unity. . . . Fears about our own weaknesses disappear when an enemy is mocked and punished—a reflex that radio shock jocks across America [like Rush Limbaugh] skillfully manipulate."[31]

Some out-groups may even be dehumanized, represented by simple, often derogatory labels instead of by their names or as unique individuals.[32] Further, as psychologist Kathleen Taylor has found, demonizing an "other" is much easier when you have limited or no interaction with members of that "othered" group. If you have never been confronted with the humanity of the enemy, it becomes easier to accept the dehumanization of the enemy by members of your own tribe.[33] In-group membership makes it easier to convince yourself that harm inflicted upon members of the out-group is acceptable or even justifiable. Studies have shown that if a member of an in-group harms a member of an out-group, other members of the in-group are unlikely to condemn them. Further, some will attempt to blame the out-group member for the harm they have suffered, perhaps characterizing them as stupid, lazy, evil, or in some other way deserving whatever happened to them.

Examples of this range from Hitler blaming the Jews for all the problems faced by Germany, or Trump denigrating mainstream news organizations—with their fact-checking, questioning, and independent investigative reporting—as "enemies of the people." In the latter case, it was hardly surprising when journalists were then physically attacked at Trump campaign rallies in recent years. While socialization typically creates a powerful barrier to doing serious harm toward others, membership in a group—particularly a strongly cohesive group—can weaken the inhibitory constraints and provide additional emotional energy to breach those barriers.[34] A similar pattern is linked to Trump's demonizing of Muslims, Mexican immigrants, Democrats, and other entities portrayed as evils of the world. Members of these "out-groups" have been attacked by Trump supporters before, during, and after his tenure in office.

In short, influencing a crowd of people is most effective when the persuader and the audience all perceive themselves to be part of the same in-group. The persuader can further solidify the commitment of being members of the in-group by "othering" the out-group as inferior, a lesser species that you don't ever want to be associated with. Trump's July 2019 rage-tweet castigating opposition politicians and calling for them to "go back to where they came from" is an excellent example of this.[35] Dividing the world into clearly marked "us" and "them" identities places much less strain on one's cognitive resources than acknowledging the details of human difference. This, by extension, is one of the more dangerous aspects of an entrenched two-party political system. The focus becomes polarization, suspicion and hatred of "them" and reverence toward "us" in a zero-sum game of winners and losers, with no regard for what's actually right or wrong and no ability to pursue or accept a negotiated compromise. As a result, political and ideological radicalization and extremism becomes almost inevitable. A typical response to the perception of being victimized and under siege involves a great deal of antagonistic "othering" and demonization, some of which may lead to violence. As Scott Atran explains, "Research on the human brain suggests that people fight when their sacred values—that is, the values that define their identity and therefore can't be compromised—are under threat."[36]

Digital influence mercenaries utilize this in-group/out-group divisiveness to both amplify fear and uncertainty, and to reinforce certainty in a position by demonizing others. Specifically, the tactics of provocation and ragebait (described in chapter 2) are meant to provoke emotional reactions about the out-group, reinforcing certainty in an individual or group identity through "othering" (e.g., turning people against "nonbelieving others") as a means of polarizing society, making people increasingly angry and defensive about what they believe to be true. Additionally, an effective influencer speaks in ways that reinforce the certainty of that chosen position, providing messages to the group that appear to align precisely with what the group's members were thinking. This in fact was one of the key advantages exploited by Trump's political campaign, particularly when saying things that some Americans were thinking about "others" but were reluctant to say out of politeness, political correctness, or inappropriateness. They relished the public insults hurled at immigrants, Democrats, liberals, elites, "globalists," and others who they believed didn't want America to be great. As Kathleen Taylor notes, "This perception of meshing minds can itself be a potent source of shared exhilaration, adding to the emotional glue which binds the movement together and makes it a coherent entity, a group, tribe, or cult rather than just a number of people."[37]

Altogether, by exploiting our tendencies toward conformity, manipulating social proof, and emphasizing in-group/out-group identities, the influencer conveys to the target a message of "you're right, because you're one of us and they are wrong." The group identity aspect of social validation also allows the influencer to identify specific individuals who are revered by that group's members, and then utilize endorsements from those individuals to bolster conformity with a particular narrative. For example, much like the ways the tobacco industry enlisted the assistance of scientists, Trump enlisted quasi-religious leaders like Florida televangelist Paula White to be public advocates on his behalf, in order to give the appearance that God was on his side.[38] This explains to some degree why—at least initially—researchers documented a large number of evangelical Christians among Trump's support base. Several of his supporters even claimed that opposing Trump is equivalent to opposing God—clearly an outrageous lie, yet believed by millions of Americans. This illustrates how social groups can validate some of the most ridiculous claims because, as Denise Winn explains, if a group of people "act on certain assumptions, those assumptions will probably gain the status of facts."[39] Further, as explained earlier in this book, repetition has a powerful impact—the more often you hear a claim, the less likely you are to assess it critically. And the longer you participate in a community of like-minded individuals, who are also unlikely to assess that claim critically as it's repeated, the higher the chances that in time the claim becomes embraced by those individuals as a fact—even though it was (and remains) completely untrue. The implications of this for the perceptions manipulation strategies pursued by digital influence mercenaries are clear.

Finally, another group identity–related strategy to manipulate and reinforce certainty involves a "demand for purity." For some, this refers to demonstrations of pure, unadulterated loyalty within the in-group. Meanwhile, as psychologist Robert Lifton explains, more extreme versions include a belief that elements outside the chosen group should be eliminated in order to prevent them from contaminating the minds of group members.[40] Trump used the demand for purity argument in many ways. He declared that any Republicans who were not adamant supporters of him and his agenda were not true Republicans and should be ostracized and punished—he even called them "human scum."[41] Federal judges who disagreed with him were called "so-called judges," and he publicly questioned their integrity and objectivity. Media outlets who disagreed with his characterization of the facts were condemned as purveyors of "fake news." Essentially, anyone who expressed a point of view not in alignment with Trump was loudly insulted in many ways, and his followers were admonished to ignore such alternative viewpoints.

As a result, individuals within the Trump supporter in-group refuse to hear or see anything that hasn't already been proven as pro-Trump. This, then, is the dangerous closing of the American mind that occurs when one falls prey to demands for purity. The demand for purity is a group-level form of the escalating commitment strategy described above, one that digital influence mercenaries can capitalize upon. To prove your conformity with the group identity, you are compelled to defend the narrative no matter how false it really is, creating opportunities for digital influence mercenaries to deploy a range of deception, disinformation, and provocation strategies.

Conclusion

Within their social groups, individuals faced with many kinds of decision-making situations will typically seek consensus, leading many to set aside their own personal beliefs and embrace the majority opinion of the group—a phenomenon often referred to as "group think."[42] Group membership thus encourages a type of conformity pressure that influences how we interpret and process information, particularly the kinds of information we seek out, accept, or reject. And due to social proof, uncertainty avoidance, cognitive biases, and other psychological dimensions described in the previous chapters of this book, we begin to see how groups influence an individual's willingness to reject inconvenient truths. Indeed, any facts that purport to show the in-group's beliefs are wrong can simply be ignored. You can push that information to the exclusionary zone outside your in-group, condemning the purveyor of inconvenient truths to purgatory, even portraying them as an evil enemy to be vanquished.

Social proof helps us navigate uncertainty and also helps us confirm what we want to believe. We look to others for suggestions and ideas about how to comprehend these complexities, what to believe, how to respond, and so forth. We thrive on social communication, and often we need it. Most people who come to believe in falsehoods do so not because of the Internet or the media but based on information provided by our friends, family, coworkers, neighbors, teachers, classmates, and so forth. These are people in whom we have placed a certain amount of trust, and in response we allow them (consciously or otherwise) to influence our perceptions and behavior. Thus, our connections with each other can be a source of strength and resilience, but also provide a sense that our shared beliefs are truth.

Social proof is also linked to reasons behind our drive to form and join groups. Research by social psychologists have found that "an opinion, a belief, an attitude is perceived as 'correct,' 'valid,' and 'proper' to the extent that it is anchored in a group of people with similar beliefs, opinions, and attitudes."[43] Further, when a subjectively held belief is socially shared, it attains the status of objectivity. In other words, "once a value is standardized and becomes common property of the group . . . it acquires objective reality."[44] This, in turn, explains how disinformation is sustained by personal relationships. If what you believe about a situation is based on false information, and I rely on your opinion, then my belief will also be influenced by the same false information. Further, when I share my belief with someone else, and she decides to agree with me, we now have three people who are convinced of something that is actually false. As the number of "believers" within our circle of contacts grows, it becomes increasingly easy (and emotionally satisfying) to dismiss as unconvincing any information that contradicts our opinion.

As discussed in the previous chapter, people have what Lee McIntyre calls "a built-in cognitive bias to agree with what others around us believe, even if the evidence before our eyes tells us otherwise. . . . If we are already motivated to *want* to believe certain things, it doesn't take much to tip us over to believing them, especially if others we care about already do so."[45] Elizabeth Kolbert agrees: "People believe that they know way more than they actually do. What allows us to persist in this belief is other people."[46] This helps explain why so many people embrace conspiracy theories, as described in chapter 4. As Deen Freelon explains, "Nearly all conspiracy theories are supported by social connections and ties. It's not just one person subscribing to this in isolation, but a network of people who support each other in their beliefs."[47] Thus, a community of like-minded people can be a vector for the spread of disinformation, and this is particularly true for online communities. Finally, when our personal contacts all believe the same facts and narratives, while rejecting other facts and narratives as invalid, the power of social proof can be significantly magnified and amplified. When a group shares similar confirmation biases and is committed to reinforcing in-group purity, it creates a gravitational force that pulls members deep into what some have called an echo chamber, a structure of mutual influence around which the Internet can now help form virtually impenetrable boundaries, as we'll examine in chapter 7.

7

ECHO CHAMBERS AND FILTER BUBBLES

The Internet—and particularly social media—allows us (and encourages us) to seek out and connect online with others who share our beliefs. However, this has had both positive and negative results. In *The Cult of the Amateur*, Andrew Keen observes how the Internet has democratized information but has also replaced genuine knowledge with "the wisdom of the crowd," dangerously blurring the lines between fact and opinion, informed argument and blustering speculation.[1] The term "the wisdom of the crowd" is, when you think of it, rather ironic; a person can be intelligent, but mobs are dangerous, unpredictable, and never intelligent. Here, then, is where we find the most rewarding avenue for spreading lies and disinformation. Once you have convinced some members of an audience to believe in your lie, and they have convinced each other (through the power of collective identity and conformity) that their belief in the lie is justified, they will become active participants in the spread of your disinformation. Further, as Kate Starbird explains, this "participatory disinformation" may have more lasting impact than so-called "top-down propaganda," because of the positive reinforcement it facilitates.[2]

Thanks to the Internet, and especially social media, we now have the ability to create and nurture what David Patrikarakos refers to as the "homophily" effect of a "cocoon in online bubbles of like-minded friends and followers."[3] Within each bubble, we believe "we are right, they are wrong," which exacerbates prejudice, bigotry, and hatred of the out-group, the "other." The comfort of certainty we find among those who share our beliefs also allows us to avoid discomforting cognitive dissonance when the facts presented to us indicate we are wrong—we can simply defend our position by claiming we're not wrong, others are just using the wrong information, the wrong "facts."[4] Social media provides the ultimate platform for creating and measuring group consensus, by encouraging likes, shares, and follows. It's a natural arena for identifying, sharing, and contributing to the social proof phenomenon described in the previous chapter.

Further, this form of collective influence on our beliefs and behaviors is often reinforced by multiple social media platforms simultaneously, where we often follow, share, and like the same kinds of people and information. As a result, our patterns of information seeking and interactions inform each social platform's algorithm, which then provides similar kinds of information to our accounts on these platforms. In other words, what we see and hear on Twitter is reinforced by what we see and hear on Facebook, Instagram, and so forth. The impact of seeing the same information in multiple formats, and on multiple social media platforms, is that it strengthens your conviction that the information must be true. And as Jason Gainous and Kevin Wagner explain, "The users of social media can opt to follow particular flows of information creating not just polarization but entire networks of reinforced beliefs."[5] These networks of reinforced beliefs are now frequently referred to in the research literature by the term "echo chambers."

Echo Chambers and Filter Bubbles: Similarities and Differences

There are several definitions and descriptions available for the term "echo chamber." My own is that an echo chamber is a form of collective influence in which all (or at least most) of the participants repeat, amplify, and reinforce the same narrative and worldview, usually based on a limited number of information sources, while differences of opinion or contradictory facts are actively suppressed, excluded, and denigrated. It is a result of people choosing to surround themselves with specific types and sources of information. Echo chambers are attractive because they help us avoid the discomforting uncertainty and cognitive dissonance described in previous chapters. And social media platforms provide an unprecedented ability to immerse ourselves within these kinds of echo chambers, providing many opportunities for the spread of disinformation.

Because we are so dependent on narratives to help us navigate a complex world, we constantly seek and welcome information that affirms or enhances the narratives we have come to embrace. This, in turn, frames the kinds of books we read, the movies and television shows we watch, the kinds of "news" we consume, and the people we follow on social media. Social bonds can be extremely influential. As Patrick Tucker notes, "The logical part of your brain really, really likes listening to the social part, which just wants to fit in."[6] People tend to weigh the opinions and behavior of their friends over those of strangers, so if your friends recommend a particular hotel, beverage, book, or whatever, it has more impact than a targeted advertisement or an endorsement by someone unfamiliar to you. The same holds true for complying with requests to join a Facebook group (for example) or respond to a survey. If the request comes from a friend, particularly one that has already complied with the same kind of request, it has more influence than if it comes from a stranger. And if the request comes to you from several of your friends or social contacts, it becomes even more likely that you will comply.[7]

The combination of certainty seeking, cognitive dissonance avoidance, cognitive biases, and in-group identity contributes to the attraction of echo chambers. People generally prefer information that supports rather than conflicts with their beliefs and worldview. We want information to provide us with a sense of confidence that we are thinking, feeling, and acting in a manner that is acceptable to others whom we respect. And studies have demonstrated that people are more likely to share information with their social networks that conforms to their existing beliefs, deepening ideological differences between individuals and groups.[8] We also don't want to face the cognitive dissonance of exposure to radically new and challenging information, and our defensive reasoning instincts lead us to construct a consistent explanation for something that appears to question what we want to believe.[9] Two concepts—elective affinity and selective exposure—help explain how we prefer to strengthen our ties to the people, information sources, and organizations we already know and like.[10] Regarding the former, studies have shown how online friend networks often perform a social filtering of content, which diminishes the diversity of information that users are exposed to. Meanwhile, as Philip Howard observes, "research on selective exposure shows that people select traditional media and broadcasting sources that they wish to be exposed to."[11] Both types of human behavior reinforce our certainty and amplify confirmation bias. Further, as Denise Winn explains, when we take in information that confirms our existing beliefs and ideas, and turn away from any information that might conflict with those beliefs and ideas, this is what psychologists call a "perceptual set"—we tend to pick up only information that we are "set" to receive.[12]

Within the echo chamber, individuals are generally unaware and unconcerned that they are cut off from competing sources of information. They risk the very real danger of herd behavior, the dangerous myth that the type of certainty provided by the "wisdom of the crowd" will ensure the right decision. Our reliance on cues from within our echo chamber appears to be a natural response to managing too much (and too conflicting) information, as they encourage the kinds of peripheral routes for processing information that were discussed in chapter 4. Social proof and in-group identity can lay the groundwork for the attractiveness of an echo chamber, while the individual's desire for certainty provides the gravitational attraction into—and interactions within—this type of collective influence community.

Echo chambers are not about abandoning our free will altogether, but rather, choosing to filter out information that we don't want to receive. We are being selective, but often fail to realize the limited, narrow way in which we are being selective. A child can learn to believe in certain things because they are unlikely to see anything else that might significantly challenge or undermine those beliefs. Echo chambers merely help us re-create that same experience by limiting our sources of information to be only that which reinforces what we believe. Meanwhile, a "filter bubble" (also called an influence bubble) is similar to an echo chamber in terms of impact, but is different in terms of design and structure. Wherein the echo chambers we inhabit are largely products of personal choices and preferences, filter bubbles are manufactured for us by the algorithms used by search engines, social media platforms, and other Internet technologies. As Richard Fletcher explains, the key difference here is that filter bubbles are formed by computer algorithms, which the user has no real control over, while echo chambers can be opted into (or out of) by the user.[13]

When Eli Pariser coined the term "filter bubble" in 2011, he defined it to be a situation in which algorithms skew the variety of information we get online in favor of stuff we like.[14] His book by this title describes how "with Google personalized for everyone, the query 'stem cells' might produce diametrically opposed results for scientists who support stem cell research and activists who oppose it. 'Proof of climate change' might turn up different results for an environmental activist and an oil company executive. In polls, a huge majority of us assume search engines are unbiased. But that may be just because they're increasingly biased to share our own views. More and more, your computer monitor is a kind of one-way mirror, reflecting your own interest while algorithmic observers watch what you click."[15]

These algorithms basically automate the creation of an echo chamber–like experience, by choosing information for us to consume that the algorithm thinks we are mostly likely to want and engage with. Further, the information that is selected and put before our eyes is influenced by our own biases. Whether we are using Facebook, Instagram, Twitter, or some other platform, the system is designed to fill our accounts with information similar to what we are already consuming and is—in all likelihood—already consistent with our beliefs.[16] And similar to the echo chamber experience, the individual is generally unaware and unconcerned with the fact that the filter bubble keeps them from seeing any competing or contradictory information they might not like. Of course, both echo chambers and filter bubbles are products of conscious (or perhaps sometimes unconscious) choices we make, particularly in terms of what we like, share, follow, and so forth. But we have a lot more direct control over our echo chambers than we do over our filter bubbles. As Laura Garcia explains, "An echo chamber is the way in which we only encounter information from like-minded people, [while] a filter bubble is a space where our previous online behavior (search history, likes, shares, and shopping habits) influences what we see online and on our social media feeds and in what order."[17]

Social media platforms are especially geared toward insulating you in bubbles of cognitive and emotional comfort, because this keeps you engaged, and in the attention economy this translates directly into profits for them. Essentially, filter bubbles play a very important attention-generating role. According to Philip Howard, "An underlying driver of attention is the social endorsement that is communicated through the act of sharing: social media users will not pay attention simply because a piece of political news is from a credible source or generated by a political party; they will pay attention because someone in their social network has signaled the importance of the content."[18] Further, as the *Wall Street Journal* demonstrated in a 2016 experiment, social media users predominately see information exclusively from like-minded friends and media sources, essentially creating an entirely different "reality" about an issue depending on their individual preferences.[19]

Importantly, these phenomena often play a mutually reinforcing role when it comes to perceptions manipulation and disinformation. The social media filter bubbles reinforce the views of the echo chamber members, while echo chamber engagement informs the filter bubble algorithms. Because the members of the echo chamber are engaging (positively or negatively) with similar kinds of information, and demonstrating similar kinds of in-group preferences and prejudices, the algorithms continually feed them more of the information that keeps them engaged. At the same time, the continual flow of this narrow scope of information reinforces the echo chamber members' convictions about how they view their world and their place within it.

Overall, these echo chambers and filter bubbles work in tandem to help us create our own personal, unique online universe of information. As Richard Fletcher notes, sometimes "we are overexposed to information that we like or agree with, potentially distorting our perception of reality because we see too much of one side, not enough of the other, and begin to assume that what we think is the only reality. This exposure could be a product of us consciously choosing to avoid or ignore what we don't want to see and hear."[20] Because consensus dictates reality,[21] the echo chamber reinforces whatever worldview and values its members want to uphold. If you do not hold those values, you are free to choose whether to remain within and eventually embrace those values, or reject the values and go find some other sources of information instead. The easier route is the former choice—individuals often adapt their beliefs in order to conform with the dominant expectations of their in-group echo chamber. In contrast, rejecting what others around you have decided to believe and going out into the world to seek a different "truth"—well, that is decidedly more difficult, and raises the kinds of uncertainty and complexity described earlier in this book.

Group dynamics within the echo chamber also exaggerate the cognitive bias effects described earlier in this chapter, as the author and legal scholar Cass Sunstein observed in his book *Going to Extremes*. Insularity often means limited information input (and usually information that reinforces preexisting views) and a desire for peer approval. Further, if a group's leader "does not encourage dissent and is inclined to an identifiable conclusion, it is highly likely that the group as a whole will move toward that conclusion."[22] And once the group has been psychologically walled off, Sunstein explains, "the information and views of those outside the group can be discredited, and hence nothing will disturb the process of polarization as group members continue to talk."[23]

Echo chambers can encourage the "bandwagoning effect" described in chapter 5. This is a type of human behavior in which social proof and conformity pressures combine to attract individuals toward supporting an idea, political candidate, product, service, sports team, and so forth. Falsehoods and conspiracy theories find safe haven within echo chambers, which insulate users from having to face the facts imposed by debunking efforts; they can simply ignore any information that contradicts what they want to believe, and take solace in the fact that others around them are doing exactly the same thing. Within the echo chamber, ignorance reinforces ignorance, while at the same time making the chamber's inhabitants feel comfortable about being ignorant. Further, they are encouraged to reject the narratives and values of those outside the bubble, offering a built-in mechanism for increasing (and capitalizing on) societal distrust, polarization, and anger. Influence efforts within each echo chamber can intensify a sense of identity through "othering" narratives that demand loyalty to the in-group and portray the out-group as inherently inferior and evil. The most extreme manifestation of this, as J. M. Berger explains, includes a "sweeping rationalization of why conflict exists and its insistence on the necessity of conflict . . . an assertion that an out-group must always be actively opposed because its fundamental identity is intrinsically harmful to the in-group."[24] Recent instances of political violence in the United States (like the January 2021 mob siege of the U.S. Capitol) reflect how ideologically oriented echo chambers that reinforce their members' beliefs, prejudices, and hatred toward "others" can be particularly dangerous.

Digital influence mercenaries can utilize echo chambers to make science denial influence efforts (like the tobacco strategy described in the previous chapter) more effective. Those who reject scientific research and empirical results, arguing that factual evidence is really open for subjective interpretation, are desperately trying to fabricate uncertainty where there is none. But when surrounded by others (humans and bots) repeating similar views within an anti-science echo chamber, they find empowerment to question any inconvenient challenges to their political beliefs. And it should be remembered that certain industries are willing to finance these kinds of digital influence efforts—there are billions of dollars in profit at stake, so investing in such forms of disinformation and perceptions manipulation simply makes good business sense.[25]

In sum, modern social media platforms have helped make us more vulnerable to the efforts of digital influence mercenaries in at least two ways.[26] First, we have a tremendous amount of freedom to actively seek out information that we believe will provide us with what we want to know, and quite often we prefer sources of information that confirm what we already tend to believe—in the process creating a wealth of opportunities for disinformation. Further, we can ignore (or even block out) other information sources that question or contradict what we want to believe, especially when these views are reinforced by an echo chamber. Meanwhile, our beliefs are shaped by an automated personalization of information involving algorithms that we have virtually no control over, and yet show us what the computer believes we will want to see. As a result, echo chambers and filter bubbles serve as digital channels through which we can be effectively influenced, by limiting the scope and breadth of information we are exposed to, and encouraging the uncritical acceptance of that information. As a result, echo chambers and filter bubbles provide channels of influence that digital influence mercenaries can capitalize upon in order to manipulate what we see and hear.

Exploiting Echo Chambers and Filter Bubbles

Earlier in this book we examined the critical importance of targeting data. Both echo chambers and filter bubbles provide useful information for the digital influence mercenary to develop a robust profile of their intended targets. However, because of their in-group collective influence nature, echo chambers are more valuable to the digital influence mercenary for achieving strategic objectives, as we'll describe below. In contrast, the filter bubble is algorithmic and more individualistic, based on things the person has done online (what they searched for, liked, shared, bought, etc.), so this creates a different sort of cookie crumb trail for the digital influence mercenary to follow in order to determine how best to influence the target. And since algorithmic data can be gathered on a specific target from multiple social media platforms, the mercenary can develop a robust picture of that target's patterns of information seeking and interaction, yielding insights that can inform a successful influence strategy. An example of how these algorithms can be used for digital influence campaigns was seen in the Trump campaign's partnership with Cambridge Analytica (described in chapter 1) to manipulate behavior using artificial intelligence–driven social media advertising that targeted specific individuals.

Echo chambers can become a vibrant means of influencing a significant number of people simultaneously. As Philip Howard notes, digital influence efforts are most effective when the messages are "delivered by a relatively enclosed network of other accounts and other content that affirms and reinforces what people are seeing."[27] Individuals prefer to communicate with in-group members; compliance with a request or command is significantly higher when the influencer is considered a credible member of the target's in-group.[28] Once an individual has embraced their membership in that in-group, it becomes easier for others within it to forge relationships with them and in some cases develop the bonds of trust that underpin influence efforts. According to Pratkanis and Aronson, this in-group membership can even lead those individuals "to purchase unwanted products, to vote for less than qualified candidates, and to hate innocent people."[29] In this environment, trust becomes something that the digital influence mercenary can leverage to their advantage. Once the target audience trusts a source of information, that source can promote a variety of falsehoods, lies, and conspiracies. On social media, the trust of others is gained by telling them what they already wanted to hear. If the target is inclined to believe something they see online, and others are seen as posting opinions favoring that as a reality, they are likely to consider it true (even if it was false to begin with, and all the corroborating opinions they saw online were actually automated "bot" social media accounts and not real people).

As discussed in the previous chapter, social proof is often important for framing the context in which an influence attempt can become effective. In the literature on the psychology of persuasion, the term "social capital manipulation" is used to describe an effort to leverage the shared norms, values, and trust within a group (or an echo chamber) as a means to connect a target's sense of identity with objectives pursued by the influencer. And as discussed in chapter 2, there are various tactics and tools through which online forms of social proof can now be manipulated. For example, it is technically possible to manufacture a huge number of those "retweets" or "shares" that amplify the perception of endorsement and support for a specific narrative. This form of engagement deception enhances perceived validity about certain views (e.g., "lots of people feel this way, so it must be true") even when based on absolutely no evidence at all. Since most of us will invariably look to others for social clues on how to navigate the various forms of uncertainty we encounter in our daily lives, the manipulation of social proof can have a significant effect on a person's decision-making, including their support of a conspiracy theory.

Members of a social media echo chamber can set their preferences, block the user accounts of "outsiders," and essentially filter out voices they don't want to hear while simultaneously finding a source of self-esteem and confirmation of their worldview from others within the echo chamber. As the collective nature of this behavior nurtures an in-group identity, trust devolves into "who you want to trust" choices based on identity and familiarity. Once a digital influence mercenary has effectively penetrated an echo chamber and gained acceptance therein, the chances are high that many of that group's members will accept the influencer's proposed narrative regardless of its merits, as long as it conforms to the group's normative values.

In order to capitalize on an echo chamber, the mercenary must first have a good sense of the target audience's attributes, as explained in chapter 2. When mapping the parameters and perceptual boundaries of an echo chamber, one important source of data is the collection of people whom the targets have chosen to surround themselves with. The digital influence mercenary can observe an easily discoverable pattern of activity that helps them understand the nature of that echo chamber, what its members believe, who has influence relative to others, and how to properly infiltrate it. The influence mercenary must also gain a thorough understanding of the in-group identity shared by those within the echo chamber, and then establish credibility as being "one of them." The effective digital influence campaign is one in which the targets share some perceived "alikeness," some similarities in background, perspective, or desires for the future that increase the likelihood that they will appreciate and accept the narrative put forth by the digital influence mercenary. As Darren Linvill and Patrick Warren explain, the first phase of infiltration thus involves messages "employed as a means of camouflage to appear more genuine, as a method of gaining followers, or a combination of both."[30] Over time, perceived credibility among the members of the echo chamber will allow the mercenary to begin infusing the discussions with information (or disinformation) geared toward achieving their overall strategic objectives.

Polarization and Targeting

Echo chambers become particularly useful to digital influence mercenaries when the targets are part of a divided, politically polarized society. Within any community there are always in-groups and out-groups, and it is increasingly easy to identify the members of each. If the digital influence mercenary's goal is to sow discord and animosity among members of a community, the data and tools are now available for identifying disagreements and seams of latent distrust that can be exploited for this purpose. Previously in this book we examined how the in-group/out-group bifurcation leads to "othering." When embracing this us-vs.-them view of reality, not only does the in-group come to blame the out-group for a wide range of grievances, but there is also a tendency to demonize and dehumanize members of the out-group. This, in turn, leads in-group members to seek out, applaud, and disseminate all manner of disinformation that portrays the out-group unfavorably. The fires of animosity are already burning, so all the influence mercenary has to do is provide some fuel and then watch as their provocation leads to further engagement.

The strategy begins by choosing a major societal issue—for example, gun control, women's rights, abortion rights, anti-racism, climate change, or whatever—something around which there are competing narratives and hotly contested opinions. Then the mercenary will pick a community of users and (after doing some data collection and analysis) begin to masquerade as an acceptable member of that community. The technical term for this is "affinity fraud," generally defined as taking advantage of people's tendency to trust others with whom they share similarities, such as religion or ethnic identity, in order to gain their trust and then influence them.[31] Once the mercenary has established a level of "street credibility" among the group, they can begin to exploit existing tensions for their own purposes. They will often switch from providing positive comments about what members of the group say to posting increasingly negative—perhaps even hostile and violent—things about "the others" (the out-group who are perceived as illegitimately supporting the opposing view). They may also deploy tactics of identity politics to convince some members of the echo chamber that they are not fully committed or being true to the in-group unless they act in some way.

These days, the strategic benefits of the echo chamber phenomenon—driven by group identities, conformity, and confirmation bias—are most visibly represented by political polarization in the United States. In 2014, according to a Pew Research report, Republicans and Democrats on Capitol Hill were "further apart from one another than at any point in modern history." The report also noted that rising polarization among elected officials was "asymmetrical, with much of the widening gap between the two parties attributable to a rightward shift among Republicans."[32] The implications for reinforcing certainty in an increasingly polarized political environment are fairly clear, as Lee McIntyre explains: "In an environment in which partisanship can be assumed, and it is often enough to 'pick a team' rather than look at the evidence, misinformation can be spread in the open and fact-checking can be disparaged. The selective use of facts that prop up one's position, and the complete rejection of facts that do not, seems part and parcel of creating the new post-truth reality. . . . When one's supporters care more about which side you're on than what the evidence says, facts truly may be subordinate to opinions."[33]

Essentially, we have seen the progression (or regression) of American society into partisan echo chambers, where uncertainty is replaced by a distinctly political interpretation of facts. For example, a poll conducted by Monmouth University in

October 2019 found that 85 percent of Democrats, 61 percent of independents, and only 40 percent of Republicans believed Trump "probably did" mention the possibility of an investigation into the Biden family during a July phone call with Ukraine's president Volodymyr Zelensky. Notably, this poll was conducted *after Trump publicly acknowledged doing this very thing*, and yet his Republican supporters were still not inclined to believe it. "This seems to be another example of partisan tribalism at work in public opinion," said Patrick Murray, director of the independent Monmouth University Polling Institute.[34]

Perhaps the most disturbing manifestation of this polarization was witnessed on January 6, 2021, when a mob of Trump supporters attacked the Capitol in Washington, D.C., forcing members of Congress to seek shelter. What began as a protest to air grievances about (unfounded and completely false) claims of voting irregularities that cost Trump his bid for reelection transformed into a violent siege against the nation's hallowed halls of democracy. Before, throughout, and even after this violent insurrection, Trump still proclaimed the election had been stolen from him, and commended the "special" and "loved" perpetrators of this attack.[35]

This incident also exemplified a unique advantage of targeting political conservatives in America with disinformation. According to the Pew Research Center, conservatives trust comparatively few information sources, while in contrast liberals tend to trust a wide (and sometimes eclectic) variety of different information sources. As a result, the nature of the conservative echo chambers are more tightly bounded, ideologically consistent, and resistant to outsiders.[36] Other researchers have found that political orientation has a significant effect on the likelihood of the number of false statements that are believed. For example, according to Hany Farid's testimony to Congress in June 2020, "The number of false statements believed by those on the right of the political spectrum is 2.15 times greater than those on the left."[37] Specifically, he notes, surveys indicate that "compared to those on the left, those on the right are: 15.44 times more likely to believe that 'asymptomatic carriers of COVID-19 who die of other medical problems are added to the coronavirus death toll to get the numbers up to justify this pandemic response;' 14.70 times more likely to believe that 'House Democrats included $25 million to boost their own salaries in their proposal for the COVID-19 related stimulus package;' 9.44 times more likely to believe that 'COVID-19 was man-made in a lab and is not thought to be a natural virus;' 7.41 times more likely to believe that 'Silver solution kills COVID-19;' and 6.97 times more likely to believe that 'COVID stands for Chinese Originated Viral Infectious Disease.'"[38] Each of these blatant falsehoods has much stronger support among conservatives than liberals in the United States, indicating that digital influence mercenaries can generate the most engagement and profits when targeting COVID-related disinformation toward those who are politically right-leaning.

As Kevin Roose explained in an August 2020 *New York Times* article, there is now a "parallel media universe" of super-conservative content on Facebook, with right-leaning pages and posts consistently generating more interaction than left-leaning ones.[39] As described earlier in this book, provoking emotional responses like outrage leads to higher levels of engagement on social media, and the algorithms used by social media platforms are geared toward pushing content that users are likely to engage with. At the same time, we have seen a trend in which fake content—and particularly that which provokes outrage—seems to be increasingly targeted toward politically conservative users.[40] With their closed loop of news sources (e.g., watching Fox News exclusively, or perhaps complemented by right-wing websites like Breitbart and Newsmax), some conservatives are apparently more prone to deception by charlatans peddling conspiracy theories, fake news, and extreme views far outside the mainstream. They have already developed the habit of avoiding (if not demonizing) other sources of information that don't seem conservative enough. Thus, all a digital influence mercenary really needs to do to convince them of some conspiracy or fake information is to make it look adequately conservative. It will be embraced enthusiastically by such people when it includes some supportive quotes (whether real or implied) from conservative icons, uses provocative and disparaging language about "liberals" and "globalists," and conveys a clear pro-Trump sentiment. Because these particular conservative social media users are already primed by confirmation bias to look for things that justify their skewed view of the world, they will be more likely than others to be tricked by fake news and conspiracies.

Further, the right-wing media ecosystem functions as an echo chamber to amplify specific interpretations (often misleading or false) of what a person actually said or did. Consider this example: David Byrne (a well-known musician living in New York) wrote an essay in 2016 about "the echo chamber" in which he was highly critical of how social media (and to an increasing degree mainstream media) work to insulate people within emotional and intellectual bubbles of comfort.[41] Doing so keeps people engaged on that social media platform, or keeps them watching that cable television channel, instead of switching to another. Adhering to a specific political narrative in how news is reported, and using algorithms to create echo chambers that make it hard to escape, translates into more advertising dollars, and more profit. Meanwhile, he notes,

> Once you've surrounded yourself with only one point of view, soon that point of view is all you hear.... The problem with Facebook and Twitter is that those platforms mostly present a point of view that you already agree with, since you only see what your "friends" are sharing.... The algorithms built into those social networks are designed to reinforce this natural human tendency and expand upon it—if you like this, you'll like this. The networks reinforce your existing point of view in order to give you more of what you like, as that will make you happy and keep you on the network—and, in turn, more ads can be accurately targeted your way. You remain blissfully happy "knowing" or, rather, believing, more and more about less and less.[42]

One of the points he made in this essay was the fact that many Trump supporters seem to turn a blind eye to—or profess complete ignorance of—the many lies Trump was promoting during his campaign appearances (e.g., his claim that he "watched in Jersey City, New Jersey, where thousands and thousands of people were cheering" on 9/11). Today, when you search on Google for "David Byrne echo chamber" you will find a lot of interesting results, which can basically be categorized on a spectrum of highly favorable versus highly critical of his essay (with just a small handful that could be considered politically neutral, neither highly favorable nor overly critical). On one end of the spectrum are the media outlets that provided a few snippets of the essay and recommended their readers to go have a look for themselves. The editors of the *Oxford Handbook of Social Influence* liked it so much they reprinted (with permission) the essay in the 2017 edition of the book.[43]

Meanwhile, at the other end of the political spectrum, Breitbart reported on the essay with a headline that reads "David Byrne: Why Can't Stupid Americans See Through Trump's Lies" and begins with the sentence, "In an [sic] lengthy new essay Scottish-born Talking Heads frontman David Byrne theorized that the main reason for the explosive political rise of Donald Trump is his supporters' inability to seek information outside of the social media 'echo chamber' to become more aware of the Republican presidential frontrunner's 'lies.'"[44] These are wildly different characterizations of what Byrne's essay says. In essence, how you felt about the essay—before even reading it—depends mainly on where you first heard about it. The impact of a "media" outlet like Breitbart is to influence a negative inclination toward it, and to exacerbate (and profit from) tensions and provocation. Anyone who is inclined to favor Breitbart's kind of "news" reporting, and decides to go read Byrne's essay, will do so with an already critical (and probably angry) opinion about it. And then, when actually reading the essay, they will look for (and likely find) confirmation within it for why they should be critical and angry. This is an example of how the whole process works to influence your opinions about something you haven't even read. And according to Gainous and Wagner, "On the Internet, this polarizing effect is maximized by providing networks containing flows of information that cater to multiple ideological positions. These networks are rewarded with increased importance by the absence of moderating influences."[45]

At some level all ideologies are an enemy of the process by which truth is discovered. No ideology—conservative or liberal, religious or atheist, capitalist or communist—has a monopoly on the truth. Furthermore, history is awash in examples of how ideological conformity—especially on a mass scale, such as found in a totalitarian state—typically produces bad outcomes. Liberals may believe the world would be better if everyone were liberal; conservatives may believe just as strongly that the world would be better if everyone were conservatives. But unanimity in political perspective does not lead to truth merely by the will of the crowd.

This is where echo chambers and filter bubbles can prove exceedingly harmful. By shutting out any dissenting opinions, individuals within the in-group manufacture their own "truth," which is then reinforced by the kinds of information they are fed by the social media algorithms. Over time this has led to certain groups of people in the United States coalescing around different points of view that they defend with greater ferocity, even though only one point of view is actually based on factual evidence, while others are emotionally based on political beliefs, desires, prejudices, and other things beyond facts. Quite often the point of view for one group is in direct opposition to that of another group. These competing and incompatible "realities" influence the behavior of the groups, in terms of both interaction within the echo chamber and rejection of (or even overt hostility toward) anyone outside the echo chamber. To the digital influence mercenary, these echo chambers provide prime opportunities for their efforts to deceive and manipulate perceptions, emotions, and behaviors.

Conclusion

As Lee McIntyre observes, it is somewhat "ironic that the Internet, which allows for immediate access to reliable information by anyone who bothers to look for it, has for some become nothing but an echo chamber."[46] We can block social media accounts expressing opinions that we disagree with or simply don't want to hear. We can choose which websites we visit, and which ones we ignore. We can—like never before—tailor our information consumption in ways that minimize the chances of uncomfortable uncertainty. Further, influencers, targets, and social media platforms all have a mutual desire for these echo chambers to exist. Target audience members are drawn to the echo chambers because of their quest for validation. They want confirmation of their beliefs, while the influencer wants to provide that confirmation as a means of achieving their own influence objectives. And social media platforms can generate profits from increasing levels of engagement, which can be a product of social capital manipulation within competing echo chambers.[47] These social media platforms also use a variety of algorithms to filter the information we see in our daily "news" feed based on what the computer believes we would "want" to read. The core business model of these platforms relies on clicks and preferences, not telling people what they "should" know. Roger McNamee, an early investor in Facebook, describes how the social media platform's algorithms give consumers "what they want" with "an unending stream of posts that confirm each user's existing beliefs. . . . Everyone sees a different version of the Internet tailored to create the illusion that everyone else agrees with them . . . while also making them more extreme and resistant to contrary facts."[48] And most importantly, filter bubbles reinforce and exacerbate the perceptions and behaviors fueled by echo chambers.

Further, as uncertainty increases with the decline of trust and faith in expertise (described in previous chapters), people gravitate toward groups in which some level of certainty is provided for them. And we now have the capability to construct digital echo chambers that protect our in-groups (and our beliefs) from any competing or contradictory sources of information. This in turn gives a significant advantage to an influencer, like a political candidate who can now utilize the aspects of conformity, confirmation bias, cognitive dissonance avoidance, and group membership to achieve their objectives. Additionally, as Gainous and Wagner explain, people who are more frequent users of social media should be more susceptible to the candidate's influence. "Individuals can select to follow the people who provide information that gives them the least amount of discomfort as a result of exposure to information contrary to their predispositions. This makes social media particularly effective in providing messages that are likely to be read and considered. Not only can candidates use social media to circumvent the media's gatekeeping function, [but] they can also control the message and direct it to the individuals who are particularly receptive to it."[49]

In sum, we must seriously consider the long-term implications of how the Internet has allowed an unprecedented strengthening of echo chambers in which like-minded people are exposed to only information that confirms their specific worldview. Because of echo chambers and filter bubbles, political conservatives in the United States increasingly see and hear only politically conservative information. Political liberals increasingly see and hear only politically liberal information. Individuals with an extremely fundamental religious orientation can surround themselves with information that is exclusively representative of that orientation. And meanwhile, falsehoods, conspiracy theories, extremist ideologies, and provocative, hateful rhetoric can echo within these chambers just as easily as any other kind of information. The implications of these phenomena include ever-growing levels of distrust and anger toward those outside our echo chambers, deepening the fissures of an already polarized society while creating opportunities for digital influence mercenaries and social media platforms to continually profit by provoking increasingly angry forms of engagement.

8

CONFRONTING THE FUTURE CHALLENGES OF DIGITAL INFLUENCE MERCENARIES

Many centuries ago, mercenaries were employed by various kings, despots, religious leaders, and others, often to fight wars or provide security, and in more recent years they have been hired by government leaders (and sometimes criminal organizations) for similar purposes. Whether they work as lone individuals or as part of an organized firm, these mercenaries are paid to use their skills for achieving the goals and wishes of their clients. And in the modern information age, they are now employed by nation-states, corporations, and even private citizens to conduct digital influence operations against targets (both foreign and domestic) selected by their clients.[1]

The goals and objectives of these clients can range across a broad spectrum, from manufacturing the appearance of grassroots support for a political candidate, policy, or narrative, to attacking the credibility of any opposition. A client's goal could be raising money by having people donate to a cause (e.g., "fight the election fraud!"), or the goal could be portraying a sociopolitical movement in an unfavorable light (e.g., "BLM and Antifa are terrorists!"). Clients may hire digital influence freelancers and firms to help them gain (or maintain) power. Clients may also want to provoke dissension, protests, animosity, hatred, and even violence. Overall, manipulating the perceptions and behaviors of large populations is made more efficient and effective by a wide range of Internet and social media platforms. It is clear now why Steve Bannon (head of Breitbart at the time) told his staff that the Internet was not just a communications medium, it was a "powerful weapon of war."[2] By mastering this weapon of war, digital influence mercenaries become highly valuable assets for any entity willing to pay them for their skills.

Whatever the client's goals, the tactics, techniques, and procedures used by these digital influence mercenaries appear similar worldwide. They will gather and analyze data about potential targets; and, as discussed in the previous chapter, the existence of echo chambers and filter bubbles can lend considerable value to these efforts. They will then seek to exploit a variety of psychological vulnerabilities in the course of their influence and persuasion efforts. These digital influence mercenaries want their targets to have greater uncertainty and fear, because emotions like these incentivize information-seeking behaviors that can be manipulated. They can also exploit a common type of anxiety generated by enviously feeling that others are experiencing better lives than you are, something often referred to as "fear of missing out."[3] This is illustrated by individuals (afraid of missing something important or stimulating) repeatedly scrolling through a continually refreshing information feed, responding to the algorithms deployed by the social media platform that are meant to promote engagement. Mercenaries also want targets to believe in falsehoods and conspiracy theories, and to be irrationally confident about what they believe, even to the point of defending those beliefs against contradictory evidence. And they want targets to construct, embrace, and reinforce digital echo chambers, because these can significantly amplify the efforts described in this book that are meant to achieve a client's goals and produce profitable online behavior.

A Brief Look Ahead

There is a healthy demand for digital influence services from various clients, from politicians to corporations, but ultimately, we—the users of social media—are providing the largest source of demand for the disinformation and provocation efforts of digital influence mercenaries. Many of us have proven that we want to be deceived and stimulated, so these mercenaries are simply providing supply to meet the demand, using tools and tactics like those described in chapter 2, combined with an appreciation for the psychological, emotional, and social vulnerabilities described in chapters 3 through 7. As a result, these digital influence mercenaries have developed what NATO (North Atlantic Treaty Organization) calls "a large, vibrant online market for buyers and sellers of tools and services for social media manipulation,"[4] and it is a market in which we are seeing growth and peer competition.

In January 2021, the Oxford Internet Institute released a report aptly titled "Industrialized Disinformation," which identifies more than sixty-five firms worldwide that we could consider digital influence mercenaries. They found that nearly $60 million has been spent on hiring these firms since 2009.[5] The report also described how politicians are increasingly hiring private companies to spread disinformation online. They identified campaigns run by third-party contractors targeting forty-eight different countries over the previous year, and concluded that "the 'disinformation-for-hire' market is booming, with advertising, marketing, and public relations companies offering to manipulate online opinion for political parties and governments."[6] Another report published that month by the Brookings Institution also found that "political actors are increasingly outsourcing their disinformation work to third-party PR and marketing firms and using AI-generated profile pictures."[7] Similarly, researchers at Princeton University identified dozens of "foreign influence efforts" in which entities engaged in state-based digital influence warfare were not government agencies, but were doing so on behalf of a country's government.[8] Their August 2020 report detailed seventy-six foreign influence efforts targeting thirty different countries from 2013 through 2019, as well as twenty domestic influence efforts in which governments targeted their own citizens.[9]

According to a 2019 report by the RAND Corporation, in the future we will continue to see states engaging in digital influence efforts against others using a variety of partner organizations. "This pattern is emerging, for example, in the complex, international network of hackers, activists, and informal propagandists being employed by Russia as part of its information campaigns, and in China's use of Chinese citizens and ethnic Chinese abroad to further its control over key narratives. State actors are likely to develop such networks to avoid attribution and also strengthen their virtual societal warfare capabilities against retaliation. It will be much more difficult to understand, maintain an accurate portrait of, and hit back against a shadowy global network."[10]

And while the traditional client-services arrangement remains an important one for these mercenaries, the attention economy has also introduced a secondary means of making profits: using the same kinds of online data analysis and perceptions manipulation efforts on social media, they can drive traffic to ad-heavy websites and Facebook pages, thereby deriving revenues from user engagement. As a result, the business model of social media platforms ensures that the online advertising strategies described in this book will remain lucrative for digital influence mercenaries for the foreseeable future. Further, as a recent report from Georgetown University's Institute for the Study of Diplomacy explains, "The current technological revolution has lowered the cost of entry for those wishing to spread misinformation and disinformation."[11] For example, advances in artificial intelligence will make fake photos and videos easier to create yet increasingly difficult to detect. As a recent UNESCO report notes, it is increasingly possible to "engineer audio and video in ways that go beyond legitimate news editing in order to make it appear that a particular individual said or did something in some place, and to pass this off as an authentic record, sending it viral in the social communications environment."[12]

As Singer and Brooking explain, "Using such technology, users will eventually be able to conjure a convincing likeness of any scene or person they or the AI can imagine. Because the image will be truly *original*, it will be impossible to identify the forgery via many of the old methods of detection," and as a result "events that never took place may nonetheless be presented online as real occurrences, documented with compelling video evidence."[13] Particularly troublesome will be entirely realistic-looking videos that show a person saying something they've never said—a fake celebrity endorsement of a political candidate, for example, or a video made to look like a surreptitious recording of a candidate doing or saying something that undermines their credibility. As Michael Mazarr and his colleagues noted in a recent RAND report, "Simply put, the ability to manufacture seemingly tangible reality from scratch has now become commonplace."[14] And as with many kinds of technological advances, over time the ability to create forged images, audio, and video will become less expensive or difficult.[15]

Along with the future growth of the digital influence industry, we will also see increasing peer competition for clients and market share within it. The digital influence mercenaries that will be most in demand in this industry are those who can demonstrate high levels of professionalism and innovation. Clients will prefer those mercenaries who can mask their identities while deceiving and provoking the targets with increasing effectiveness and without getting caught. It is also highly likely that the more lucrative contracts will go to firms and freelancers who can show evidence of effectiveness, based on the goals and objectives of those efforts (which will vary according to client and target). Operators within this industry can monitor and assess the impact of their influence efforts by gathering and analyzing data on the target's reception and reaction to the information they were exposed to. Success in digital influence operations can be measured by the target's behavior, focusing on questions like: Did they do something that the influencer wanted them to (e.g., like, share, forward, retweet, vote, buy, protest, join, reject, or some other behavioral response)? Did they express some kind of emotional response (outrage, anger, sympathy, encouragement, etc.)? With these kinds of assessment in hand, the digital influence mercenaries can then refine their efforts to maximize effectiveness, while also using their assessment data to convince potential clients to hire them.

With no accountability, responsibility, or self-constraints, digital influence mercenaries may also become exceedingly ruthless in this unregulated environment. Some will probably be hired to conduct character assassinations, or for hacking operations to digitally destroy their targets. A recently published RAND Corporation report suggests that the future will bring "new forms of widespread cyber-harassment, and in time this will result in the Internet becoming a notably crueler and more intimidating space."[16] The strategies and tactics pursued here could include creating fake websites and social media accounts that provide deceptively negative or even compromising information, "generating faked videos using high-grade digital mimicry programs that allegedly show the targets stealing, killing, or in intimate contexts, and hacking official databases to corrupt the targets' tax or police records."[17] Cyber-harassment tactics could also involve hacking into the target's social media or email accounts and then firing off a flurry of offensive or self-incriminating messages in order to embarrass the account's true owner.[18]

There is already a wide variety of potential clients for the different services provided by digital influence mercenaries, who will likely work for whoever is willing to pay. This is surely a growth industry, with virtually no limits on targeting possibilities. Future scenarios could include attempts to influence stock prices by flooding social media with provocative or controversial information, like a faked announcement posted by the hacked account of a CEO. As we have seen in years past, fake news about senior government or business leaders could wreak havoc on the stock market. A fabricated video of a plane crash could damage that airline's stock prices, at least temporarily, until enough people are convinced the video was fabricated.

Ordinary individuals could feasibly hire these digital influence mercenaries to launch attacks against someone they don't like. One could imagine using fake photos and videos in all kinds of smear campaigns against ex-boyfriends, celebrities, even professors. Are there any laws preventing you or me from hiring a digital influence mercenary firm or freelancer to spread this kind of disinformation?

The implications of algorithmically generated face-swapping videos are fairly clear for boosting (or undermining) support for a political candidate. As Will Knight observed in a recent article about one of the world's top deepfake video experts, "When fake video footage is as easy to make as fake news articles, it is a virtual guarantee that it will be weaponized. Want to sway an election, ruin the career and reputation of an enemy, or spark ethnic violence? It's hard to imagine a more effective vehicle than a clip that *looks* authentic, spreading like wildfire through Facebook, WhatsApp, or Twitter, faster than people can figure out they've been duped."[19]

As conspiracy theory communities and extremists move to new social media platforms, their track record for being good targets for influence operations will attract mercenaries to follow them there. Influential members of Parler, Gab, Rumble, and WhatsApp communities (for example) will be targeted with messages that the mercenaries want to get amplified. And it is also likely that we will see politicians, corporations, media commentators, and others amplify conspiracy theories along with a broad range of disinformation and provocation efforts for their own gain, both on and offline.

In sum, the future for this industry is disturbingly wide open. Digital influence mercenaries have significant advantages over their victims and those trying to protect the general public from their malicious efforts. They can mask their efforts behind various technological smokescreens that provide levels of anonymity and operational security. They can get paid to exploit fear and uncertainty, overconfidence, and other human traits described in this book. They can generate profits from social media algorithms that reward their efforts to deceive and provoke emotional responses of users. And in addition to their digital influence efforts, mercenary firms and freelancers can also incorporate offline measures (newspapers, personal proxies) as additional means of influencing local audiences. How we—individually and collectively—respond to these challenges will determine the impacts of digital influence efforts in the future.

Responding to Digital Influence Mercenaries

In response to the projected forecast for this global industry, there are certain things that social media platforms can do to make things more difficult for digital influence mercenaries. For example, while social media platforms have historically "prioritized growth, profit, and market dominance over creating a safe and healthy online ecosystem," as Hany Farid described in his June 2020 testimony before Congress, they could instead "decide that they value trusted information over untrusted information, respectful over hateful, and unifying over divisive, and in turn fundamentally change the divisiveness-fueling and misinformation-distributing machine that is social media today."[20] Unfortunately, some observers believe these companies are unlikely to change in this way because of the negative impact it would have on their profits. It is literally not in the platforms' best interests to encourage reasoned debate or nuanced, difficult conversations, because those are slow and boring by their very nature and can prove distinctly unprofitable in the attention economy. However, within the past few years we have seen increasingly aggressive efforts by Internet companies to identify disinformation with warning labels, remove potentially harmful content, and block "coordinated inauthentic behavior" described in this book. Websites, Facebook pages, and YouTube channels are being shut down, and social media accounts are being suspended, often permanently.

For example, in early August 2020, Facebook announced it had removed more than 7 million pieces of content with false claims about COVID-19 since January of that year.[21] In December the company announced plans to remove misinformation about COVID-19 vaccines from the site. They specifically targeted claims about COVID-19 vaccines "that have been debunked by public health experts," to include "false claims about the safety, efficacy, ingredients or side effects of the vaccines," as well as false conspiracy theories about them, such as the claim that "specific populations are being used without their consent to test the vaccine's safety."[22] One of their targets was a public Facebook group called "REFUSE CORONA V@X AND SCREW BILL GATES" (referring to the billionaire whose foundation was helping to fund the development of vaccines) that had been launched by a city contractor in Waukesha, Wisconsin. The group grew to 14,000 members in under four months, one of more than a dozen groups that were dedicated to opposing the COVID-19 vaccine and the idea that it might be mandated by governments.[23]

COVID-19 disinformation has also been banned by YouTube and Twitter, some of which promoted such claims as "social distancing does not work" and that children are "almost immune."[24] In May 2020, Twitter "introduced a new label for Tweets containing synthetic and manipulated media" and announced that "similar labels will now appear on Tweets containing potentially harmful and misleading information related to COVID-19. . . . Depending on the propensity for harm and type of misleading information, warnings may also be applied to a Tweet. These warnings will inform people that the information in the Tweet conflicts with public health experts' guidance before they view it."[25] YouTube's *Community*

Guidelines policy revision, released in May 2020, states that it will not allow misinformation "that poses a serious risk of egregious harm" or that "spreads medical misinformation that contradicts the World Health Organization's (WHO) or local health authorities' medical information about COVID-19."[26]

Social media platforms have also been encouraged to revise their algorithms to stop promoting accounts and pages that frequently spread misinformation. Of course, while there may not be a completely technical solution to the challenges posed by digital influence mercenaries, independent researchers have been working with some online platforms to develop forms of artificial intelligence or human-machine detection of malign information.[27] Facebook is funding the efforts of several academic researchers who are trying to develop a computer algorithm that may detect deepfakes.[28] Similarly, a collaboration between researchers at the University of California and the software company Adobe produced a tool that correctly identifies altered images 99 percent of the time.[29] And in addition to identifying and banning pages or accounts that spread harmful disinformation, companies are also being encouraged to stop funding fake news websites. For example, the Gateway Pundit site is funded by Google Ads, and Breitbart carries advertising from several corporations. Generating advertising revenue is one of the core profit-generation models of digital influence mercenaries, so if this is made increasingly difficult it could incentivize at least some to go do other things with their skills instead.

Some platforms have also been increasingly active in identifying and banning individuals responsible for the spread of disinformation. For example, in May 2019, Facebook closed the accounts of several controversial figures, including Alex Jones, the conspiracy theorist and founder of Infowars.[30] Twitter had already banned Jones in 2018, along with Louis Farrakhan and others who had been using the social media platform to disseminate hateful and false information.[31] And one of the most impactful responses of this kind was banning Donald Trump from Twitter, Facebook, Instagram, and YouTube in January 2021 following his incitement of a mob that physically attacked the nation's Capitol and sent members of Congress fleeing to shelter.

Dangerous groups and movements have also been removed from major social media platforms, although many of their members simply migrated to less-regulated platforms casting themselves as "censorship-free" alternatives—including MeWe, Parler, or Gab—leading to an emerging ecosystem of niche conspiracy communities on those platforms.[32] Twitter began cracking down in July 2020 on fans of the right-wing QAnon conspiracy, removing thousands of accounts that engaged in targeted harassment, and announcing a plan to keep QAnon information from appearing in trending topics or search results.[33] In October 2020, a spokesperson for Facebook announced that the company had "expanded our Dangerous Individuals and Organizations policy to address militarized social movements and violence-inducing conspiracy networks, such as QAnon . . . we've identified over 600 militarized social movements, removing about 2,400 Pages, 14,200 Groups and about 1,300 Instagram accounts they maintained, and in addition, we've removed about 1,700 Pages, 5,600 Groups and about 18,700 Instagram accounts representing QAnon."[34] And in 2021, Twitter suspended more than 70,000 accounts linked to QAnon following the violent siege of the U.S. Capitol in Washington, D.C.,[35] while Facebook began imposing restrictions on dozens of "groups" (forums for like-minded users), particularly after the company's own research found that these had become "a vector for the rabid partisanship and even calls for violence that inflamed the country after the election."[36]

These and many similar efforts can have some positive impact on the long-term prospects of digital influence mercenaries. The so-called "deplatforming" of accounts and groups because of content that violates the company's terms of service may lead to a reduced audience of conspiracy believers on the major social media platforms that they can target with their provocation and deception efforts. However, a much more impactful response from the social media platforms has involved removing accounts (and networks of accounts) because of specific patterns of behavior. Twitter uses the term "platform manipulation" to describe the act of using a social media platform "in a manner intended to amplify or suppress information or engage in behavior that manipulates or disrupts people's experience."[37] Most of the account "takedowns" involving digital influence mercenaries have been in response to these identifiable patterns of activity, rather than for the specific information they posted.

Over the past few years, millions of accounts on Twitter, Facebook, Instagram, YouTube, and other platforms have been suspended or deleted following these companies' own internal monitoring and investigations into such activity. Some investigations have focused on botnets, like Facebook's April 2017 suspension of more than 30,000 accounts in France that they suspected were automated and linked to Russia.[38] In June 2018, Facebook unveiled new measures aimed at reducing the reach of pages run by foreign-based publishers like those in Veles, Macedonia (described in chapter 1).[39] And in September 2020, Facebook announced that since 2017 they had "removed over 100 networks worldwide for engaging in coordinated inauthentic behavior . . . [noting that] with each takedown, threat actors lose their infrastructure across many platforms, forcing them to adjust their techniques, and further reducing their ability to reconstitute and gain traction."[40]

Another important way that social media platforms could counter these malicious efforts to manipulate perceptions is by providing significant amounts of high-quality corporate data to scientific and scholarly researchers. Without sufficient data, it is impossible to determine the extent of disinformation or hate speech problems and to craft appropriate corresponding policy responses.[41] One promising idea, promoted by technology experts Jon Bateman and Craig Newark, is that a collection of social media platforms could form a partnership with universities and governments to create an independent research initiative, providing it with adequate data, money, and other resources as well as guaranteed independence, with a core mission of tackling key questions about how influence operations work and what is effective against them. In their view, "Disinformation and other influence operations are among the greatest challenges facing democracies. We can't stand still until we fully understand this threat, but we also can't keep flying blind forever. The battle for truth requires arming ourselves with knowledge."[42]

Governments also have a role to play in responding to the digital influence mercenary firms and freelancers described in this book. As the Institute for the Study of Diplomacy observes, "To truly combat and mitigate against information operations, there needs to be an approach that has the government, tech, and civil society sectors working in unison."[43] While a democratic government can only do so much to constrain the forces of supply and demand that fuel the growth of the digital influence mercenary industry, political leaders have issued threats against social media platforms, and some European countries have even passed laws attempting to regulate the behavior of at least some Internet companies (like Google). Governments throughout Europe and North America have launched numerous investigations, and in some cases have brought criminal charges (like the United States did against individuals involved in attempts to influence the 2016 presidential election). In one example, Douglass Mackey was arrested in January 2021 and charged with interfering in the 2016 election by tricking nearly five thousand supporters of Hillary Clinton into trying to vote through illegitimate means such as text message or online.[44]

Meanwhile, the Cybersecurity and Infrastructure Security Agency (CISA), within the Department of Homeland Security, launched a public education campaign in January 2021 with a particular focus on supporting COVID-19 response organizations and K-12 educational institutions.[45] More forceful measures have also been taken. For example, in 2018, the U.S. Cyber Command conducted a series of operations against the Russia-based firm formerly known as the Internet Research Agency (described in chapter 1), in order to undermine their capability to influence the midterm elections that year. While the overall damage inflicted on these digital influence mercenaries was limited to just a few days, the operations sent a clear signal of the U.S. government's recognition of the threat, and its willingness to confront such attempts in the future.[46]

But the most frequent type of U.S. government response has been sanctions against foreign entities proven to be involved in influence operations against American targets. Sometimes sanctions have targeted specific firms and individuals (like Yevgeny Prighozhin and the Russia-based Internet Research Agency),[47] though sanctions against countries or individuals who sponsor the efforts of digital influence mercenaries have been rare, as illustrated by the Rally Forge incident described in chapter 1. In that instance, the marketing firm was found to be running a domestic "troll farm" involving hundreds of Facebook and Instagram users—many of them teenagers in the Phoenix, Arizona, area—who had been hired to post comments largely sympathetic to Trump and other conservative causes across social media, as well as spread false information about COVID-19 and cast doubt on the integrity of mail-in ballots.[48] The pages and accounts removed by Facebook had developed a following of nearly 400,000 people. Twitter also acted against the Rally Forge operation, suspending 262 accounts involved in "platform manipulation and spam." However, these social media platforms did not punish the funding sources that paid Rally Forge for these operations, including the conservative pro-Trump youth organization Turning Point Action.[49] One would think perhaps the government could step in and punish these organizations somehow for their role in this incident—but alas, there appear to be no legal measures for doing so. Perhaps this is an area where thoughtful legislation by Congress could have a positive impact.

Obviously, finding ways to punish or otherwise hold people accountable would be a useful strategy for deterring this kind of behavior in the future. But in the absence of a legal framework, social media platforms and government agencies are at a significant disadvantage when trying to confront the issues addressed in this book. In the future, it won't really matter whether the client is an individual, organization, or even a government. The digital influence firms and freelancers will carry out the tasks for which they were hired, and if they happen to get caught and deplatformed or sanctioned, they—not the sponsoring clients who paid them for their work—will have to face the consequences. As the Stanford Internet Observatory notes, "The use of marketing agencies and social consultancies to carry out influence operations has become quite common now, worldwide. Hiring an agency may afford the client plausible deniability in the event of discovery."[50] And naturally, the clients can simply look around and hire some other digital influence mercenaries to take their place.

Finally, in addition to encouraging more effective responses by social media platforms and governments, there are things that ordinary individuals can do to make the digital influence efforts described in this book more difficult for the perpetrators. There is already much greater public attention focusing on digital influence threats to security and society than there was a decade ago. A flurry of new research articles, reports, and books have shed light on the problems of fake social media accounts, troll farms, fake news, manipulated photos and videos, and the threats these and other things pose to the health and prosperity of a democratic society. But in addition to raising awareness and educating ourselves, there are also behavioral changes that we as citizens of a democratic society must consider. In truth, the number one advantage that digital influence mercenaries have is not lax governance or lack of accountability on social media platforms, it is the willing participation of every individual user who amplifies disinformation simply because it confirms their prejudices about how they believe the world should be. Our egos thrive on being convinced we are right, so reinforcing a person's perspective (through disinformation) naturally becomes a prominent and effective digital influence strategy, which can amplify our cognitive biases and confirm our beliefs about something untrue. As mentioned earlier, many of us actively seek disinformation, and the digital influence mercenaries are all too willing to provide it—and make a handsome profit while doing so.

In fact, many human traits are being exploited by these digital influence mercenaries. They can capitalize on ignorance, media illiteracy, superstition, prejudice, arrogance, greed, carelessness, lack of empathy, selfishness, gullibility, illusions of superiority, and rigidity in our views (to name just a handful). A critical barrier to more effective resistance against these digital influence efforts is the "not me" syndrome. Some individuals will insist that "others can be made to carry out evil deeds, but not me"—an orientation that is dangerous because, as Philip Zimbardo and his colleagues observed, "we become most vulnerable to influence attempts when our false pride in our ability to resist them reduces vigilance toward external forces."[51]

Further complicating matters is the fact that an increasing amount of the news people are seeing is inaccurate or suspicious—according to one recent report, Americans consumed twice as much dubious news in 2020 as they did in 2019.[52] The burden lies heavily upon each of us to recognize the harmful effects of this socially mediated flood of disinformation, and to do our part to repel these influence efforts through critical thinking before sharing/retweeting or responding to messages we see online. Perhaps some self-reflection about our biases and prejudices is needed as well. Overall, we must become more effective at monitoring and filtering out disinformation and emotionally provocative messages on our own; we have to adapt our behavior using new tools of social media literacy. In an effort to help us in this regard, Facebook has posted guidelines for how its users can spot fake news.[53] Eugene Kiely and Lori Robertson of FactCheck.org published a brief summary for how to spot fake news,[54] and the Atlantic Council's Digital Forensic Research Lab has partnered with Google Jigsaw to provide a compelling visualization that explains the threat of disinformation around the world.[55] The BBC offers a brief guide, developed by Laura Garcia, on what we all need to be aware of when consuming news online,[56] along with a short list from Carl Miller on how to identify a bot (automated account).[57]

The U.S. Department of Homeland Security has published an array of resources, infographics, and even a graphic novel as part of its effort to educate the public about the threats of disinformation.[58] Other information resources of value include books like Brooke Borel's *The Chicago Guide to Fact-Checking*, Bill Kovach and Tom Rosenstiel's *Blur: How to Know What's True in the Age of Information Overload*, Daniel Levitin's *Weaponized Lies: How to Think Critically in the Post-truth Era*, and Sarah Harrison Smith's *The Fact Checker's Bible*.[59] And the recently published book *True or False*, by former CIA analyst Cindy Otis, takes readers through the history and impact of fake news over the centuries and then provides a wealth of useful tips (and illustrations) for how to spot fake news.[60]

In addition to educating ourselves and improving our own social media literacy, each of us can also try to address the emotional and psychological vulnerabilities that digital influence mercenaries are looking to take advantage of. For example, instead of allowing ourselves to engage in lazy reasoning, we should exert more effort in critical analysis and fact-checking. When we are uncertain about something important, we should be more judicious in the information we rely upon to mitigate that uncertainty. And since a lot of influence efforts focus on emotional provocation, we should try to resist the knee-jerk reaction to something we see on social media, whether we really like it or are outraged by it. The more we react, the more vulnerable we are to further emotional manipulation, and thus the more attractive a target we become to the digital influence mercenaries. Managing our negative emotional responses more effectively is particularly important—ragebait and outrage fatigue are far less likely when we are not so quick to hate others. And of course, some people need to really take some time and reflect on the more repugnant views they embrace—like racism, sexism, and misogyny—which lend oxygen to the flames of digital influence provocation strategies. As disinformation researcher Claire Wardle explains, "Simply saying what the facts are is not going to convince minds that aren't already open."[61]

Another major problem exists in how we interact with high-quality information. For most people, access to fact-checked professional journalism, academic journals, and scientific research requires costly subscriptions and fees to get beyond the publisher's paywalls. In contrast, we can all freely access enormous amounts of fake news, disinformation, and conspiracy theories each day. Without a massive sea change in the ways ordinary citizens interact with fact-based information, and with social media and other Internet-based forms of communication, the mercenaries' ability to deceive, provoke, and manipulate our perceptions will only grow stronger. Additionally, we must decide whether we will continue to tolerate prolific lying, particularly among political leaders and media outlets. If there was a widespread effort to hold people accountable for upholding the truth at all times and punish them when they refuse to do so, digital influence mercenaries would have a much more difficult time achieving their objectives. But alas, no such efforts currently exist nor are any on the horizon. Thus, when assessing why the digital influence tactics described in this book can be so effective in the modern era, it becomes clear that we are often our own worst enemy.

Final Thoughts

As this book goes to press, we are already seeing new developments in the landscape of digital influence mercenaries. A shift in the political climate in the United States has had only a minimal impact on decentralized but vocal movements from the extreme left and the extreme right blaming moderate Democratic politicians for virtually everything wrong in the country. For some on the left, expectations (often unreasonable) for swift progress on matters of social justice, economic growth, and public health have not been met, fueling anxiety and frustration. On the right, the conspiracies and frustrations that fueled the January 6, 2021, attack on the U.S. Capitol remain entrenched among millions of nationalist conservatives, militias, and extremists, seething for revenge against those they blame for perceived injustices. Across the political spectrum, groups and individuals are still making good use of social media platforms, which continue to provide a safe haven for conspiracy theories and falsehoods, both new and old, aiming to increase our uncertainty or remedy it. And our foreign adversaries (both state and non-state actors) continue amplifying disunity and polarization among target audiences. As a result of all these trends, we will continue to see examples of online deception, provocation, and perceptions manipulation for the foreseeable future. There will likely be some new influence aggressors and different targets, along with new technological developments that enhance the effectiveness of their efforts. Overall, in the absence of unimaginably huge changes in America and worldwide, the future looks promising for digital influence mercenaries to continue generating profits and power through information warfare.

NOTES

CHAPTER 1. THE DIVERSE LANDSCAPE OF DIGITAL INFLUENCE MERCENARIES

1. Soufan Center, *IntelBrief: The Social Media Weapons of Authoritarian States*, September 13, 2019, https://thesoufancenter.org/intelbrief-the-social-media-weapons-of-authoritarian-states/ (accessed January 16, 2021).
2. An algorithm is defined as a fixed series of steps that a computer performs in order to solve a problem or complete a task. Claire Wardle et al., *Information Disorder: Toward an Interdisciplinary Framework for Research and Policymaking*, Council of Europe, Shorenstein Center (Harvard University), and First Draft, October 31, 2017, https://shorensteincenter.org/information-disorder-framework-for-research-and-policymaking/ (accessed July 14, 2021).
3. Hannah Ritchie, "Read All about It: The Biggest Fake News Stories of 2016," CNBC, December 20, 2016, https://www.cnbc.com/2016/12/30/read-all-about-it-the-biggest-fake-news-stories-of-2016.html (accessed January 16, 2021); and Claire Wardle, "6 Types of Misinformation Circulated This Election Season," *Columbia Journalism Review*, November 18, 2016, https://www.cjr.org/tow_center/6_types_election_fake_news.php (accessed January 16, 2021).
4. Dan Evon, "Pope Francis Shocks World," Snopes, July 10, 2016, https://www.snopes.com/fact-check/pope-francis-donald-trump-endorsement/ (accessed January 16, 2021). Also, on October 2, Pope Francis spoke publicly about the U.S. election for the first time, saying, "I never say a word about electoral campaigns." See Ritchie, "Read All about It."

5. Ritchie, "Read All about It," and Wardle, "6 Types of Misinformation."
6. Lee McIntyre, *Post-truth* (Cambridge, MA: MIT Press, 2018), 105, citing Andrew Higgins et al., "Inside a Fake News Sausage Factory," *New York Times*, November 25, 2016, https://www.nytimes.com/2016/11/25/world/europe/fake-news-donald-trump-hillary-clinton-georgia.html (accessed January 16, 2021).
7. McIntyre, *Post-truth*, 105, citing Higgins et al., "Inside a Fake News Sausage Factory."
8. Emma Jane Kirby, "The City Getting Rich from Fake News," *BBC News*, December 5, 2016, https://www.bbc.com/news/magazine-38168281 (accessed January 16, 2021).
9. Samanth Subramanian, "Inside the Macedonian Fake-News Complex," *Wired*, February 2017, https://www.wired.com/2017/02/veles-macedonia-fake-news/ (accessed January 16, 2021).
10. Subramanian, "Inside the Macedonian Fake-News Complex."
11. Saska Cvetkovska et al., *The Secret Players behind Macedonia's Fake News Sites*, Organized Crime and Corruption Reporting Project, July 18, 2018, https://www.occrp.org/en/spooksandspin/the-secret-players-behind-macedonias-fake-news-sites (accessed January 16, 2021).
12. Cvetkovska et al., *The Secret Players*.
13. Carl Miller, "Meeting Kosovo's Clickbait Merchants," *BBC News*, November 10, 2018, https://www.bbc.com/news/technology-46136513 (accessed January 16, 2021).
14. Facebook announcement: https://newsroom.fb.com/news/2019/08/cib-uae-egypt-saudi-arabia/ (accessed January 16, 2021).
15. Declan Walsh and Nada Rashwan, "'We're at War': A Covert Social Media Campaign Boosts Military Rulers," *New York Times*, September 6, 2019, https://www.nytimes.com/2019/09/06/world/middleeast/sudan-social-media.html (accessed January 16, 2021).
16. Michiko Kakutani, *The Death of Truth: Notes on Falsehood in the Age of Trump* (New York: Tim Duggan Books, 2018), 156, citing Laura Sydell, "We Tracked Down a Fake-News Creator in the Suburbs. Here's What We Learned," *All Tech Considered*, NPR, November 23, 2016, https://www.npr.org/sections/alltechconsidered/2016/11/23/503146770/npr-finds-the-head-of-a-covert-fake-news-operation-in-the-suburbs (accessed January 16, 2021).
17. Kakutani, *The Death of Truth*, 156, citing Sydell, "We Tracked Down."
18. Kakutani, *The Death of Truth*, 156, citing Sydell, "We Tracked Down."

19. Kakutani, *The Death of Truth*, 156, citing Sydell, "We Tracked Down."
20. Miles O'Brien, "Online Anger Is Gold to This Junk-News Pioneer," *PBS News Hour*, May 2, 2018, https://www.pbs.org/newshour/show/online-anger-is-gold-to-this-junk-news-pioneer (accessed January 16, 2021).
21. McIntyre, *Post-truth*, 107, citing Scott Shane, "From Headline to Photograph, a Fake News Masterpiece," *New York Times*, January 18, 2017, https://www.nytimes.com/2017/01/18/us/fake-news-hillary-clinton-cameron-harris.html (accessed January 16, 2021).
22. McIntyre, *Post-truth*, citing Shane, "From Headline to Photograph."
23. Eli Saslow, "'Nothing on This Page Is Real': How Lies Become Truth in Online America," *Washington Post*, November 17, 2018, https://www.washingtonpost.com/national/nothing-on-this-page-is-real-how-lies-become-truth-in-online-america/2018/11/17/edd44cc8-e85a-11e8-bbdb-72fdbf9d4fed_story.html (accessed January 16, 2021).
24. Saslow, "'Nothing on This Page Is Real.'"
25. *The Price of Influence: Disinformation in the Private Sector, Report CTA-2019-0930* (Boston: Insikt Group and Recorded Future, 2019), https://go.recordedfuture.com/hubfs/reports/cta-2019-0930.pdf (accessed January 16, 2021).
26. Craig Silverman, "Disinformation for Hire: How a New Breed of PR Firms Is Selling Lies Online," *Buzzfeed News*, January 6, 2020, https://www.buzzfeednews.com/article/craigsilverman/disinformation-for-hire-black-pr-firms (accessed January 16, 2021).
27. Cherilyn Ireton and Julie Posetti, *Journalism, Fake News, and Disinformation* (Paris: UNESCO, 2018), 15.
28. Philip N. Howard, *Lie Machines: How to Save Democracy from Troll Armies, Deceitful Robots, Junk News Operations, and Political Operatives* (New Haven, CT: Yale University Press, 2020), 74.
29. Sebastian Bay and Rolf Fredheim, *Falling Behind: How Social Media Companies Are Failing to Combat Inauthentic Behaviour Online*, NATO Strategic Communications Centre of Excellence (December 2019), https://www.stratcomcoe.org/how-social-media-companies-are-failing-combat-inauthentic-behaviour-online (accessed January 16, 2021).
30. Samantha Bradshaw and Philip N. Howard, *Challenging Truth and Trust: A Global Inventory of Organized Social Media Manipulation* (working paper, Project on Computational Propaganda, Oxford, UK, July 20, 2018), 7.
31. Bradshaw and Howard, *Challenging Truth*, 7.

32. Victoria Kwan, "Facebook's Ex–Security Chief on Disinformation Campaigns: 'The Sexiest Explanation Is Usually Not True,'" First Draft, July 9, 2019, https://firstdraftnews.org/latest/alex-stamos-interview-disinformation-campaigns/ (accessed January 16, 2021).
33. Miller, "Meeting Kosovo's Clickbait Merchants."
34. Bay and Fredheim, *Falling Behind*.
35. Bay and Fredheim, *Falling Behind*.
36. Howard, *Lie Machines*, 104.
37. Bay and Fredheim, *Falling Behind*.
38. Davey Alba, "Fake 'Likes' Remain Just a Few Dollars Away, Researchers Say," *New York Times*, December 6, 2019, https://www.nytimes.com/2019/12/06/technology/fake-social-media-manipulation.html (accessed January 16, 2021).
39. Howard, *Lie Machines*, 64.
40. Howard, *Lie Machines*, 64.
41. Craig Timberg and Tony Romm, "Bipartisan Senate Report Calls for Sweeping Effort to Prevent Russian Interference in 2020 Election," *Washington Post*, October 8, 2019, https://www.washingtonpost.com/technology/2019/10/08/bipartisan-senate-report-calls-sweeping-effort-prevent-russian-interference-election/ (accessed January 16, 2021); United States Senate, 116th Congress (2019), *Report of the Select Committee on Intelligence, United States Senate, on Russian Active Measures Campaigns and Interference in the 2016 U.S. Election* (S. Rep. 116-XX), vol. 1, *Russian Efforts against Election Infrastructure with Additional Views*, https://www.intelligence.senate.gov/sites/default/files/documents/Report_Volume1.pdf (accessed January 16, 2021), and vol. 5, *Counterintelligence Threats and Vulnerabilities* (August 2020), https://intelligence.senate.gov/sites/default/files/documents/report_volume5.pdf (accessed January 16, 2021).
42. Ben Nimmo and Alec Toler, *The Russians Who Exposed Russia's Trolls*, Atlantic Council Digital Forensics Lab, March 8, 2018, https://medium.com/dfrlab/the-russians-who-exposed-russias-trolls-72db132e3cd1 (accessed January 16, 2021).
43. Thomas Rid, *Active Measures: The Secret History of Disinformation and Political Warfare* (New York: Farrar, Straus and Giroux, 2020), 409.
44. For a detailed account of the origins and early years of the Internet Research Agency, see Rid, *Active Measures*, 399–409.
45. Nimmo and Toler, *The Russians Who Exposed Russia's Trolls*.

46. The article is available in Russian at https://mr-7.ru/articles/112478/ (accessed January 16, 2021). Source: Nimmo and Toler, *The Russians Who Exposed Russia's Trolls.*
47. In another example, Internet activist Lyudmila Savchuk recounts her experiences infiltrating the Internet Research Agency in St. Petersburg, now widely known as a "troll farm" spreading disinformation around the world, in a video published by Disinfo Portal at https://disinfoportal.org/stratcomdc-ms-lyudmila-savchuk-on-infiltrating-the-internet-research-agency/ (accessed January 16, 2021).
48. Office of the Director of National Intelligence (DNI), *Background to "Assessing Russian Activities and Intentions in Recent US Elections,"* January 6, 2017, 4, https://www.dni.gov/files/documents/ICA_2017_01.pdf (accessed January 16, 2021). A recent Graphika report about "the business and influence operations of Russian oligarch Yevgeny Prigozhin" also refers to this IRA as a "troll farm," https://graphika.com/reports/more-troll-kombat/ (accessed January 16, 2021).
49. The official indictment is available online: *United States of America v. Internet Research Agency LLC a/k/a/ Mediasintez LLC et al., Criminal No. (18 U.S.C. SS 2, 371, 1349, 1028A)*, United States District Court for the District of Columbia, filed 2/16/18, https://www.justice.gov/file/1035477/download (accessed January 16, 2021). For analysis, see Rachel Wolfe, "Read Deputy Attorney General Rod Rosenstein's Remarks on the Russia Indictment," Vox, February 16, 2018, https://www.vox.com/2018/2/16/17020872/rosenstein-russia-indictments-transcript (accessed January 16, 2021); and Michael V. Hayden, *The Assault on Intelligence: American National Security in an Age of Lies* (New York: Penguin, 2018), 254.
50. Peter Pomerantsev, *This Is Not Propaganda* (New York: Public Affairs, 2018), 23.
51. Philip N. Howard, Bharath Ganesh, Dimitra Liotsiou, John Kelly, and Camille François, *The IRA, Social Media, and Political Polarization in the United States, 2012–2018* (working paper, Project on Computational Propaganda, Oxford, UK, 12/2018, https://demtech.oii.ox.ac.uk/research/posts/the-ira-and-political-polarization-in-the-united-states/ (accessed July 14, 2021).
52. Davey Alba and Sheera Frenkel, "Russia Tests New Disinformation Tactics in Africa to Expand Influence," *New York Times*, October 30, 2019, https://www.nytimes.com/2019/10/30/technology/russia-facebook-disinformation-africa.html (accessed January 16, 2021).

53. Alba and Frenkel, "Russia Tests"; see also "Facebook Suspends Accounts Tied to Putin Ally for Political Meddling," *New York Post*, October 30, 2019, https://nypost.com/2019/10/30/facebook-suspends-accounts-tied-to-putin-ally-for-political-meddling/ (accessed January 16, 2021).
54. Shelby Grossman et al., *Stoking Conflicts by Keystroke*, Stanford Internet Observatory, December 15, 2020, https://cyber.fsi.stanford.edu/content/ira-takedown-20201215 (accessed July 14, 2021).
55. Nathaniel Gleicher et al., "Removing Coordinated Inauthentic Behavior from France and Russia," Facebook Newsroom, December 15, 2020, https://about.fb.com/news/2020/12/removing-coordinated-inauthentic-behavior-france-russia/ (accessed January 16, 2021).
56. P. W. Singer and Emerson T. Brooking, *LikeWar: The Weaponization of Social Media* (Boston: Houghton Mifflin Harcourt, 2018), 107.
57. DNI, *Background to "Assessing Russian Activities,"* 4–6.
58. DNI, *Background to "Assessing Russian Activities,"* 12.
59. Jakub Kalenský, *A Change of Tactics: Blurring Disinformation's Source*, Disinfo Portal, June 6, 2019, https://disinfoportal.org/a-change-of-tactics-blurring-disinformations-source (accessed January 16, 2021).
60. Kalenský, *A Change of Tactics*.
61. Shelby Grossman, Khadeja Ramali, Renee DiResta, *Blurring the Lines of Media Authenticity: Prigozhin-Linked Group Funding Libyan Broadcast Media*, Stanford Internet Observatory, March 20, 2020, https://cyber.fsi.stanford.edu/io/news/libya-prigozhin (accessed January 16, 2021).
62. Clint Watts, "Disinformation: A Primer in Russian Active Measures and Influence Campaigns," Statement Prepared for the U.S. Senate Select Committee on Intelligence, March 30, 2017, https://bit.ly/2oJ0hZV (accessed January 16, 2021).
63. Donie O'Sullivan and Kaya Yurieff, "Facebook Bans Company It Says Ran Fake Accounts for Turning Point," *CNN Business*, October 9, 2020, https://www.cnn.com/2020/10/08/tech/facebook-rally-forge-ban/index.html (accessed January 16, 2021); Isaac Stanley-Becker, "Facebook Bans Marketing Firm Running 'Troll Farm' for Pro-Trump Youth Group," *Washington Post*, October 8, 2020, https://www.washingtonpost.com/technology/2020/10/08/facebook-bans-media-consultancy-running-troll-farm-pro-trump-youth-group/ (accessed January 16, 2021); and *Analysis of an October 2020 Facebook Takedown*

Linked to U.S. Political Consultancy Rally Forge, Stanford Internet Observatory, October 8, 2020, https://cyber.fsi.stanford.edu/io/news/oct-2020-fb-rally-forge (accessed January 16, 2021).

64. O'Sullivan and Yurieff, "Facebook Bans Company."
65. Diego A. Martin and Jacob N. Shapiro, *Trends in Online Foreign Influence Efforts*, Woodrow Wilson School of Public and International Affairs, Princeton University, July 8, 2019, 8, https://scholar.princeton.edu/jns/research-reports (accessed January 16, 2021).
66. Martin and Shapiro, *Trends in Online Foreign Influence Efforts*, 7.
67. Martin and Shapiro, *Trends in Online Foreign Influence Efforts*, 8.
68. Sebastian Bay et al., *The Black Market for Social Media Manipulation*, NATO StratCom COE and Singularex, November 2018, 16, https://www.stratcomcoe.org/black-market-social-media-manipulation (accessed January 16, 2021).
69. Bay et al., *The Black Market for Social Media Manipulation*.
70. Andy Greenberg, "Alphabet-Owned Jigsaw Bought a Russian Troll Campaign as an Experiment," *Wired*, June 12, 2019, https://www.wired.com/story/jigsaw-russia-disinformation-social-media-stalin-alphabet/ (accessed January 16, 2021).
71. *The Price of Influence: Disinformation in the Private Sector, Report CTA-2019-0930*.
72. Ben Popken, "Trolls for Hire: Russia's Freelance Disinformation Firms Offer Propaganda with a Professional Touch," NBC News, October 1, 2019, https://www.nbcnews.com/tech/security/trolls-hire-russia-s-freelance-disinformation-firms-offer-propaganda-professional-n1060781 (accessed January 16, 2021); *The Price of Influence: Disinformation in the Private Sector, Report CTA-2019-0930*.
73. *The Price of Influence: Disinformation in the Private Sector, Report CTA-2019-0930*.
74. Popken, "Trolls for Hire."
75. *The Price of Influence: Disinformation in the Private Sector, Report CTA-2019-0930*.
76. Popken, "Trolls for Hire."
77. Michael Erbschloe, *Social Media Warfare: Equal Weapons for All* (Boca Raton, FL: CRC Press, 2017), 149–50.
78. Erbschloe, *Social Media Warfare*, 149–50.
79. Stanley-Becker, "Facebook Bans Marketing Firm."
80. Stanley-Becker, "Facebook Bans Marketing Firm."

81. Davey Alba and Adam Satariano, "At Least 70 Countries Have Had Disinformation Campaigns, Study Finds," *New York Times*, September 26, 2019, https://www.nytimes.com/2019/09/26/technology/government-disinformation-cyber-troops.html (accessed January 16, 2021).
82. Howard, *Lie Machines*, 96.
83. Howard, *Lie Machines*, 43–44.
84. Howard, *Lie Machines*, 96; and Isa Soares, "The Fake News Machine: Inside a Town Gearing Up for 2020," CNN Money, 2017, https://money.cnn.com/interactive/media/the-macedonia-story/ (accessed January 16, 2021).
85. Howard, *Lie Machines*, 97.
86. Howard, *Lie Machines*, 87.
87. Christian Davies, "Undercover Reporter Reveals Life in a Polish Troll Farm," *Guardian*, November 1, 2019, https://www.theguardian.com/world/2019/nov/01/undercover-reporter-reveals-life-in-a-polish-troll-farm (accessed January 16, 2021).
88. Singer and Brooking, *LikeWar*, 111.
89. Howard, *Lie Machines*, 88–89.
90. Howard, *Lie Machines*, 88–89.
91. Silverman, "Disinformation for Hire."
92. Howard, *Lie Machines*, 88–89.
93. Howard, *Lie Machines*, 88–89.
94. Silverman, "Disinformation for Hire."
95. Silverman, "Disinformation for Hire."
96. Silverman, "Disinformation for Hire."
97. Silverman, "Disinformation for Hire."
98. Emily Taylor et al., *Follow the Money: How the Online Advertising Ecosystem Funds COVID-19 Junk News and Disinformation*, Comprop Working Paper 2020.1, Oxford Internet Institute, August 3, 2020, 2, https://comprop.oii.ox.ac.uk/research/posts/follow-the-money-how-the-online-advertising-ecosystem-funds-covid-19-junk-news-and-disinformation/ (accessed January 16, 2021).
99. McIntyre, *Post-truth*, 105.
100. Ireton and Posetti, *Journalism, Fake News and Disinformation*, 17.
101. Bay and Fredheim, *Falling Behind*.
102. For more on digital influence silos, see James J. F. Forest, *Digital Influence Warfare in the Age of Social Media* (Santa Barbara, CA: Praeger Security International, 2021).

103. Robert B. Cialdini, *Influence: The Psychology of Persuasion*, rev. ed. (New York: HarperCollins, 2007), 163.
104. Singer and Brooking, *LikeWar*, 119–20; Craig Silverman, "This Analysis Shows How Viral Fake Election News Stories Outperformed Real News on Facebook," *BuzzFeed News*, November 16, 2016, https://www.buzzfeednews.com/article/craigsilverman/viral-fake-election-news-outperformed-real-news-on-facebook (accessed January 16, 2021).
105. Sydell, "We Tracked Down a Fake-News Creator"; McIntyre, *Post-truth*, 107; Ritchie, "Read All about It"; and Wardle, "6 Types of Misinformation."
106. McIntyre, *Post-truth*, 105.
107. Howard, *Lie Machines*, 70.
108. Howard, *Lie Machines*, 70.
109. Howard, *Lie Machines*, 70.
110. Howard, *Lie Machines*, 12.
111. Naomi Oreskes and Erik M. Conway, *Merchants of Doubt: How a Handful of Scientists Obscured the Truth on Issues from Tobacco Smoke to Global Warming* (New York: Bloomsbury, 2010), 57.
112. A more detailed account of Rush Limbaugh, and his impact on the rise of the Fox cable network, is provided in chapter 5 of Forest, *Digital Influence Warfare in the Age of Social Media*.
113. Lisa Kaplan, "The Biggest Social Media Operation You've Never Heard of Is Run Out of Cyprus by Russians," Lawfare, December 18, 2019, https://www.lawfareblog.com/biggest-social-media-operation-youve-never-heard-run-out-cyprus-russians (accessed January 16, 2021).
114. Kaplan, "The Biggest Social Media Operation."
115. Daisuke Wakabayashi and Sapna Maheshwari, "YouTube Advertiser Exodus Highlights Perils of Online Ads," *New York Times*, March 23, 2017, https://www.nytimes.com/2017/03/23/business/media/youtube-advertisers-offensive-content.html (accessed January 16, 2021).
116. Gilad Edelman, "Why YouTube Won't Ban Trump's Misleading Ads about Biden," *Wired*, December 3, 2019, https://www.wired.com/story/youtube-trump-biden-political-ads/ (accessed January 16, 2021).
117. Drew Harwell, "Faked Pelosi Videos, Slowed to Make Her Appear Drunk, Spread across Social Media," *Washington Post*, May 24, 2019, https://www.washingtonpost.com/technology/2019/05/23/faked-pelosi-videos-slowed-make-her-appear-drunk-spread-across-social-media/ (accessed January 16, 2021).

118. Taylor et al., "Follow the Money," 6.
119. Alba, "Fake 'Likes' Remain."
120. Ryan Holiday, *Trust Me, I'm Lying: Confessions of a Media Manipulator*, rev. ed. (New York: Portfolio/Penguin, 2017), 47.
121. Ireton and Posetti, *Journalism, Fake News and Disinformation*, 17.
122. Kalenský, *A Change of Tactics*.
123. Erbschloe, *Social Media Warfare*, 151.
124. Singer and Brooking, *LikeWar*, 210.
125. Singer and Brooking, *LikeWar*, 210.
126. Charlie Kirk (@charliekirk11), "Breaking: Legal group finds hundreds of double voting cases, thousands of deceased voters on rolls in Palm Beach County. A new discovery shows 24,000 instances of irregularities among the voter rolls in Palm Beach County, Fla., according to a new report. Voter fraud is real," Twitter, November 10, 2019, 12:41 p.m., https://mobile.twitter.com/charliekirk11/status/1193584417723342848. Kirk's account at that time indicated that he had 1.4 million followers.
127. Christopher Knaus et al., "Inside the Hate Factory: How Facebook Fuels Far-Right Profit," *Guardian*, December 5, 2019, https://www.theguardian.com/australia-news/2019/dec/06/inside-the-hate-factory-how-facebook-fuels-far-right-profit (accessed January 16, 2021).
128. Knaus et al., "Inside the Hate Factory."
129. Knaus et al., "Inside the Hate Factory."
130. For example, see *Portrait of a Troll*, Organized Crime and Corruption Reporting Project (OCCRP), June 19, 2016, https://www.occrp.org/en/other/5369-portrait-of-a-troll (accessed January 16, 2021).
131. Cindy C. Combs, "The Media as a Showcase for Terrorism," in *Teaching Terror: Strategic and Tactical Learning in the Terrorist World*, ed. James J. F. Forest (Lanham, MD: Rowman & Littlefield, 2006), 133–54.
132. For more on this, see Howard, *Lie Machines*, 106.
133. Bay and Fredheim, *Falling Behind*.
134. Leonid Bershidsky, "Facebook Just Can't Seem to Beat the Russians," Bloomberg, December 6, 2019, https://www.bloomberg.com/opinion/articles/2019-12-06/facebook-just-can-t-seem-to-beat-the-russians (accessed January 16, 2021).
135. McIntyre, *Post-truth*, 105.

CHAPTER 2. DIGITAL INFLUENCE METHODS

1. Jarol B. Manheim, *Strategy in Information and Influence Campaigns* (New York: Routledge, 2011), 185.
2. Susan Barnes, "A Privacy Paradox: Social Networking in the United States," *First Monday* 11, no. 9 (2006), 5, http://doi.org/10.5210/fm.v11i9.1394 (accessed January 16, 2021); cited in Ciaran McMahon, *The Psychology of Social Media* (London: Routledge, 2019), 17.
3. For example, see Temple University's guide to Webscraping, https://guides.temple.edu/mining-twitter/scraping (accessed January 16, 2021); and Allen Zeng, "A Beginner's Guide to Collecting Twitter Data," Knight Lab Ideas, March 15, 2014, https://knightlab.northwestern.edu/2014/03/15/a-beginners-guide-to-collecting-twitter-data-and-a-bit-of-web-scraping/ (accessed January 16, 2021).
4. An algorithm is defined as a fixed series of steps that a computer performs in order to solve a problem or complete a task. Wardle, *Information Disorder*.
5. Manheim, *Strategy in Information and Influence Campaigns*, 52.
6. For an excellent description and explanation of algorithms, see Carl Miller, *The Death of the Gods: The New Global Power Grab* (London: Windmill Books, 2018), 272–81.
7. Wardle, *Information Disorder*.
8. Howard, *Lie Machines*, 173–74.
9. Kakutani, *The Death of Truth*, 127; Matthew Rosenberg and Gabriel J. X. Dance, "'You Are the Product': Targeted by Cambridge Analytica on Facebook," *New York Times*, April 8, 2018, https://www.nytimes.com/2018/04/08/us/facebook-users-data-harvested-cambridge-analytica.html (accessed January 16, 2021); Carole Cadwalladr and Emma Graham-Harrison, "Revealed: 50 Million Facebook Profiles Harvested for Cambridge Analytica in Major Data Break," *Guardian*, March 17, 2018, https://www.theguardian.com/news/2018/mar/17/cambridge-analytica-facebook-influence-us-election (accessed January 16, 2021); Olivia Solon, "Facebook Says Cambridge May Have Gained 37m More Users' Data," *Guardian*, April 4, 2018, https://www.theguardian.com/technology/2018/apr/04/facebook-cambridge-analytica-user-data-latest-more-than-thought (accessed January 16, 2021).
10. For example, see S. Rep. No. 116-XX, vol. 5, *Counterintelligence Threats and Vulnerabilities*, 663 (2020).

11. Matthew Rosenberg and Nicholas Confessore, "Justice Department and F.B.I. Are Investigating Cambridge Analytica," *New York Times*, May 15, 2018, https://www.nytimes.com/2018/05/15/us/cambridge-analytica-federal-investigation.html (accessed January 16, 2021).
12. Brittany Kaiser, *Targeted: The Cambridge Analytica Whistleblower's Inside Story of How Big Data, Trump, and Facebook Broke Democracy and How It Can Happen Again* (New York: Harper, 2019), 98.
13. Carole Cadwalladr, "The Great British Brexit Robbery," *Guardian*, May 7, 2017, https://www.theguardian.com/technology/2017/may/07/the-great-british-brexit-robbery-hijacked-democracy (accessed January 16, 2021).
14. Rosenberg and Dance, "'You Are the Product.'"
15. Rosenberg and Dance, "'You Are the Product.'"
16. Kaiser, *Targeted*, 145.
17. Rosenberg and Confessore, "Justice Department and F.B.I. Are Investigating Cambridge Analytica."
18. Kaiser, *Targeted*, 39–40.
19. Emma L. Briant, "Leave.EU: Dark Money, Dark Ads and Data Crimes," in *The Sage Handbook of Propaganda*, ed. Paul Baines, Nicholas O'Shaughnessy, and Nancy Snow (London: Routledge, 2019); Emma L. Briant, *Evidence for the US Senate Judiciary Committee on Cambridge Analytica and SCL Group*, June 2018, https://www.judiciary.senate.gov/imo/media/doc/Professor%20Emma%20L.%20Briant%20Report%20on%20Cambrige%20Analytica.pdf (accessed January 16, 2021); and Jane Mayer, "New Evidence Emerges of Steve Bannon and Cambridge Analytica's Role in Brexit," *New Yorker*, November 17, 2018, https://www.newyorker.com/news/news-desk/new-evidence-emerges-of-steve-bannon-and-cambridge-analyticas-role-in-brexit (accessed January 16, 2021).
20. Ellen Berry, "Cambridge Analytica Whistleblower Contends Data-Mining Swung Brexit Vote," *New York Times*, March 27, 2018, https://www.nytimes.com/2018/03/27/world/europe/whistle-blower-data-mining-cambridge-analytica.html (accessed January 16, 2021).
21. Rachel Leah, "Steve Bannon Tried to Suppress Black Vote, Cambridge Analytica Whistleblower Says," *Salon*, May 18, 2018, https://www.salon.com/2018/05/18/steve-bannon-tried-to-suppress-black-votes-cambridge-analytica-whistleblower-says/ (accessed January 16, 2021); Cadwalladr and Graham-Harrison, "Revealed."

22. Kaiser, *Targeted*, 70
23. Kaiser, *Targeted*, 70.
24. Kaiser, *Targeted*, 195.
25. Kaiser, *Targeted*, 146.
26. Igor Derysh, "Robert and Rebekah Mercer Bail on Trump Campaign—They Spent $49 Million in 2016," Salon, June 18, 2019, https://www.salon.com/2019/06/18/robert-and-rebekah-mercer-bail-on-trump-campaign-they-spent-49-million-in-2016/ (accessed January 16, 2021).
27. The series of tweets begins on January 2, 2020: Hindsight is 2020, (@HindsightFiles), "CAMBRIDGE ANALYTICA—EXPOSED: The document release includes previously unreleased emails, project plans, case studies, negotiations and more spanning at least 65 countries. Democracy has been hacked. Let's learn from our mistakes," Twitter, January 2, 2020, 3:30 p.m., https://twitter.com/HindsightFiles/status/1212848706619351060 (accessed July 16, 2021).
28. Carole Cadwalladr, "Fresh Cambridge Analytica Leak 'Shows Global Manipulation Is Out of Control,'" *Guardian*, January 4, 2020, https://www.theguardian.com/uk-news/2020/jan/04/cambridge-analytica-data-leak-global-election-manipulation (accessed January 16, 2021).
29. Kaiser, *Targeted*.
30. Emma Briant's book is due to be published in 2021 and is tentatively titled *Propaganda Machine: Inside Cambridge Analytica and the Digital Influence Industry* (London: Bloomsbury, 2022).
31. Singer and Brooking, *LikeWar*, 123.
32. Katarzyna Pruszkiewicz, Wojciech Ciesla, and Konrad Szczygiel, *Undercover at a Troll Farm*, Investigate Europe, November 1, 2019, https://www.investigate-europe.eu/undercover-at-a-troll-farm/ (accessed January 16, 2021).
33. Wardle, *Information Disorder*.
34. Miller, "Meeting Kosovo's Clickbait Merchants."
35. Lion Gu, Vladimir Kropotov, and Fyodor Yarochkin, *The Fake News Machine: How Propagandists Abuse the Internet and Manipulate the Public*, TrendLabs (R&D Center of Trend Micro, 2017), 32, https://documents.trendmicro.com/assets/white_papers/wp-fake-news-machine-how-propagandists-abuse-the-internet.pdf (accessed July 16, 2021).
36. Michael Newberg, "As Many as 48 Million Twitter Accounts Aren't People, Says Study," CNBC, March 10, 2017, https://www.cnbc.com/2017/03/10/nearly-48-million-twitter-accounts-could-be-bots-says-study.html (accessed

January 16, 2021); Scott Shane and Mike Isaac, "Facebook Says It's Policing Fake Accounts. But They're Still Easy to Spot," *New York Times*, November 3, 2017, https://www.nytimes.com/2017/11/03/technology/facebook-fake-accounts.html (accessed January 16, 2021).

37. Sara Fischer, "How Bots and Fake Accounts Work," Axios, October 31, 2017, https://www.axios.com/how-bots-and-fake-accounts-work-1513306547-4b0214b2-3277-422a-b492-06a1c0e2c61e.html (accessed January 16, 2021).

38. Howard, *Lie Machines*, 172–73.

39. Carl Miller, "What Are 'Bots' and How Can They Spread Fake News?," BBC News, December 2020, https://www.bbc.co.uk/bitesize/articles/zjhg47h (accessed January 16, 2021).

40. Wardle, *Information Disorder*.

41. Howard, *Lie Machines*, 80–81.

42. For example, see Shelly Palmer, "How to Build Your Own Troll Bot Army," March 18, 2018, https://www.shellypalmer.com/2018/03/build-troll-farm/ (accessed January 16, 2021); and "Build the Best Free Instagram Automation Bot 15 Minutes," https://medium.com/@rohanarun/how-to-build-an-instagram-bot-farm-in-15-minutes-for-free-14468c844f7a (accessed January 16, 2021).

43. Anthony R. Pratkanis and Elliot Aronson, *Age of Propaganda: The Everyday Use and Abuse of Persuasion*, rev. ed. (New York: Henry Holt, 2001), 182.

44. For details about Facebook's policies on this, see https://www.facebook.com/communitystandards/inauthentic_behavior (accessed January 16, 2021).

45. Howard, *Lie Machines*, 88–89.

46. Robert Walker, "Combating Weapons of Influence on Social Media," master's thesis, Naval Postgraduate School, June 2019, https://apps.dtic.mil/sti/pdfs/AD1080481.pdf (accessed January 16, 2021).

47. Pomerantsev, *This Is Not Propaganda*, 54.

48. Jane Mayer, "How Russia Helped Swing the Election for Trump," *New Yorker*, September 24, 2018, https://www.newyorker.com/magazine/2018/10/01/how-russia-helped-to-swing-the-election-for-trump (accessed January 16, 2021).

49. Mayer, "How Russia Helped Swing the Election for Trump."

50. Walker, "Combating Weapons of Influence on Social Media."

51. Jack Stubbs and Christopher Bing, "Facebook Suspends Russian Instagram Accounts Targeting U.S. Voters," Reuters, October 21, 2019, https://www

.reuters.com/article/us-facebook-accounts-russia/facebook-suspends-russian-instagram-accounts-targeting-u-s-voters-idUSKBN1X01YP (accessed January 16, 2021).

52. Camille François, Ben Nimmo, and C. Shawn Eib, *The IRA CopyPasta Campaign*, Graphika, October 2019, 1–2, https://graphika.com/reports/copypasta/ (accessed January 16, 2021).

53. Tony Romm and Craig Timberg, "Facebook, Twitter Suspend Russian-Linked Operation Targeting African Americans on Social Media," *Washington Post*, March 12, 2020, https://www.washingtonpost.com/technology/2020/03/12/facebook-russia-african-americans-2020/ (accessed January 16, 2021).

54. Vidhi Choudhary, "Facebook Shuts Down Romania-Linked Accounts Posing as Trump Supporters," *Forbes*, August 6, 2020, https://www.forbes.com/sites/vidhichoudhary/2020/08/06/facebook-shuts-down-romania-linked-accounts-posing-as-trump-supporters/#253dca843536 (accessed January 16, 2021).

55. Rachel Sandler, "Facebook Bans Marketing Firm That Made Fake Accounts for Conservative Nonprofit Turning Point Action," *Forbes*, October 8, 2020, https://www.forbes.com/sites/rachelsandler/2020/10/08/facebook-bans-marketing-firm-that-made-fake-accounts-for-conservative-nonprofit-turning-point-action/?sh=16b1d8135dae (accessed January 16, 2021).

56. Alba and Frenkel, "Russia Tests."

57. Darren L. Linvill and Patrick L. Warren, "Troll Factories: Manufacturing Specialized Disinformation on Twitter," *Political Communication* 37, no. 4 (February 5, 2020): 448.

58. Linvill and Warren, "Troll Factories," 447–67.

59. Erbschloe, *Social Media Warfare*, 279.

60. Howard, *Lie Machines*, 174.

61. J.-B. Jeangène Vilmer, A. Escorcia, M. Guillaume, J. Herrera, *Information Manipulation: A Challenge for Our Democracies*, report by the Policy Planning Staff (CAPS) of the Ministry for Europe and Foreign Affairs and the Institute for Strategic Research (IRSEM) of the Ministry for the Armed Forces (Paris, August 2018), 20.

62. Vilmer et al., *Information Manipulation*, 20.

63. Linvill and Warren, "Troll Factories," 452.

64. Linvill and Warren, "Troll Factories," 452.

65. Tim Hwang, *Deepfakes: Primer and Forecast*, NATO Strategic Communications Centre of Excellence, June 2020, 12, https://www.stratcomcoe.org/deepfakes-primer-and-forecast (accessed January 16, 2021).
66. Robert Chesney and Danielle Citron, "Deepfakes and the New Disinformation War," *Foreign Affairs*, January/February 2019, 147–55, https://www.foreignaffairs.com/articles/world/2018-12-11/deepfakes-and-new-disinformation-war (accessed January 16, 2021).
67. Michael J. Mazarr et al., *The Emerging Risk of Virtual Societal Warfare* (Santa Monica, CA: RAND Corporation, 2019), 99.
68. Zamira Rahim, "'Deepfake' Queen Delivers Alternative Christmas Speech, in Warning about Misinformation," CNN, December 25, 2020, https://www.cnn.com/2020/12/25/uk/deepfake-queen-speech-christmas-intl-gbr/index.html (accessed January 16, 2021). The video aired on Britain's Channel 4, https://www.channel4.com/programmes/alternative-christmas-message (accessed January 16, 2021), and is also available on YouTube, https://www.youtube.com/watch?v=IvY-Abd2FfM (accessed January 16, 2021).
69. Renee Diresta et al., *Telling China's Story: The Chinese Communist Party's Campaign to Shape Global Narratives*, Stanford Internet Observatory and Hoover Institution, Stanford University, July 20, 2020, 13, https://cyber.fsi.stanford.edu/io/news/new-whitepaper-telling-chinas-story (accessed January 16, 2021).
70. Yochai Benkler et al., *Network Propaganda* (Oxford: Oxford University Press, 2018), 9.
71. Walker, "Combating Weapons of Influence on Social Media."
72. Zarine Kharazian and Tessa Knight, "Why the Debunked COVID-19 Conspiracy Video 'Plandemic' Won't Go Away," Atlantic Council's Digital Forensics Research Lab, May 14, 2020, https://medium.com/dfrlab/why-the-debunked-covid-19-conspiracy-video-plandemic-wont-go-away-c9dd36c2037c (accessed January 16, 2021).
73. Linvill and Warren, "Troll Factories," 453.
74. Isaac Stanley-Becker, "Disinformation for Profit: How a Florida 'Dealmaker' Turns Conservative Outrage into Cash," *Washington Post*, August 11, 2020, https://www.washingtonpost.com/technology/2020/08/11/evans-disinformation-florida-email/ (accessed January 16, 2021).
75. Stanley-Becker, "Disinformation for Profit."

76. House Committee on Energy and Commerce, *Disinformation Online and a Country in Crisis*, 116th Cong. (June 24, 2020), (testimony of Hany Farid, PhD), https://www.hsdl.org/?view&did=840913 (accessed January 16, 2021).
77. For example, a team of researchers identified a list of key topics amplified by Russian mercenary accounts, as described in their report *Tactics and Tropes of the Internet Research Agency*, New Knowledge, December 2018, https://www.newknowledge.com/disinforeport (accessed January 16, 2021).
78. Linvill and Warren, "Troll Factories," 453.
79. Linvill and Warren, "Troll Factories," 453.
80. "Flaming," *TechTerms*, https://techterms.com/definition/flaming (accessed January 16, 2021).
81. Walker, "Combating Weapons of Influence on Social Media"; also, see Howard, *Lie Machines*, 174.
82. Judith S. Donath, "Identity and Deception in the Virtual Community," in *Communities in Cyberspace*, ed. P. Kollock and M. Smith (London: Routledge, 1998), http://vivatropolis.org/papers/Donath/IdentityDeception/IdentityDeception.pdf (accessed January 16, 2021).
83. Alice Marwick and Rebecca Lewis, *Media Manipulation and Disinformation Online*, Data and Society (May 2017), https://datasociety.net/output/media-manipulation-and-disinfo-online/ (accessed January 16, 2021).
84. Shelly Banjo, "Facebook, Twitter, and the Digital Disinformation Mess," *Washington Post*, October 31, 2019, https://www.washingtonpost.com/business/facebook-twitter-and-the-digital-disinformation-mess/2019/10/31/3f81647c-fbd1-11e9-9e02-1d45cb3dfa8f_story.html (accessed October 1, 2020).
85. Samantha Bradshaw and Philip N. Howard, *Troops, Trolls and Troublemakers: A Global Inventory of Organized Social Media Manipulation*, working paper No. 2017.12, Project on Computational Propaganda, Oxford, UK, July 17, 2017, https://demtech.oii.ox.ac.uk/research/posts/troops-trolls-and-troublemakers-a-global-inventory-of-organized-social-media-manipulation/ (accessed July 16, 2021); Kakutani, *The Death of Truth*, 132.
86. Donath, "Identity and Deception in the Virtual Community."
87. Wardle, *Information Disorder*.
88. Rosanna E. Guadagno, "Compliance: A Classic and Contemporary Review," in *The Oxford Handbook of Social Influence*, ed. Stephen G. Harkins et al. (New York: Oxford University Press, 2017), 123.
89. Wardle, *Information Disorder*; and Gu et al., *The Fake News Machine*.

90. Atlantic Council Digital Forensic Research Lab, *Confronting the Threat of Disinformation: The Problem*, Google Jigsaw Data Visualizer (February 2020), https://jigsaw.google.com/the-current/disinformation/dataviz/.
91. Franziska B. Keller, David Schoch, Sebastian Stier, and JungHwan Yang, "Political Astroturfing on Twitter: How to Coordinate a Disinformation Campaign," *Political Communication* 37, no. 2 (October 26, 2019): 256–80.
92. Howard, *Lie Machines*, 171.
93. Walker, "Combating Weapons of Influence on Social Media."
94. Singer and Brooking, *LikeWar*, 142, citing Marion R. Just et al., "'It's Trending on Twitter': An Analysis of the Twitter Manipulations in the Massachusetts 2010 Special Senate Election," 2012, https://www.academia.edu/24640252/It_s_Trending_on_Twitter_-_An_Analysis_of_the_Twitter_Manipulations_in_the_Massachusetts_2010_Special_Senate_Election (accessed January 16, 2021).
95. *Analysis of an October 2020 Facebook Takedown Linked to U.S. Political Consultancy Rally Forge*, Stanford Internet Observatory, October 8, 2020, https://cyber.fsi.stanford.edu/io/news/oct-2020-fb-rally-forge (accessed January 16, 2021).
96. Zack Beauchamp, "Trump's Allies in the National Security Council Are Being Taken Out," Vox, August 2, 2017, https://www.vox.com/world/2017/8/2/16087434/ezra-cohen-watnick-fired (accessed January 16, 2021).
97. An "amplifier account" is typically a bot whose sole purpose is to boost the spread of content by automatically liking, sharing, and reposting (or retweeting) the original message. An "automated retweet" is a type of amplifier bot account unique to the social media platform Twitter, which is programmed to automatically repost messages received from specific accounts.
98. *Oxford English Dictionary*, (2020), s.v. "hashtag."
99. ZionWarrior (@ZionWarrior6), "This is what happens when you think politics is a party: - Wars - Injustice - Failed Economies - Homeless - Drug epidemics *** Meeting lots of 'cool' people and having fun! #DemocratsAreDestroyingAmerica and BAD for the world!" Twitter, May 28, 2021, 1:46 p.m., https://twitter.com/ZionWarrior6/status/1398349998312628228.
100. Caroline Orr, "How Russian and Alt-Right Twitter Accounts Worked Together to Skew the Narrative about Berkeley," Arc Digital, September 1, 2017, https://medium.com/arc-digital/how-russian-alt-right-twitter-accounts-worked-together-to-skew-the-narrative-about-berkeley-f03a3d04ac5d (accessed July 16, 2021).

101. Marwick and Lewis, *Media Manipulation and Disinformation Online.*
102. Marwick and Lewis, *Media Manipulation and Disinformation Online.*
103. Marwick and Lewis, *Media Manipulation and Disinformation Online,* 39.
104. Paraphrasing Marwick and Lewis, *Media Manipulation and Disinformation Online,* 50, who cite Kelly Weill, "Racist Trolls Are behind NYU's 'White Student Union' Hoax," Daily Beast, November 23, 2015, https://www.the dailybeast.com/racist-trolls-are-behind-nyus-white-student-union-hoax (accessed January 16, 2021); Andrew Anglin, "White Student Unions Rise across America," Daily Stormer, November 24, 2015, http://www.dailystormer .com/white-student-unions-rise-across-america/ (accessed January 16, 2021; site has since been taken offline); Walbert Castillo, "'Illini White Student Union' Challenges 'Black Lives Matter,'" *USA Today,* November 21, 2015, http:// www.usatoday.com/story/news/nation-now/2015/11/21/illini-white-student -union-challenges-black-lives-matter/76165878/ (accessed January 16, 2021); Bears for Equality, "Racists Probably Started a White Student Union at Your School. They're All Fake," Medium, November 23, 2015, https://medium .com/@b4e2015/racists-probably-started-a-white-student-union-at-your -school-they-re-all-fake-5d1983a0b229#.hv09kobey (accessed January 16, 2021); Brendan O'Connor, "Who's behind the Fake 'Union of White NYU Students'?" Gawker, November 23, 2015, http://gawker.com/who-s-behind -the-fake-union-of-white-nyu-students-1744300282 (accessed January 16, 2021); and Yanan Wang, "More Than 30 Purported 'White Student Unions' Pop Up across the Country," *Washington Post,* November 24, 2015, https:// www.washingtonpost.com/news/morning-mix/wp/2015/11/24/more-than -30-questionably-real-white-students-unions-pop-up-across-the-country /(accessed January 16, 2021).
105. Bruce Bartlett, *The Truth Matters* (New York: Ten Speed Press, 2017), 19.
106. Whitney Phillips, *The Oxygen of Amplification,* Data and Society, May 2, 2018, https://datasociety.net/library/oxygen-of-amplification/ (accessed January 16, 2021).
107. Claire Wardle, "5 Lessons for Reporting in an Age of Disinformation," First Draft, December 27, 2018, https://firstdraftnews.org/latest/5-lessons-for -reporting-in-an-age-of-disinformation/ (accessed January 16, 2021).
108. Phillips, *The Oxygen of Amplification.*
109. Wardle, "5 Lessons for Reporting in an Age of Disinformation."
110. Craig Silverman, *Lies, Damn Lies, and Viral Content,* Tow Center for Digital Journalism, Columbia Journalism School, February 10, 2015, https://www

.cjr.org/tow_center_reports/craig_silverman_lies_damn_lies_viral_content.php (accessed January 16, 2021), and at https://academiccommons.columbia.edu/doi/10.7916/D8Q81RHH (accessed January 16, 2021).
111. Wardle, "5 Lessons for Reporting in an Age of Disinformation."
112. Paraphrasing Bartlett, *The Truth Matters*, 19.
113. Bartlett, *The Truth Matters*, 19.
114. Shelby Grossman, Khadeja Ramali, and Renee DiResta, *Blurring the Lines of Media Authenticity: Prigozhin-Linked Group Funding Libyan Broadcast Media*, Stanford Internet Observatory, March 20, 2020, https://cyber.fsi.stanford.edu/io/news/libya-prigozhin (accessed January 16, 2021).
115. Grossman et al., *Blurring the Lines*.
116. Emerson T. Brooking and Suzanne Kianpour, *Iranian Digital Influence Efforts: Guerrilla Broadcasting for the Twenty-First Century* (Washington, D.C.: Atlantic Council, 2020), 15. https://www.atlanticcouncil.org/in-depth-research-reports/report/iranian-digital-influence-efforts-guerrilla-broadcasting-for-the-twenty-first-century/.
117. Dorothy Denning, "Activism, Hacktivism and Cyberterrorism: The Internet as a Tool for Influencing Foreign Policy," in *Networks and Netwars: The Future of Terror, Crime, and Militancy*, ed. John Arquilla and David Ronfeldt (Santa Monica, CA: RAND Corporation, 2001), 239–88, https://www.rand.org/pubs/monograph_reports/MR1382.html (accessed January 16, 2021).
118. David Nikel, "Norwegian Newspaper Website Taken Offline after Content Hack," *Forbes*, October 19, 2019, https://www.forbes.com/sites/davidnikel/2019/10/19/norwegian-newspaper-website-taken-offline-after-content-hack/amp/ (accessed January 16, 2021).
119. Mihir Zaveri, "Government Website Is Hacked with Pro-Iran Messages," *New York Times*, January 6, 2020, https://www.nytimes.com/2020/01/06/us/iran-hack-federal-depository-library.html (accessed January 16, 2021).
120. Paul Mozur and Alexandra Stevenson, "Chinese Cyberattack Hits Telegram, App Used by Hong Kong Protesters," *New York Times*, June 13, 2019, https://www.nytimes.com/2019/06/13/world/asia/hong-kong-telegram-protests.html (accessed January 16, 2021).
121. Tom Uren, Elise Thomas, and Jacob Wallis, *Tweeting through the Great Firewall: Preliminary Analysis of PRC-linked Information Operations on the Hong Kong Protests*, Australian Strategic Policy Institute, September 3, 2019, https://www.aspi.org.au/report/tweeting-through-great-firewall (accessed January 16, 2021).

122. Cyberbullying is a type of bullying that takes place using electronic devices and equipment such as cell phones, computers, and tablets as well as communication tools including social media sites, text messages, chat, and websites. Michael Erbschloe, *Social Media Warfare*, 282.
123. Brooke Jarvis, "How One Woman's Digital Life Was Weaponized against Her," *Wired*, November 14, 2017, https://www.wired.com/story/how-one-womans-digital-life-was-weaponized-against-her/amp (accessed January 16, 2021).
124. Claire Wardle, *Information Disorder*.
125. Esther Chan and Rachel Blundy, "'Bulletproof' China-Backed Site Attacks HK Democracy Activists," AFP (Agence France Presse), November 1, 2019, https://news.yahoo.com/bulletproof-china-backed-attacks-hk-democracy-activists-070013463.html (accessed January 16, 2021).
126. Kakutani, *The Death of Truth*, 121.
127. McMahon, *The Psychology of Social Media*, 36–37, citing research by John Suler.
128. McMahon, *The Psychology of Social Media*, 36–37, citing research by John Suler.
129. Bradshaw and Howard, "Challenging Truth and Trust," 12.
130. Bay et al., *The Black Market for Social Media Manipulation*, 15.
131. John Scott-Railton et al., "Dark Basin: Uncovering a Massive Hack-for-Hire Operation," Citizen Lab, June 9, 2020, https://citizenlab.ca/2020/06/dark-basin-uncovering-a-massive-hack-for-hire-operation/ (accessed January 16, 2021).
132. Gu et al., *The Fake News Machine*.
133. Oreskes and Conway, *Merchants of Doubt*, 7; McIntyre, *Post-truth*.

CHAPTER 3. FEAR AND UNCERTAINTY

1. Kakutani, *The Death of Truth*, 54.
2. McIntyre, *Post-truth*, 125.
3. Hayden, *The Assault on Intelligence*, 221–22.
4. McIntyre, *Post-truth*, 126.
5. Kakutani, *The Death of Truth*, 35, citing Tom Nichols, *The Death of Expertise: The Campaign against Established Knowledge and Why It Matters* (Oxford: Oxford University Press, 2017).
6. Kakutani, *The Death of Truth*, citing Nichols, *The Death of Expertise*.
7. Rohit Bhargava, *Likeonomics: The Unexpected Truth behind Earning Trust, Influencing Behavior, and Inspiring Action* (Hoboken, NJ: Wiley, 2012), 14–15.
8. Bhargava, *Likeonomics*, 14–15.

9. Marwick and Lewis, *Media Manipulation and Disinformation Online*, citing Art Swift, "Americans' Trust in Mass Media Sinks to New Low," Gallup, September 14, 2016, http://www.gallup.com/poll/195542/americans-trust-mass-media-sinks-new-low.aspx (accessed January 16, 2021).
10. Marwick and Lewis, *Media Manipulation and Disinformation Online*, 38.
11. Bhargava, *Likeonomics*, 16.
12. Jennifer Kavanagh and Michael D. Rich, *Truth Decay* (Santa Monica, CA: RAND Corporation, 2019), 5, 31, 97–100, https://www.rand.org/pubs/research_reports/RR2314.html (accessed January 16, 2021).
13. Kakutani, *The Death of Truth*, 1.
14. Kavanagh and Rich, *Truth Decay*, xi.
15. Kavanagh and Rich, *Truth Decay*, xi.
16. Al Gore, *The Assault on Reason* (New York: Penguin Press, 2007), 1–2.
17. Kavanagh and Rich, *Truth Decay*, xi.
18. Aubrey De Grey, "Society's Parlous Inability to Reason about Uncertainty," in *What Should We Be Worried About*, ed. John Brockman (New York: Harper, 2014), 289.
19. While this quote has been attributed to Aristotle and several others, the basic point being made is that all things may be knowable, but in a specific individual's journey toward complete knowledge, there will be times that new knowledge shows there are more things to learn. A similar quote frequently attributed to Albert Einstein is "The more I learn, the more I realize how much I don't know."
20. Denise Winn, *The Manipulated Mind: Brainwashing, Conditioning, and Indoctrination* (Los Altos, CA: Malor Books, 2000), 44.
21. Ken Booth and Nicholas J. Wheeler, "Uncertainty," in *Security Studies*, ed. Paul Williams and Matt McDonald, 3rd ed. (London: Routledge, 2018), 132.
22. Hannah Murphy, "Inside Facebook's Information Warfare Team," *Financial Times*, July 5, 2019, https://www.ft.com/content/70b86214-9e77-11e9-9c06-a4640c9feebb (accessed January 16, 2021).
23. Alex Romero, "An Ecosystem of Mistrust and Disinformation," Disinfo Portal, June 19, 2019, https://disinfoportal.org/an-ecosystem-of-mistrust-and-disinformation/ (accessed January 16, 2021).
24. Richard Stengel, *Information Wars: How We Lost the Global Battle against Disinformation and What We Can Do about It* (Washington, D.C.: Atlantic Monthly Press, 2019).

25. Sean Illing, "A Giant Fog Machine: How Right-Wing Media Obscures Mueller and Other Inconvenient Stories," Vox, October 31, 2017. Also cited in Hayden, *Assault on Intelligence*, 189.
26. "The Statistical Shark," *New York Times*, September 6, 2001, https://www.nytimes.com/2001/09/06/opinion/the-statistical-shark.html (accessed January 16, 2021).
27. Philip G. Zimbardo, Ebbe B. Ebbesen, and Christina Maslach, *Influencing Attitudes and Changing Behavior*, 2nd ed. (New York: Random House, 1977), 98–99.
28. Olivia Gazis, "Feds Release New Processes of Notifying Public about Foreign Election Interference," CBS News, November 8, 2019, https://www.dni.gov/index.php/newsroom/news-articles/item/2068-feds-release-new-processes-of-notifying-public-about-foreign-election-interference (accessed January 16, 2021).
29. Singer and Brooking, *LikeWar*, 150.
30. Caroline Jack, *Lexicon of Lies: Terms for Problematic Information*, Data and Society, August 9, 2017, 9, citing C. Gibson, "What We Talk about When We Talk about Donald Trump and 'Gaslighting,'" *Washington Post*, January 27, 2017, https://www.washingtonpost.com/lifestyle/style/what-we-talk-about-when-we-talk-about-donald-trump-and-gaslighting/2017/01/27/b02e6de4-e330-11e6-ba11-63c4b4fb5a63_story.html (accessed January 16, 2021); V. Calef and E. M. Weinshel, "Some Clinical Consequences of Introjection: Gaslighting," *Psychoanalytic Quarterly* 50 (1981): 44–66.
31. Walker, "Combating Strategic Weapons of Influence on Social Media."
32. Oreskes and Conway, *Merchants of Doubt*; see also Allan Brandt, *The Cigarette Century: The Rise, Fall, and Deadly Persistence of the Product that Defined America* (New York: Basic Books, 2007), 220, 228–30.
33. Kakutani, *The Death of Truth*, 74.
34. Oreskes and Conway, *Merchants of Doubt*, 20–21, citing Mark Parascandola, "Public Health Then and Now: Cigarettes and the US Public Health Service in the 1950s," *American Journal of Public Health* 91, no. 2 (February 2001): 196–205.
35. Oreskes and Conway, *Merchants of Doubt*, 20–21, citing Mark Parascandola, "Two Approaches to Etiology: The Debate over Smoking and Lung Cancer in the 1950s," *Endeavor* 28, no. 2 (June 2008): 81–86.

36. Oreskes and Conway, *Merchants of Doubt*, 20–21, citing Dean F. Davies, "A Statement on Lung Cancer," *CA: A Cancer Journal for Clinicians* 9, no. 6 (1959): 207–8.
37. Oreskes and Conway, *Merchants of Doubt*, 23.
38. McIntyre, *Post-truth*, 23, citing Ari Rabin-Havt, *Lies, Incorporated: The World of Post-truth Politics* (New York: Anchor Books, 2016), 26–27; and Oreskes and Conway, *Merchants of Doubt*, 16.
39. Lee McIntyre, *Post-truth*, 23.
40. Oreskes and Conway, *Merchants of Doubt*, 23.
41. Michael J. Mazarr et al., *The Emerging Risk of Virtual Societal Warfare* (Santa Monica, CA: RAND Corporation, 2019), 100; see also Rabin-Havt, *Lies, Incorporated*.
42. Oreskes and Conway, *Merchants of Doubt*, 34.
43. Oreskes and Conway, *Merchants of Doubt*, 24.
44. Oreskes and Conway, *Merchants of Doubt*, 32.
45. McIntyre, *Post-truth*, 23–24.
46. Oreskes and Conway, *Merchants of Doubt*, 32; see the 1994 congressional report, House Committee on Energy and Commerce, Subcommittee on Health and the Environment, chaired by Henry Waxman, *The Hill and Knowlton Documents, Waxman Report: How the Tobacco Industry Launched Its Disinformation Campaign*, Majority Staff Report, May 26, 1994, 103rd Cong., 2nd sess., Serial No. 103-153; also see David Michaels, *Doubt Is Their Product: How Industry's Assault on Science Threatens Your Health* (New York: Oxford University Press, 2008).
47. Oreskes and Conway, *Merchants of Doubt*, 38.
48. Oreskes and Conway, *Merchants of Doubt*, 66–72.
49. Oreskes and Conway, *Merchants of Doubt*, 84.
50. Oreskes and Conway, *Merchants of Doubt*, 105.
51. Oreskes and Conway, *Merchants of Doubt*, 111.
52. Oreskes and Conway, *Merchants of Doubt*, 129.
53. S. Fred Singer, "My Adventures in the Ozone Layer," *National Review*, June 30, 1989, 36, cited in Oreskes and Conway, *Merchants of Doubt*, 128.
54. Laura Eggerston, "*Lancet* Retracts 12-Year-Old Article Linking Autism to MMR Vaccines," *Canadian Medical Association Journal* 182, no. 4 (2010): 199–200, https://www.ncbi.nlm.nih.gov/pmc/articles/PMC2831678/ (accessed January 16, 2021).

55. McIntyre, *Post-truth*, 29, citing Chris Mooney, *The Republican War on Science* (New York: Basic Books, 2005), 81; see also James Lawrence Powell, "Why Climate Deniers Have No Scientific Credibility: Only 1 of 9,136 Recent Peer-Reviewed Authors Rejects Global Warming," DeSmog, January 8, 2014, https://www.desmog.com/2014/01/08/why-climate-deniers-have-no-scientific-credibility-only-1-9136-study-authors-rejects-global-warming/ (accessed July 17, 2021).
56. Matt McGrath, "Climate Change: 'Clear and Unequivocal' Emergency, Say Scientists," BBC News, November 6, 2019, https://www.bbc.com/news/science-environment-50302392 (accessed January 16, 2021).
57. McIntyre, *Post-truth*, 30–31, citing James Hogan and Richard Littlemore, *Climate Cover-Up: The Crusade to Deny Global Warming* (Vancouver: Greystone, 2009), 43.
58. McIntyre, *Post-truth*, 29.
59. McIntyre, *Post-truth*, 28, citing Justin Gillis and Leslie Kaufman, "Leak Offers Glimpse of Campaign against Climate Change," *New York Times*, February 12, 2012.
60. McIntyre, *Post-truth*, 28, citing Heartland's website, http://www.heartland.org/Center-Climate-Environment/index.html (accessed January 16, 2021).
61. Rabin-Havt, *Lies, Incorporated*, 7.
62. Judith Warner, "Fact-Free Science," *New York Times Magazine*, February 25, 2011, https://www.nytimes.com/2011/02/27/magazine/27FOB-WWLN-t.html (accessed January 16, 2021).
63. For a brief description of this, see Kakutani, *The Death of Truth*, 74–75.
64. Kakutani, *The Death of Truth*, 74–75.
65. McIntyre, *Post-truth*, 150.
66. Kakutani, *The Death of Truth*, 141.
67. McIntyre, *Post-truth*, 78.
68. McIntyre, *Post-truth*, 77–82.
69. McIntyre, *Post-truth*, 84.
70. Phil Helsel, Ariana Brookington, and Marianna Sotomayor, "Trump Takes Heat for Blaming Charlottesville Violence on 'Many Sides,'" NBC News, August 12, 2017, https://www.nbcnews.com/politics/white-house/trump-politicians-condemn-white-nationalist-rally-charlottesville-virginia-n792096 (accessed January 16, 2021).
71. Kakutani, *The Death of Truth*, 73.

72. McIntyre, *Post-truth*, xiv.
73. Kakutani, *The Death of Truth*, 142–43.
74. McKay Coppins, "The Billion-Dollar Disinformation Campaign to Reelect the President," *The Atlantic*, February 10, 2020, https://www.theatlantic.com/magazine/archive/2020/03/the-2020-disinformation-war/605530/ (accessed January 16, 2021).
75. McIntyre, *Post-truth*, 87.

CHAPTER 4. COMFORTING FALSEHOODS AND CONSPIRACIES

1. Lois Becket, "Facts Won't Fix This: Experts on How to Fight America's Disinformation Crisis," *Guardian*, January 1, 2021, https://www.theguardian.com/us-news/2021/jan/01/disinformation-us-election-covid-pandemic-trump-biden (accessed January 16, 2021).
2. Richard E. Petty and John T. Cacioppo, *Communication and Persuasion: Central and Peripheral Routes to Attitude Change* (New York: Springer-Verlag, 1986); Manheim, *Strategy in Information and Influence Campaigns*, 75–76.
3. Manheim, *Strategy in Information and Influence Campaigns*, 75–76.
4. S. T. Fiske and S. E. Taylor, *Social Cognition* (New York: McGraw-Hill, 1991). Cited in Anthony R. Pratkanis and Elliot Aronson, *Age of Propaganda: The Everyday Use and Abuse of Persuasion* (New York: Henry Holt and Company, 1992), 38.
5. Pratkanis and Aronson, *Age of Propaganda*, 39.
6. Kathleen Taylor, *Brainwashing: The Science of Thought Control* (Oxford: Oxford University Press, 2004), 317.
7. Paraphrasing Pratkanis and Aronson, *Age of Propaganda*, 46.
8. Pratkanis and Aronson, *Age of Propaganda*, 66.
9. Pankaj Mishra, *Age of Anger: A History of the Present* (New York: Farrar, Straus and Giroux, 2017), 343.
10. Cherilyn Ireton and Julie Posetti, *Journalism, Fake News, and Disinformation* (Paris: UNESCO, 2018), 17.
11. Ireton and Posetti, *Journalism, Fake News, and Disinformation*, 9.
12. Mazarr et al., *The Emerging Risk of Virtual Societal Warfare*, 103, citing Stephan Lewandowsky, Ullrich K. H. Ecker, and John Cook, "Beyond Misinformation: Understanding and Coping with the 'Post-truth' Era," *Journal of Applied Research in Memory and Cognition* 6, no. 4 (December 2017): 354, 356.

13. For a detailed description of this, see chapter 2 of *Digital Influence Warfare in the Age of Social Media* by James J. F. Forest (Santa Barbara, CA: Praeger, 2021); and see also Peter Pomerantsev, *Nothing Is True and Everything Is Possible: The Surreal Heart of the New Russia* (New York: Public Affairs, 2014).
14. Kakutani, *The Death of Truth*, 37, paraphrasing George Orwell, *1984*.
15. Transcripts, CNN, July 22, 2016, http://transcripts.cnn.com/TRANSCRIPTS/1607/22/nday.06.html (accessed January 16, 2021).
16. Norman Mailer, *Marilyn* (New York: Garland Books, 1973), 18. Cited in Pratkanis and Aronson, *Age of Propaganda*, 104.
17. Pratkanis and Aronson, *Age of Propaganda*, 104.
18. Pratkanis and Aronson, *Age of Propaganda*, 112–13.
19. Pratkanis and Aronson, *Age of Propaganda*, 113.
20. David Matthews, "Rush Limbaugh Denied Health Risks of Smoking Years before Lung Cancer Diagnosis," *New York Daily News*, February 3, 2020, https://www.nydailynews.com/news/national/ny-rush-limbaugh-smoking-effects-cancer-diagnosis-20200203-4ma66mowazektovzh7hg2aynhq-story.html (accessed January 16, 2021).
21. Matthews, "Rush Limbaugh Denied Health Risks of Smoking."
22. Karen M. Douglas, Robbie M. Sutton, and Aleksandra Cichocka, "The Psychology of Conspiracy Theories," *Current Directions in Psychological Science* 26, no. 6 (2017): 538–42.
23. Douglas et al., "The Psychology of Conspiracy Theories."
24. Joel Achenbach, "50 Years after Apollo, Conspiracy Theorists Are Still Howling at the 'Moon Hoax,'" *Washington Post*, May 24, 2019, https://www.washingtonpost.com/national/health-science/50-years-after-apollo-conspiracy-theorists-are-still-howling-at-the-moon-hoax/2019/05/23/ca5b4a3a-700e-11e9-9f06-5fc2ee80027a_story.html (accessed January 16, 2021).
25. Pomerantsev, *This Is Not Propaganda*, 48.
26. Pomerantsev, *This Is Not Propaganda*, 48.
27. Nancy L. Rosenblum and Russell Muirhead, *A Lot of People Are Saying: The New Conspiracism and the Assault on Democracy* (Princeton, NJ: Princeton University Press, 2019).
28. Brian Resnick, "The Dark Allure of Conspiracy Theories, Explained by a Psychologist," Vox, May 25, 2017, https://www.vox.com/science-and-health/2017/4/25/15408610/conspiracy-theories-psychologist-explained (accessed January 16, 2021).

29. Resnick, "The Dark Allure of Conspiracy Theories."
30. Resnick, "The Dark Allure of Conspiracy Theories."
31. Nicole Karlis, "Why QAnon Followers Believe," Salon, August 11, 2018, https://www.salon.com/2018/08/11/how-qanon-believers-think-the-psychology-of-embracing-far-right-conspiracy-theories/ (accessed January 16, 2021).
32. Robert Chesney and Danielle Keats Citron, "Deep Fakes: A Looming Challenge for Privacy, Democracy, and National Security," *California Law Review* 1753 (July 14, 2018): 107; University of Texas Law, Public Law Research Paper No. 692; University of Maryland Legal Studies Research Paper No. 2018–21, https://ssrn.com/abstract=3213954 (accessed January 16, 2021) or http://dx.doi.org/10.2139/ssrn.3213954 (accessed January 16, 2021).
33. Chesney and Citron, "Deep Fakes," 107.
34. Singer and Brooking, *LikeWar*, 108.
35. For example, see Pomerantsev, *Nothing Is True and Everything Is Possible*.
36. For more, see the website http://smokershistory.com (accessed January 16, 2021).
37. http://smokershistory.com.
38. Karlis, "Why QAnon Followers Believe."
39. Nichols, *The Death of Expertise*, 59.
40. Tom Jensen, "Democrats and Republicans Differ on Conspiracy Theory Beliefs," Public Policy Polling, April 2, 2013, http://www.publicpolicypolling.com/polls/democrats-and-republicans-differ-on-conspiracy-theory-beliefs/(accessed January 16, 2021); also, see Douglas et al., "The Psychology of Conspiracy Theories," 538–42.
41. For details, see Andrew Breiner, "Pizzagate, Explained: Everything You Want to Know about the Comet Ping Pong Pizzeria Conspiracy Theory but Are Too Afraid to Search For on Reddit," Salon, December 10, 2016, https://www.salon.com/2016/12/10/pizzagate-explained-everything-you-want-to-know-about-the-comet-ping-pong-pizzeria-conspiracy-theory-but-are-too-afraid-to-search-for-on-reddit/ (accessed January 16, 2021); and Gregor Aisch, Jon Huang, and Cecilia Kang, "Dissecting the #PizzaGate Conspiracy Theories," *New York Times*, December 10, 2016, https://www.nytimes.com/interactive/2016/12/10/business/media/pizzagate.html (accessed January 16, 2021).
42. Faiz Siddiqui and Susan Svrluga, "N.C. Man Told Police He Went to D.C. Pizzeria with Gun to Investigate Conspiracy Theory," *Washington Post*, December 5, 2016, https://www.washingtonpost.com/news/local/wp/2016/12/04/

d-c-police-respond-to-report-of-a-man-with-a-gun-at-comet-ping-pong-restaurant/ (accessed January 16, 2021).

43. Marco Chown Oved, "Anatomy of a Manufactured Election Scandal," *The Star* (Canada), October 9, 2019, https://www.thestar.com/politics/federal/2019/10/09/anatomy-of-a-manufactured-election-scandal.html (accessed January 16, 2021).
44. Joel Mathis, "The Making of Coronavirus Denialism," *The Week*, May 11, 2020, https://theweek.com/articles/913730/making-coronavirus-conspiracy-theory (accessed January 16, 2021).
45. Jennifer S. Hunt, *The COVID-19 Pandemic vs. Post-truth*, Global Health Security Network, September 1, 2020, 20–21, https://www.ghsn.org/Policy-Reports (accessed January 16, 2021).
46. Kharazian and Knight, "Why the Debunked COVID-19 Conspiracy Video 'Plandemic' Won't Go Away."
47. Darren L. Linvill and Patrick Warren, "Yes, Russia Spreads Coronavirus Lies. But They Were Made in America," *Washington Post*, April 2, 2020, https://www.washingtonpost.com/outlook/2020/04/02/yes-russia-spreads-coronavirus-lies-they-were-made-america/ (accessed January 16, 2021).
48. Karlis, "Why QAnon Followers Believe."
49. Karlis, "Why QAnon Followers Believe."
50. Adrienne LaFrance, "The Prophecies of Q," *The Atlantic*, June 2020, https://www.theatlantic.com/magazine/archive/2020/06/qanon-nothing-can-stop-what-is-coming/610567/ (accessed January 16, 2021).
51. LaFrance, "The Prophecies of Q."
52. LaFrance, "The Prophecies of Q."
53. LaFrance, "The Prophecies of Q."
54. Mark Scott, "Conspiracy Theories Run Wild on Amazon," Politico, December 22, 2020, https://www.politico.eu/article/amazon-qanon-covid19-coronavirus-disinformation-conspiracy-theories/ (accessed January 16, 2021).
55. LaFrance, "The Prophecies of Q."
56. Alex Kaplan, "Trump Has Repeatedly Amplified QAnon Twitter Accounts," Media Matters, January 2, 2020, https://www.mediamatters.org/twitter/fbi-calls-qanon-domestic-terror-threat-trump-has-amplified-qanon-supporters-twitter-more-20 (accessed January 16, 2021).
57. Amarnath Amarasingam and Marc-André Argentino, "The QAnon Conspiracy Theory: A Security Threat in the Making?," *CTC Sentinel*, July 2020, 39–40.

58. Amarasingam and Argentino, "The QAnon Conspiracy Theory," 40.
59. Amarasingam and Argentino, "The QAnon Conspiracy Theory," 40–41.
60. Don Sweeney, "'We Don't Want to Die' Kids Beg as Ranting Dad Livestreams Police Chase," *Charlotte Observer*, June 14, 2020, https://www.charlotteobserver.com/news/nation-world/national/article243527722.html (accessed January 16, 2021).
61. Kaplan, "Trump Has Repeatedly Amplified QAnon Twitter Accounts."
62. Rob Stein, "Fauci Reveals He Has Received Death Threats and His Daughters Have Been Harassed," NPR, August 5, 2020, https://www.npr.org/sections/coronavirus-live-updates/2020/08/05/899415906/fauci-reveals-he-has-received-death-threats-and-his-daughtershave-been-harassed (accessed January 16, 2021).
63. Steve Gorman and Rebecca Spalding, "Wisconsin Pharmacist Arrested on Charges of Sabotaging COVID Vaccine Doses," Reuters, December 31, 2020, https://www.reuters.com/article/us-health-coronavirus-usa-pharmacist/wisconsin-pharmacist-arrested-on-charges-of-sabotaging-covid-vaccine-doses-idUSKBN2961YF (accessed January 16, 2021).
64. Shaila Dewan and Kay Nolan, "Pharmacist Accused of Tampering with Vaccine Was Conspiracy Theorist, Police Say," *New York Times*, January 4, 2021, https://www.nytimes.com/2021/01/04/us/pharmacist-accused-of-tampering-with-vaccine-was-conspiracy-theorist-police-say.html (accessed January 16, 2021).
65. Vanessa Romo, "Pharmacist Arrested, Accused of Destroying More Than 500 Moderna Vaccine Doses," NPR, December 31, 2020, https://www.npr.org/2020/12/31/952536531/pharmacist-arrested-accused-of-destroying-more-than-500-moderna-vaccine-doses (accessed January 16, 2021).
66. Hunt, *The COVID-19 Pandemic vs. Post-truth*.
67. Audrey Kurth Cronin, "The Nashville Bombing and Threats to Critical Infrastructure: We Saw This Coming," War on the Rocks, December 31, 2020, https://warontherocks.com/2020/12/the-nashville-bombing-and-threats-to-critical-infrastructure-we-saw-this-coming/ (accessed January 16, 2021).
68. Jordan Freiman, "Nashville Bomber Sent Writings Espousing Conspiracy Theories to Multiple People Days before Blast," CBS News, January 3, 2021, https://www.cbsnews.com/news/nashville-bomber-anthony-quinn-sent-conspiracy-theories-to-people-before-explosion/ (accessed January 16, 2021).

69. Elise Thomas, "QAnon Deploys 'Information Warfare' to Influence the 2020 Election," *Wired*, February 17, 2020, https://www.wired.com/story/qanon-deploys-information-warfare-influence-2020-election/ (accessed January 16, 2021).
70. "Donations under $8K to Trump 'Election Defense' Instead Go to President, RNC," Reuters, November 11, 2020, https://www.reuters.com/article/us-usa-election-trump-fundraising-insigh/donations-under-8k-to-trump-election-defense-instead-go-to-president-rnc-idUSKBN27R309 (accessed January 16, 2021); and Kelsey Vlamis, "Donations to Trump's Election Legal Fund Would Also Go towards Paying Off His Campaign's Debt," Business Insider, November 7, 2020, https://www.businessinsider.com/donations-trump-legal-fund-spent-on-paying-off-campaign-debt-2020-11 (accessed January 16, 2021).
71. Craig Silverman, "This Pro-Trump YouTube Network Sprang Up Just After He Lost," Buzzfeed, January 8, 2021, https://www.buzzfeednews.com/article/craigsilverman/epoch-times-trump-you-tube (accessed January 16, 2021).
72. https://support.google.com/youtube/answer/2801973?hl=en (accessed January 16, 2021).
73. J. M. Berger, *Extremism* (Cambridge, MA: MIT Press, 2019).
74. Glenn Kessler et al., "A Term of Untruths," *Washington Post*, January 23, 2021, https://www.washingtonpost.com/politics/interactive/2021/timeline-trump-claims-as-president/?tid=ss_tw (accessed April 22, 2021).
75. Kakutani, *The Death of Truth*, 132.

CHAPTER 5. OVERCONFIDENCE AND CONFIRMATION BIAS

1. Daniel J. Levitin, *Weaponized Lies: How to Think Critically in the Post-truth Era* (New York: Dutton, 2017), 205–6.
2. O'Brien, "Online Anger Is Gold to This Junk-News Pioneer."
3. David Lazer et al., "The Science of Fake News," *Science* 359, no. 6380 (March 9, 2018): 1095.
4. McIntyre, *Post-truth*, 114, citing Charles Simic, "Expendable America," *New York Review of Books*, November 19, 2016, https://www.nybooks.com/daily/2016/11/19/trump-election-expendable-america/ (accessed January 16, 2021).
5. C. S. Lewis, *The Four Loves* (San Diego, CA: Harcourt Brace, 1960), 61.
6. Cailin O'Connor and James Owen Weatherall, *The Misinformation Age: How False Beliefs Spread* (New Haven, CT: Yale University Press, 2019), 43.
7. Winn, *The Manipulated Mind*, 45.

8. Elliot Aronson, *The Social Animal* (San Francisco: W. H. Freeman, 1976), cited in Winn, *The Manipulated Mind*, 36.
9. Susan T. Fiske and Shelley E. Taylor, *Social Cognition* (New York: McGraw-Hill, 1991), cited in Pratkanis and Aronson, *Age of Propaganda*, 38.
10. Martie G. Haselton, Daniel Nettle, and Paul W. Andrews, "The Evolution of Cognitive Bias," in *The Handbook of Evolutionary Psychology*, ed. David M. Buss (Hoboken, NJ: Wiley, 2005), 724–46. Also, see Marcus Lu, "50 Cognitive Biases in the Modern World," *Visual Capitalist*, February 1, 2020, https://www.visualcapitalist.com/50-cognitive-biases-in-the-modern-world/ (accessed January 16, 2021); and for an excellent graphic illustration of 188 biases, see the "Cognitive Bias Codex" developed by John Manoogian III and Buster Benson, https://www.visualcapitalist.com/wp-content/uploads/2017/09/cognitive-bias-infographic.html (accessed January 16, 2021).
11. Howard, *Lie Machines*, 174.
12. Elizabeth Kolbert, "Why Facts Don't Change Our Minds," *New Yorker*, February 27, 2017, https://www.newyorker.com/magazine/2017/02/27/why-facts-dont-change-our-minds (accessed January 16, 2021), cited in Kakutani, *The Death of Truth*, 113.
13. Raymond Nickerson, "Confirmation Bias: A Ubiquitous Phenomenon in Many Guises," *Review of General Psychology* 2, no. 2 (1998): 175–220, https://www.researchgate.net/publication/280685490_Confirmation_Bias_A_Ubiquitous_Phenomenon_in_Many_Guises.
14. Bert H. Hodges, "Conformity and Divergence in Interactions, Groups and Cultures," in *The Oxford Handbook of Social Influence*, ed. Stephen G. Harkins et al. (New York: Oxford University Press, 2017), 100.
15. Donald Trump, on *Morning Joe*, MSNBC, March 16, 2016. See Eliza Collins, "Trump: I Consult Myself on Foreign Policy," Politico, March 16, 2016, https://www.politico.com/blogs/2016-gop-primary-live-updates-and-results/2016/03/trump-foreign-policy-adviser-220853 (accessed January 16, 2021); Jim Swift, "Donald Trump Talks to Himself for Foreign Policy Advice," *Weekly Standard*, March 16, 2016, https://www.weeklystandard.com/donald-trump-talks-to-himself-for-foreign-policy-advice/article/2001601/ (accessed January 16, 2021).
16. Marc Fisher, "Donald Trump Doesn't Read Much. Being President Probably Wouldn't Change That," *Washington Post*, July 17, 2016, https://www.washingtonpost.com/politics/donald-trump-doesnt-read-much-being-president

-probably-wouldnt-change-that/2016/07/17/d2ddf2bc-4932-11e6-90a8-fb84201e0645_story.html (accessed January 16, 2021).
17. McIntyre, *Post-truth*, 51.
18. McIntyre, *Post-truth*, 52, citing Justin Kruger and David Dunning, "Unskilled and Unaware of It: How Difficulties in Recognizing One's Own Incompetence Lead to Inflated Self-Assessments," *Journal of Personality and Social Psychology* 77, no. 6 (1999): 1121, https://www.ncbi.nlm.nih.gov/pubmed/10626367 (accessed January 16, 2021).
19. McIntyre, *Post-truth*, 62.
20. Pratkanis and Aronson, *Age of Propaganda*, 281, citing Lance Canon, "Self-Confidence and Selective Exposure to Information," in *Conflict, Decision, and Dissonance*, ed. Leon Festinger (Palo Alto, CA: Stanford University Press, 1964), 83–96.
21. Kolbert, "Why Facts Don't Change Our Minds."
22. Kakutani, *The Death of Truth*, xi.
23. Leon Festinger, *A Theory of Cognitive Dissonance* (Palo Alto, CA: Stanford University Press, 1957). Also, see Frantz Fanon, *Black Skin, White Masks* (New York: Grove Press, 1952), and McIntyre, *Post-truth*, 36.
24. McIntyre, *Post-truth*, 35.
25. McIntyre, *Post-truth*, 35.
26. Eddie Harmon-Jones, David M. Amodio, and Cindy Harmon-Jones, "Action-Based Model of Dissonance: A Review, Integration, and Expansion of Conceptions of Cognitive Conflict," in *Advances in Experimental Social Psychology*, vol. 41, ed. Mark P. Zanna (Burlington, VT: Academic Press, 2009), 119–66.
27. Philip G. Zimbardo, Ebbe B. Ebbesen, and Christina Maslach, *Influencing Attitudes and Changing Behavior*, 2nd ed. (New York: Random House, 1977), 168.
28. Zimbardo et al., *Influencing Attitudes and Changing Behavior*, 168.
29. Pratkanis and Aronson, *Age of Propaganda*, 266.
30. Monika Taddicken and Laura Wolff, "'Fake News' in Science Communication: Emotions and Strategies of Coping with Dissonance Online," *Media and Communication* 8, no. 1 (2020): 206–17, https://www.cogitatiopress.com/mediaandcommunication/article/view/2495/2495 (accessed January 16, 2021).
31. Sydell, "We Tracked Down a Fake-News Creator," and Scott Shane, "From Headline to Photograph, a Fake News Masterpiece," *New York Times*, January 18, 2017, https://www.nytimes.com/2017/01/18/us/fake-news-hillary-clinton-cameron-harris.html (accessed January 16, 2021).

32. Manheim, *Strategy in Information and Influence Campaigns*, 72.
33. Joseph Kahne and Benjamin Bowyer, "Educating for Democracy in a Partisan Age: Confronting the Challenges of Motivated Reasoning and Misinformation," *American Educational Research Journal* 54, no. 1 (February 2017).
34. McIntyre, *Post-truth*, 45.
35. National Endowment for Democracy, "How the Way We Think Drives Disinformation: An International Forum Working Paper," January 8, 2020, https://www.ned.org/demand-for-deceit-how-way-we-think-drives-disinformation-samuel-woolley-katie-joseff/ (accessed January 16, 2021).
36. National Endowment for Democracy, "How the Way We Think Drives Disinformation."
37. Winn, *The Manipulated Mind*, 206.
38. McIntyre, *Post-truth*, 45.
39. Gordon Pennycook and David Rand, "Lazy, Not Biased: Susceptibility to Partisan Fake News Is Better Explained by Lack of Reasoning Than by Motivated Reasoning," *Cognition*, June 2018, 40, https://doi.org/10.1016/j.cognition.2018.06.011; and Gordon Pennycook and David Rand, "Why Do People Fall for Fake News?," *New York Times*, January 19, 2019, https://www.nytimes.com/2019/01/19/opinion/sunday/fake-news.html (accessed January 16, 2021).
40. Pennycook and Rand, "Lazy, Not Biased," 40.
41. McIntyre, *Post-truth*, 48, citing Brendan Nyhan and Jason Reifler, "When Corrections Fail: The Persistence of Political Misperceptions," *Political Behavior* 32 (March 2010): 303–30, https://doi.org/10.1007/s11109-010-9112-2 and https://www.dartmouth.edu/~nyhan/nyhan-reifler.pdf (accessed January 16, 2021).
42. Nyhan and Reifler, "When Corrections Fail."
43. Pennycook and Rand, "Why Do People Fall for Fake News?"
44. Samantha Bradshaw, "Disinformation Optimised: Gaming Search Engine Algorithms to Amplify Junk News," *Internet Policy Review* 8, no. 4 (December 2019), https://policyreview.info/articles/analysis/disinformation-optimised-gaming-search-engine-algorithms-amplify-junk-news (accessed January 16, 2021).
45. Nyhan and Reifler, "When Corrections Fail," and Pennycook and Rand, "Lazy, Not Biased."

46. Pennycook and Rand, "Lazy, Not Biased," 40, citing April Strickland, Charles Taber, and Milton Lodge, "Motivated Reasoning and Public Opinion," *Journal of Health Politics, Policy, and Law* 36, no. 6: 89–122, https://doi.org/10.1215/03616878-1460524 (accessed January 16, 2021).
47. Francis Fukuyama, "Against Identity Politics: The New Tribalism and the Crisis of Democracy," *Foreign Affairs*, September/October 2018, 102.
48. Pennycook and Rand, "Why Do People Fall for Fake News?"
49. Fiske and Taylor, *Social Cognition*, cited in Pratkanis and Aronson, *Age of Propaganda*, 38.
50. Alice H. Eagly and Shelly Chaiken, *The Psychology of Attitudes* (San Diego, CA: Harcourt Brace Jovanovich College Publishers, 1993); and Miriam J. Metzger and Andrew J. Flanagin, "Credibility and Trust of Information in Online Environments: The Use of Cognitive Heuristics," *Journal of Pragmatics* 59 (2013), https://www.sciencedirect.com/science/article/abs/pii/S0378216613001768 (accessed January 16, 2021).
51. Pennycook and Rand, "Lazy, Not Biased," 44.
52. Robert J. Lifton, *Thought Reform and the Psychology of Totalism: A Study of "Brainwashing" in China* (London: Victor Gollancz, 1961), 420–35; described and explained in Kathleen Taylor, *Brainwashing: The Science of Thought Control* (Oxford: Oxford University Press, 2004), 23–25.
53. For example, in a Fox News interview in July 2020, Trump was asked whether he would carry out his threat to veto a bill in Congress, supported by the military's leadership, that would rename army bases named for Confederate generals. His response: "I don't care what the military says." "Transcript, 'Fox News Sunday' Interview with President Trump," Fox News, July 19, 2020, https://www.foxnews.com/politics/transcript-fox-news-sunday-interview-with-president-trump (accessed January 16, 2021).
54. Friedrich Nietzsche, *On Truth and Untruth: Selected Writings*, trans. and ed. Taylor Carman (New York: HarperPerennial, 2010), 24, cited in Mazarr et al., *The Emerging Risk of Virtual Societal Warfare*, 101.
55. Mazarr et al., *The Emerging Risk of Virtual Societal Warfare*, 101.
56. Cialdini, *Influence*, 167–207; and Taylor, *Brain Washing*, 74–76.
57. Pratkanis and Aronson, *Age of Propaganda*, 239.
58. Howard, *Lie Machines*, 102.
59. Pratkanis and Aronson, *Age of Propaganda*, 237.
60. Manheim, *Strategy and Information in Influence Campaigns*, 27.

61. McIntyre, *Post-truth*, 48, citing Nyhan and Reifler, "When Corrections Fail."
62. McIntyre, *Post-truth*, 42.
63. Pennycook and Rand, "Lazy, Not Biased," 40.
64. For a discussion of these tactics and strategies, see Forest, *Digital Influence Warfare in the Age of Social Media*.

CHAPTER 6. COLLECTIVE IDENTITY AND CONFORMITY

1. Elihu Katz and Paul Lazarsfeld, *Personal Influence* (Glencoe, IL: Free Press of Glencoe, 1955), cited in Limor Shifman, *Memes in Digital Culture* (Cambridge, MA: MIT Press, 2014), 124.
2. Arie W. Kruglanski and Edward Orehek, "The Need for Certainty as a Psychological Nexus for Individuals and Society," in *Extremism and the Psychology of Uncertainty*, ed. Michael A. Hogg and Danielle L. Blaylock (London: Blackwell, 2012), 3.
3. Amber M. Gaffney and Michael A. Hogg, "Social Identity and Social Influence," in *The Oxford Handbook of Social Influence*, 261.
4. Kruglanski and Orehek, "The Need for Certainty," 3.
5. Michael A. Hogg, "Self-Uncertainty, Social Identity, and the Solace of Extremism," in *Extremism and the Psychology of Uncertainty*, ed. Michael Hogg and Danielle Blaylock (Malden, MA: Wiley, 2012), 19–30; and Berger, *Extremism*, 136–83.
6. Berger, *Extremism*, 60–64.
7. Kruglanski and Orehek, "The Need for Certainty," 8.
8. Pratkanis and Aronson, *Age of Propaganda*, 217.
9. Gaffney and Hogg, "Social Identity and Social Influence," 261.
10. Bert H. Hodges, "Conformity and Divergence in Interactions, Groups and Cultures," in *The Oxford Handbook of Social Influence*, 87.
11. Hodges, "Conformity and Divergence," 100.
12. Em Griffin, *A First Look at Communication Theory*, 7th ed. (New York: McGraw-Hill, 2008); Elisabeth Noelle-Neumann, *The Spiral of Silence: Public Opinion—Our Social Skin*, 2nd ed. (Chicago: University of Chicago Press, 1993), cited in Pomerantsev, *This Is Not Propaganda*, 58.
13. Winn, *The Manipulated Mind*, 38.
14. Cialdini, *Influence*, 163.
15. Cialdini, *Influence*, 163.
16. Pratkanis and Aronson, *Age of Propaganda*, 150.

17. Mazarr et al., *The Emerging Risk of Virtual Societal Warfare*, 118.
18. Taylor, *Brainwashing*, 312–13.
19. Gaffney and Hogg, "Social Identity and Social Influence," 262; Michael A. Hogg and Janice Adelman, "Uncertainty-Identity Theory: Extreme Groups, Radical Behavior, and Authoritarian Leadership," *Journal of Social Issues* 69, no. 3 (2013): 436–54; Michael A. Hogg, "Uncertainty-Identity Theory," in *Handbook of Theories of Social Psychology*, ed. P. A. M. van Lange, A. W. Kruglanski, and E. T. Higgins, 5th ed. (London: Sage, 2012), 2:1166–1207.
20. Zimbardo et al., *Influencing Attitudes and Changing Behavior*, 169.
21. Gaffney and Hogg, "Social Identity and Social Influence," 261.
22. Tina Gaudette, Ryan Scrivens, Garty Davies, and Richard Frank, "Upvoting Extremism: Collective Identity Formation and the Extreme Right on Reddit," *New Media and Society*, September 12, 2020, https://doi.org/10.11 77/1461 444820958123 (accessed January 16, 2021).
23. Pratkanis and Aronson, *Age of Propaganda*, 220.
24. For more on cults (and their similarities with terrorists), see Marc Galanter and James J. F. Forest, "Cults, Charismatic Groups, and Social Systems: Understanding the Behavior of Terrorist Recruits," in *The Making of a Terrorist*, ed. James J. F. Forest (Westport, CT: Praeger Security International), 2:34–50.
25. LaFrance, "The Prophecies of Q."
26. Berger, *Extremism*, 84–89.
27. Berger, *Extremism*, 85.
28. For an excellent, detailed explanation of this in-group/out-group framing and its implications, see Berger, *Extremism*, 51–56, 62–63, 84–89.
29. Pratkanis and Aronson, *Age of Propaganda*, 112–13.
30. Taylor, *Brainwashing*, 295, citing Frank Fincham and Miles Hewstone, "Attribution Theory and Research: From Basic to Applied," in *Introduction to Social Psychology*, ed. Miles Hewstone and Wolfgang Stroebe, 3rd ed. (Oxford: Blackwell, 2001), 197–238.
31. David Bodanis, "Technology-Generated Fascism," in *What Should We Be Worried About?*, 166–67.
32. Pratkanis and Aronson, *Age of Propaganda*, 217.
33. Taylor, *Brainwashing*, 384 (paraphrasing).
34. Taylor, *Brainwashing*, 391 (paraphrasing).
35. Amelia Lucas, "Trump Tells Progressive Congresswomen to 'Go Back' to Where They Came From," CNBC, July 14, 2019, https://www.cnbc.com

/2019/07/14/trump-tells-progressive-congresswomen-to-go-back-to-where-they-came-from.html (accessed April 17, 2021); Colin Dwyer and Andrew Limbong, "'Go Back Where You Came From': The Long Rhetorical Roots of Trump's Racist Tweets," NPR, July 15, 2019, https://www.npr.org/2019/07/15/741827580/go-back-where-you-came-from-the-long-rhetorical-roots-of-trump-s-racist-tweets (accessed April 17, 2021); and Margaret Talev and Ros Krasny, "Trump Continues Attack on Congresswomen After Telling Them to 'Go Back,'" Bloomberg, July 14, 2019, https://www.bloomberg.com/news/articles/2019-07-14/trump-to-progressive-democrats-go-back-to-where-you-came-from (accessed April 17, 2021).

36. Scott Atran, "This Is Your Brain on Terrorism," *Foreign Affairs*, December 2, 2019, https://www.foreignaffairs.com/articles/2019-12-02/your-brain-terrorism (accessed January 16, 2021).
37. Taylor, *Brainwashing*, 312–13.
38. Orlando Sentinel Editorial Board, "Paula White Is an Example of Religious Leaders Weaponizing Faith for Politics," *Orlando Sentinel*, October 31, 2019, https://www.orlandosentinel.com/opinion/editorials/os-op-paula-white-weaponizing-religion-politics-20191031-opb6zdcauvhszmzhvrht63zwla-story.html (accessed July 17, 2021).
39. Winn, *The Manipulated Mind*, 45.
40. Lifton, *Thought Reform*, 420–35; described and explained in Taylor, *Brainwashing*, 23–25.
41. David Jackson, "'Human Scum': Donald Trump Has Harsh Comments for 'Never Trumper' Republicans," *USA Today*, October 23, 2019, https://www.usatoday.com/story/news/politics/2019/10/23/donald-trump-describes-republican-critics-human-scum/4076555002/ (accessed January 16, 2021).
42. "Groupthink" definition, *Psychology Today*, https://www.psychologytoday.com/us/basics/groupthink (accessed January 16, 2021).
43. Kruglanski and Orehek, "The Need for Certainty," 3, citing Leon Festinger, "Informal Social Communication," *Psychological Review* 57 (1950): 272–73.
44. Kruglanski and Orehek, "The Need for Certainty," 3, citing Muzafer Sherif, *The Psychology of Social Norms* (New York: Harper, 1936), 124.
45. McIntyre, *Post-truth*, 62.
46. Kolbert, "Why Facts Don't Change Our Minds."
47. Becket, "Facts Won't Fix This."

CHAPTER 7. ECHO CHAMBERS AND FILTER BUBBLES

1. Kakutani, *The Death of Truth*, 35.
2. Becket, "Facts Won't Fix This."
3. David Patrikarakos, *War in 140 Characters: How Social Media Is Reshaping Conflict in the Twenty-First Century* (New York: Basic Books, 2017), 12–13.
4. Patrikarakos, *War in 140 Characters*, 12–13.
5. Jason Gainous and Kevin M. Wagner, *Tweeting to Power: The Social Media Revolution in American Politics* (Oxford: Oxford University Press, 2014), 14, citing Cass Sunstein, *Republic.com* (Princeton, NJ: Princeton University Press, 2002).
6. Patrick Tucker, "Why Fake News Spreads: A Neurological Explanation," *Defense One*, March 23, 2017, https://www.defenseone.com/technology/2017/03/why-fake-news-spreads-neurological-explanation/136417/ (accessed January 16, 2021).
7. Guadagno, "Compliance: A Classic and Contemporary Review"; also citing Kwon et al., "Social Network Influence on Online Behavioral Choices Exploring Group Formation on Social Network Sites," *American Behavioral Scientist* 58 (2014): 1345–60.
8. Howard, *Lie Machines*, 101; Walter Quattrociochi, Antonio Scala, and Cass R. Sunstein, *Echo Chambers on Facebook* (Rochester, NY: Social Science Research Network, June 13, 2016), https://papers.ssrn.com/sol3/papers.cfm?abstract_id=2795110 (accessed January 16, 2021); Seth Flaxman, Sharad Goel, and Justin M. Rao, "Filter Bubbles, Echo Chambers, and Online News Consumption," *Public Opinion Quarterly* 80, no. S1 (2016): 298–320, https://5harad.com/papers/bubbles.pdf (accessed January 16, 2021).
9. Howard, *Lie Machines*, 102; and John L. Cotton and Rex A. Heiser, "Selective Exposure to Information and Cognitive Dissonance," *Journal of Research in Personality* 14, no. 4 (1980): 518–27.
10. Howard, *Lie Machines*, 100–105; Solomon Messing and Sean J. Westwood, "Selective Exposure in the Age of Social Media," *Communication Research* 41, no. 8 (2014): 1042–63, https://doi.org/10.1177/0093650212466406 (accessed January 16, 2021).
11. Howard, *Lie Machines*, 101.
12. See Winn, *The Manipulated Mind*, 42–43.
13. Richard Fletcher, *The Truth behind Filter Bubbles: Bursting Some Myths*, Reuters Institute, University of Oxford, January 22, 2020, https://reutersinstitute

.politics.ox.ac.uk/risj-review/truth-behind-filter-bubbles-bursting-some-myths (accessed January 16, 2021). In this piece, Fletcher explains how "this distinction is important because echo chambers could be a result of filtering or they could be the result of other processes, but filter bubbles have to be the result of algorithmic filtering."

14. Eli Pariser, "Beware Online 'Filter Bubbles,'" TED talk, March 10, 2011, https://www.ted.com/talks/eli_pariser_beware_online_filter_bubbles/transcript (accessed January 16, 2021); also, see Rani Molla, "Social Media Is Making a Bad Political Situation Worse," Vox, November 10, 2020, https://www.vox.com/recode/21534345/polarization-election-social-media-filter-bubble (accessed January 16, 2021).
15. Eli Pariser, *The Filter Bubble: How the New Personalized Web Is Changing What We Read and How We Think* (New York: Penguin Books, 2011), 3; Kakutani, *The Death of Truth*, 116–17.
16. Kavanagh and Rich, *Truth Decay*, 118–19.
17. Laura Garcia, "Why the News We See Online Isn't Always What We Think It Is," BBC, December 22, 2020, https://www.bbc.co.uk/bitesize/articles/zd7f382 (accessed January 16, 2021).
18. Howard, *Lie Machines*, 105.
19. Jon Keegan, "Blue Feed, Red Feed: See Liberal Facebook and Conservative Facebook, Side by Side," *Wall Street Journal*, May 18, 2016, https://graphics.wsj.com/blue-feed-red-feed/ (accessed January 16, 2021).
20. Fletcher, *The Truth behind Filter Bubbles*.
21. For an excellent description of this, see J. M. Berger, *Optimal* (Cambridge, MA: Multifaceted Media Group, 2020), 291.
22. Cass Sunstein, *Going to Extremes: How Like Minds Unite and Divide* (New York: Oxford University Press, 2009), 87, cited in Kakutani, *The Death of Truth*, 114.
23. Sunstein, *Going to Extremes*, 4, cited in Kakutani, *The Death of Truth*, 114–15. Also, regarding extremism and the in-group/out-group framework, see Berger, *Extremism*.
24. Berger, *Extremism*, 75–76.
25. For more, see Oreskes and Conway, *Merchants of Doubt*; Rabin-Havt, *Lies, Incorporated*; O'Connor and Weatherall, *The Misinformation Age*; McIntyre, *Post-truth*; and Kakutani, *The Death of Truth*.
26. Fletcher, *The Truth behind Filter Bubbles*.
27. Howard, *Lie Machines*, 81.

28. Guadagno, "Compliance: A Classic and Contemporary Review," 118.
29. Pratkanis and Aronson, *Age of Propaganda*, 223.
30. Linvill and Warren, "Troll Factories," 452.
31. Erbschloe, *Social Media Warfare*, 279.
32. Kakutani, *The Death of Truth*, 110.
33. McIntyre, *Post-truth*, 33–34.
34. Maureen Groppe, "Poll: Only 4 in 10 Republicans Think Trump Mentioned Biden on Ukraine Call Even Though He Acknowledged Doing So," *USA Today*, October 1, 2019, https://www.usatoday.com/story/news/politics/2019/10/01/poll-gop-doesnt-believe-trump-talked-biden-ukrainians/3829338002/ (accessed January 16, 2021).
35. Julia Jacobs, "A Visual Timeline on How the Attack on Capitol Hill Unfolded," ABC News, January 10, 2021, https://abcnews.go.com/US/visual-timeline-attack-capitol-hill-unfolded/story?id=75112066 (accessed January 16, 2021); and Doha Madani, "Trump Tells Mob at Capitol 'We Love You' but 'Go Home,'" NBC News, January 6, 2021, https://www.nbcnews.com/politics/congress/live-blog/electoral-college-certification-updates-n1252864/ncrd1253120#blogHeader (accessed January 16, 2021).
36. Amy Mitchell et al., *Political Polarization and Media Habits: From Fox News to Facebook, How Liberals and Conservative Keep Up with Politics*, Pew Research Center, October 24, 2014, https://www.journalism.org/2014/10/21/political-polarization-media-habits/ (accessed January 16, 2021).
37. House Committee on Energy and Commerce, *Disinformation Online and a Country in Crisis*.
38. House Committee on Energy and Commerce, *Disinformation Online and a Country in Crisis*.
39. Kevin Roose, "What if Facebook Is the Real 'Silent Majority'?," *New York Times*, August 27, 2020, https://www.nytimes.com/2020/08/27/technology/what-if-facebook-is-the-real-silent-majority.html (accessed January 16, 2021); cited in Emily Stewart, "America's Growing Fake News Problem, in One Chart," Vox, December 22, 2020, https://www.vox.com/policy-and-politics/2020/12/22/22195488/fake-news-social-media-2020 (accessed January 16, 2021).
40. Sara Fischer, "'Unreliable' News Sources Got More Traction in 2020," Axios, December 22, 2020, https://www.axios.com/unreliable-news-sources-social-media-engagement-297bf046-c1b0-4e69-9875-05443b1dca73.html (accessed

January 16, 2021); and Stewart, "America's Growing Fake News Problem, in One Chart."
41. David Byrne, "The Echo Chamber," February 1, 2016, http://davidbyrne.com/journal/the-echo-chamber (accessed January 16, 2021).
42. Byrne, "The Echo Chamber."
43. Harkins et al., *The Oxford Handbook of Social Influence*, 457–60.
44. Daniel Nussbaum, "David Byrne: Why Can't Stupid Americans See Through Trump's Lies and Bullsh*t?," Breitbart, February 12, 2016, https://www.breitbart.com/entertainment/2016/02/12/david-byrne-blames-social-media-for-rise-of-donald-trump/ (accessed January 16, 2021).
45. Gainous and Wagner, *Tweeting to Power*, 14.
46. McIntyre, *Post-truth*, 95.
47. For more on this, see Joshua Tucker et al., *Social Media, Political Polarization, and Political Disinformation: A Review of the Scientific Literature*, Hewlett Foundation, March 2018, https://www.hewlett.org/wp-content/uploads/2018/03/Social-Media-Political-Polarization-and-Political-Disinformation-Literature-Review.pdf (accessed January 16, 2021).
48. Roger McNamee, "How to Fix Facebook—Before It Fixes Us," *Washington Monthly* (January–March 2018), https://washingtonmonthly.com/magazine/january-february-march-2018/how-to-fix-facebook-before-it-fixes-us/ (accessed January 16, 2021), cited in Hayden, *The Assault on Intelligence*, 223.
49. Gainous and Wagner, *Tweeting to Power*, 26.

CHAPTER 8. CONFRONTING THE FUTURE CHALLENGES OF DIGITAL INFLUENCE MERCENARIES

1. For more on this topic, see Forest, *Digital Influence Warfare in the Age of Social Media*.
2. Singer and Brooking, *LikeWar*, 133, citing Joseph Bernstein, "Alt-White: How the Breitbart Machine Laundered Racist Hate," Buzzfeed, October 5, 2017, https://www.buzzfeednews.com/article/josephbernstein/heres-how-breitbart-and-milo-smuggled-white-nationalism#.grEVqB2aa (accessed July 14, 2021).
3. Elizabeth Scott, "How to Deal with FOMO in Your Life," Very Well Mind, February 19, 2020, https://www.verywellmind.com/how-to-cope-with-fomo-4174664 (accessed January 16, 2021).
4. Bay et al., *The Black Market for Social Media Manipulation*.

5. Samantha Bradshaw, Hannah Bailey, and Philip N. Howard, *Industrialized Disinformation: 2020 Global Inventory of Organized Social Media Manipulation*, Oxford Internet Institute, Program on Democracy and Technology, January 13, 2021, https://demtech.oii.ox.ac.uk/research/posts/industrialized-disinformation/ (accessed April 22, 2021).
6. Hannah Murphy and Siddharth Venkataramakrishnan, "Boom in Private Companies Offering Disinformation-for-Hire," *Financial Times*, January 12, 2021, https://www.ft.com/content/cb6b3342-a320-486e-b54c-a49ad32f2166 (accessed January 16, 2021).
7. Josh A. Goldstein and Shelby Grossman, "How Disinformation Evolved in 2020," Brookings Institution, January 4, 2021, https://www.brookings.edu/techstream/how-disinformation-evolved-in-2020/ (accessed January 16, 2021).
8. Martin and Shapiro, *Trends in Online Foreign Influence Efforts*.
9. Diego A. Martin, Jacob N. Shapiro, and Julia G. Ilhardt, *Trends in Online Influence Efforts*, Empirical Studies of Conflict Project, 2020, https://esoc.princeton.edu/publications/trends-online-influence-efforts (accessed January 16, 2021).
10. Mazarr et al., *The Emerging Risk of Virtual Societal Warfare*, 159.
11. Barbara K. Bodine et al., *The New Weapon of Choice: Technology and Information Operations Today*, Working Group Report, Institute for the Study of Diplomacy, Georgetown University, October 2020.
12. Ireton and Posetti, *Journalism, Fake News, and Disinformation*, 17.
13. Singer and Brooking, *LikeWar*, 255.
14. Mazarr et al., *The Emerging Risk of Virtual Societal Warfare*, 99.
15. Chesney and Citron, "Deepfakes and the New Disinformation War."
16. Chesney and Citron, "Deepfakes and the New Disinformation War," 124.
17. Chesney and Citron, "Deepfakes and the New Disinformation War," 127–28.
18. Chesney and Citron, "Deepfakes and the New Disinformation War," 127–28. Many of these examples are drawn from the case described in Brooke Jarvis, "Me Living Was How I Was Going to Beat Him," *Wired*, December 2017. It cites one statistic that by 2016 more than 10 million Americans reported that they had been threatened with, or had experienced, the unauthorized sharing of explicit images online.
19. Will Knight, "The World's Top Deepfake Artist Is Wrestling with the Monster He Created," *Technology Review*, August 16, 2019, https://www.technology

review.com/s/614083/the-worlds-top-deepfake-artist-is-wrestling-with-the-monster-he-created/ (accessed January 16, 2021).

20. House Committee on Energy and Commerce, *Disinformation Online and a Country in Crisis*.

21. House Committee on Energy and Commerce, *Disinformation Online and a Country in Crisis*.

22. Kang-Xing Jin, "Removing False Claims about COVID-19 Vaccines," Facebook, December 3, 2020, https://about.fb.com/news/2020/12/coronavirus/#removing-covid-vaccine-misinformation (accessed January 16, 2021).

23. Elizabeth Culliford and Gabriella Borter, "Facebook's Dilemma: How to Police Claims about Unproven COVID-19 Vaccines," Reuters, August 7, 2020, https://www.reuters.com/article/us-health-coronavirus-facebook-insight/facebooks-dilemma-how-to-police-claims-about-unproven-covid-19-vaccines-idUSKCN253OI8 (accessed January 16, 2021).

24. Culliford and Borter, "Facebook's Dilemma."

25. Yoel Roth and Nick Pickles, "Updating Our Approach to Misleading Information," Twitter Press Release, May 11, 2020, https://blog.twitter.com/en_us/topics/product/2020/updating-our-approach-to-misleading-information.html (accessed January 16, 2021).

26. Center for Countering Digital Hate, "What Promises Have Tech Giants Made on Removing Covid Misinformation?," June 1, 2020, https://www.counterhate.co.uk/post/what-promises-have-tech-giants-made-on-removing-covid-misinformation (accessed January 16, 2021).

27. William Marcellino et al., *Human-Machine Detection of Online-Based Malign Information* (Santa Monica, CA: RAND Corporation, 2020), https://www.rand.org/pubs/research_reports/RRA519-1.html (accessed January 16, 2021); and Shelley Cazares, Jenny Holzer, and Emily Parrish, "Weaponized Tweets: AI Could Help Defend against Adversary Attacks in Social Media," War on the Rocks, October 16, 2020, https://warontherocks.com/2020/10/weaponized-tweets-artificial-intelligence-could-help-defend-against-adversary-attacks-in-social-media/ (accessed January 16, 2021).

28. David Ingram and Jacob Ward, "Digitally Altered 'Deepfake' Videos a Growing Threat as 2020 Election Approaches," NBC News, December 14, 2019, https://www.nbcnews.com/tech/tech-news/little-tells-why-battle-against-deepfakes-2020-may-rely-verbal-n1102881 (accessed January 16, 2021).

29. James Vincent, "Adobe's Prototype AI Tool Automatically Spots Photoshopped Faces," The Verge, June 14, 2019, https://www.theverge.com/2019/6/14/18678782/adobe-machine-learning-ai-tool-spot-fake-facial-edits-liquify-manipulations (accessed January 16, 2021).
30. Mike Isaac and Kevin Roose, "Facebook Bars Alex Jones, Louis Farrakhan, and Others from Its Services," *New York Times*, May 2, 2019, https://www.nytimes.com/2019/05/02/technology/facebook-alex-jones-louis-farrakhan-ban.html (accessed January 16, 2021).
31. Kate Conger and Jack Nicas, "Twitter Bars Alex Jones and Infowars, Citing Harassing Messages," *New York Times*, September 6, 2018, https://www.nytimes.com/2018/09/06/technology/twitter-alex-jones-infowars.html (accessed January 16, 2021).
32. Kharazian and Knight, "Why the Debunked COVID-19 Conspiracy Video 'Plandemic' Won't Go Away."
33. Ben Collins and Brandy Zadrozny, "Twitter Bans 7,000 QAnon Accounts, Limits 150,000 Others as Part of Broad Crackdown," NBC News, July 21, 2020, https://www.nbcnews.com/tech/tech-news/twitter-bans-7-000-qanon-accounts-limits-150-000-others-n1234541 (accessed January 16, 2021).
34. Facebook Newsroom, "An Update to How We Address Movements and Organizations Tied to Violence," October 27, 2020, https://about.fb.com/news/2020/08/addressing-movements-and-organizations-tied-to-violence/ (accessed January 16, 2021).
35. "Twitter Suspends 70,000 Accounts Linked to QAnon," BBC News, January 12, 2020, https://www.bbc.com/news/technology-55638558 (accessed January 16, 2021).
36. Jeff Horwitz, "Facebook Knew Calls for Violence Plagued 'Groups,' Now Plans Overhaul," *Wall Street Journal*, January 31, 2021, https://www.wsj.com/articles/facebook-knew-calls-for-violence-plagued-groups-now-plans-overhaul-11612131374 (accessed April 22, 2021).
37. Twitter, "Platform Manipulation and Spam Policy," September 2019, https://help.twitter.com/en/rules-and-policies/platform-manipulation (accessed January 16, 2021).
38. Eric Auchard and Joseph Menn, "Facebook Cracks Down on 30,000 Fake Accounts in France," Reuters, April 13, 2017, https://www.reuters.com/article/us-france-security-facebook/facebook-cracks-down-on-30000-fake-accounts-in-france-idUSKBN17F25G (accessed January 16, 2021).

39. Cvetkovska et al., *The Secret Players behind Macedonia's Fake News Sites*.
40. Facebook, *August 2020 Coordinated Inauthentic Behavior Report*, September 1, 2020, https://about.fb.com/news/2020/09/august-2020-cib-report/ (accessed January 16, 2021).
41. Victoria Smith and Natalie Thompson, *Survey on Countering Influence Operations Highlights Steep Challenges, Great Opportunities*, Partnership for Countering Influence Operations (PCIO), Carnegie Endowment for International Peace, December 7, 2020, https://carnegieendowment.org/2020/12/07/survey-on-countering-influence-operations-highlights-steep-challenges-great-opportunities-pub-83370 (accessed April 22, 2021).
42. Jon Bateman and Craig Newark, "Social Media Disinformation Discussions Are Going in Circles. Here's How to Change That," *Slate*, March 24, 2021, https://slate.com/technology/2021/03/online-disinformation-congressional-hearing-amazon-google-twitter-ceos.html (accessed April 22, 2021).
43. Bodine et al., *The New Weapon of Choice*.
44. Shayna Jacobs, "Trump Supporter Charged in 2016 Twitter Scheme to Undermine Hillary Clinton," *Washington Post*, January 27, 2021, https://www.washingtonpost.com/national-security/douglass-mackey-ricky-vaughn-donald-trump-hillary-clinton/2021/01/27/78a37940-60c8-11eb-afbe-9a11a127d146_story.html (accessed April 22, 2021).
45. Cybersecurity and Infrastructure Security Agency press release, "CISA Launches Campaign to Reduce the Risk of Ransomware," U.S. Department of Homeland Security, January 21, 2021, https://www.cisa.gov/news/2021/01/21/cisa-launches-campaign-reduce-risk-ransomware (accessed April 22, 2021).
46. Ellen Nakashima, "U.S. Cyber Command Operation Disrupted Internet Access of Russian Troll Factory on Day of 2018 Midterms," *Washington Post*, February 27, 2019, https://www.washingtonpost.com/world/national-security/us-cyber-command-operation-disrupted-internet-access-of-russian-troll-factory-on-day-of-2018-midterms/2019/02/26/1827fc9e-36d6-11e9-af5b-b51b7ff322e9_story.html (accessed April 22, 2021).
47. Craig Timberg and Tony Romm, "Bipartisan Senate Report Calls for Sweeping Effort to Prevent Russian Interference in 2020 Election," *Washington Post*, October 8, 2019, https://www.washingtonpost.com/technology/2019/10/08/bipartisan-senate-report-calls-sweeping-effort-prevent-russian-interference-election/ (accessed January 16, 2021); United States Senate, 116th Congress (2019), *Report of the Select Committee on Intelligence, United States Senate,*

on *Russian Active Measures Campaigns and Interference in the 2016 U.S. Election* (S. Rep. 116-XX), vol. 1, *Russian Efforts against Election Infrastructure with Additional Views*, https://www.intelligence.senate.gov/sites/default/files/documents/Report_Volume1.pdf (accessed January 16, 2021); and vol. 5, *Counterintelligence Threats and Vulnerabilities* (August 2020), https://intelligence.senate.gov/sites/default/files/documents/report_volume5.pdf (accessed January 16, 2021).

48. O'Sullivan and Yurieff, "Facebook Bans Company It Says Ran Fake Accounts for Turning Point"; Stanley-Becker, "Facebook Bans Marketing Firm Running 'Troll Farm' for Pro-Trump Youth Group"; and Stanford Internet Observatory, *Analysis of an October 2020 Facebook Takedown Linked to U.S. Political Consultancy Rally Forge*.
49. O'Sullivan and Yurieff, "Facebook Bans Company It Says Ran Fake Accounts for Turning Point."
50. Stanford Internet Observatory, *Analysis of an October 2020 Facebook Takedown Linked to U.S. Political Consultancy Rally Forge*.
51. Zimbardo, Ebbesen, and Maslach, *Influencing Attitudes and Changing Behavior*, 3–4.
52. Stewart, "America's Growing Fake News Problem, in One Chart."
53. Facebook guidelines for how its users can spot fake news: https://www.facebook.com/help/188118808357379 (accessed January 16, 2021).
54. Eugene Kiely and Lori Robertson, "How to Spot Fake News," FactCheck, November 18, 2016, https://www.factcheck.org/2016/11/how-to-spot-fake-news/ (accessed January 16, 2021).
55. Atlantic Council Digital Forensic Research Lab, *Confronting the Threat of Disinformation: The Problem*, Google Jigsaw Data Visualizer, February 2020, https://jigsaw.google.com/the-current/disinformation/dataviz/ (accessed January 16, 2021).
56. Laura Garcia, "What We All Need to Be Aware of When Consuming News Online," BBC, https://www.bbc.co.uk/bitesize/articles/zd7f382 (accessed January 16, 2021).
57. Miller, "What Are 'Bots' and How Can They Spread Fake News?"
58. Cybersecurity and Infrastructure Security Agency, Mis-, Dis-, Malinformation (MDM) team (formerly known as the "Countering Foreign Influence Task Force"), U.S. Department of Homeland Security, https://www.cisa.gov/mdm (accessed July 14, 2021).

59. Brooke Borel, *The Chicago Guide to Fact-Checking* (Chicago: University of Chicago Press, 2016); Bill Kovach and Tom Rosenstiel, *Blur: How to Know What's True in the Age of Information Overload* (New York: Bloomsbury, 2010); Daniel J. Levitin, *Weaponized Lies: How to Think Critically in the Post-truth Era* (New York: Dutton, 2017); Sarah Harrison Smith, *The Fact Checker's Bible: A Guide to Getting It Right* (New York: Anchor Books, 2004).
60. Cindy L. Otis, *True or False: A CIA Analyst's Guide to Spotting Fake News* (New York: Feiwel and Friends, 2020).
61. Becket, "Facts Won't Fix This."

SELECTED BIBLIOGRAPHY

BOOKS

Arquilla, John, and David Ronfeld. *Networks and Netwars*. Santa Monica, CA: RAND Corporation, 2001.

Bartlett, Bruce. *The Truth Matters*. New York: Ten Speed Press, 2017.

Benkler, Yochai, Robert Faris, and Hal Roberts. *Network Propaganda: Manipulation, Disinformation, Radicalization in American Politics*. Oxford: Oxford University Press, 2018.

Berger, J. M. *Extremism*. Cambridge, MA: MIT Press, 2018.

Berger, J. M. *Optimal*. Cambridge, MA: Multifaceted Media Group, 2020.

Bhargava, Rohit. *Likeonomics: The Unexpected Truth Behind Earning Trust, Influencing Behavior, and Inspiring Action*. Hoboken, NJ: Wiley, 2012.

Borel, Brooke. *The Chicago Guide to Fact-Checking*. Chicago: University of Chicago Press, 2016.

Braddock, Kurt. *Weaponized Words*. London: Cambridge University Press, 2020.

Briant, Emma L. *Propaganda Machine: The Hidden Story of Cambridge Analytica and the Digital Influence Industry*. London: Bloomsbury, forthcoming.

Brooking, Emerson T., and Suzanne Kianpour. *Iranian Digital Influence Efforts: Guerrilla Broadcasting for the Twenty-First Century*. Washington, D.C.: Atlantic Council, 2020.

Brose, Christian. *The Kill Chain: Defending America in the Future of High-Tech Warfare*. Boston, MA: Hachette Books, 2020.

Cialdini, Robert B. *Influence: The Psychology of Persuasion*. Rev. ed. New York: HarperCollins, 2007.

Clarke, Richard A., and Robert K. Knake. *The Fifth Domain: Defending Our Country, Our Companies, and Ourselves in the Age of Cyber Threats*. New York: Penguin Press, 2020.

Erbschloe, Michael. *Social Media Warfare: Equal Weapons for All*. New York: CRC Press, 2017.

Forest, James J. F. *Digital Influence Warfare in the Age of Social Media*. Santa Barbara, CA: ABC-CLIO/Praeger Security International, 2021.

Forest, James J. F., ed. *The Making of a Terrorist*. Santa Barbara, CA: ABC-CLIO/Praeger Security International, 2005.

Fridman, Ofer, Vitaly Kabernik, and James C. Pearce, eds. *Hybrid Conflicts and Information Warfare: New Labels, Old Politics*. Boulder, CO: Lynne Rienner, 2018.

Gainous, Jason, and Kevin M. Wagner. *Tweeting to Power: The Social Media Revolution in American Politics*. Oxford: Oxford University Press, 2014.

Galeotti, Mark. *Russian Political War: Moving Beyond the Hybrid*. London: Routledge, 2019.

Gass, Robert H., and John S. Seiter. *Persuasion: Social Influence and Compliance Gaining*. London: Routledge, 2013.

Hadnagy, Christopher. *Social Engineering: The Science of Human Hacking*. 2nd ed. New York: Wiley, 2018.

Hadnagy, Christopher, and Michele Fincher. *Phishing Dark Waters: The Offensive and Defensive Sides of Malicious Emails*. New York: Wiley, 2015.

Hobbes, Renee. *Mind Over Media: Propaganda Education for a Digital Age*. New York: W. W. Norton, 2020.

Holiday, Ryan. *Trust Me, I'm Lying: Confessions of a Media Manipulator*. Rev. ed. New York: Portfolio, 2017.

Howard, Philip N. *Lie Machines: How to Save Democracy from Troll Armies, Deceitful Robots, Junk News Operations, and Political Operatives*. New Haven, CT: Yale University Press, 2020.

Jackson, Brooks, and Kathleen Hall Jamieson. *UnSpun: Finding Facts in a World of Disinformation*. New York: Random House, 2007.

Jamieson, Kathleen Hall. *Cyberwar: How Russian Hackers and Trolls Helped Elect a President*. New York: Oxford University Press, 2018.

Jankowicz, Nina. *How to Lose the Information War: Russia, Fake News and the Future of Conflict*. New York: I. B. Tauris, 2020.

Jasper, Scott. *Russian Cyber Operations: Coding the Boundaries of Conflict.* Washington, D.C.: Georgetown University Press, 2020.

Kaiser, Brittany. *Targeted: The Cambridge Analytica Whistleblower's Inside Story of How Big Data, Trump, and Facebook Broke Democracy and How It Can Happen Again.* New York: Harper, 2019.

Kakutani, Michiko. *The Death of Truth: Notes on Falsehood in the Age of Trump.* New York: Tim Duggan Books, 2018.

Kavanagh, Jennifer, William Marcellino, Jonathan S. Blake, Shawn Smith, Steven Davenport, and Mahlet G. Tebeka. *News in a Digital Age: Comparing the Presentation of News Information over Time and across Media Platforms.* Santa Monica, CA: RAND Corporation, 2019.

Kavanagh, Jennifer, and Michael D. Rich. *Truth Decay.* Santa Monica, CA: RAND Corporation, 2019.

Kovach, Bill, and Tom Rosenstiel. *Blur: How to Know What's True in the Age of Information Overload.* New York: Bloomsbury, 2010.

Krieg, Andreas, and Jean-Marc Rickli. *Surrogate Warfare: The Transformation of War in the Twenty-First Century.* Washington, D.C.: Georgetown University Press, 2019.

Levitin, Daniel J. *Weaponized Lies: How to Think Critically in the Post-truth Era.* New York: Dutton, 2017.

Manheim, Jarol B. *Strategy in Information and Influence Campaigns.* New York: Routledge, 2011.

Mazarr, Michael J., Ryan Michael Bauer, Abigail Casey, Sarah Anita Heintz, and Luke J. Matthews. *The Emerging Risk of Virtual Societal Warfare: Social Manipulation in a Changing Information Environment.* Santa Monica, CA: RAND Corporation, 2019.

Mazarr, Michael J., Abigail Casey, Alyssa Demus, Scott W. Harold, Luke J. Matthews, Nathan Beauchamp-Mustafaga, and James Sladden. *Hostile Social Manipulation: Present Realities and Emerging Trends.* Santa Monica, CA: RAND Corporation, 2019.

McCorquodale, Sara. *Influence: How Social Media Influencers Are Shaping Our Digital Future.* London: Bloomsbury, 2020.

McFate, Sean. *The New Rules of War: How America Can Win Against Russia, China, and Other Threats.* New York: William Morrow, 2020.

McFate, Sean. *The Modern Mercenary: Private Armies and What They Mean for World Order.* Oxford: Oxford University Press, 2017.

McIntyre, Lee. *Post-truth*. Cambridge, MA: MIT Press, 2018.

McMahon, Ciaran. *The Psychology of Social Media*. London: Routledge, 2019.

Merlan, Anna. *Republic of Lies: American Conspiracy Theorists and Their Surprising Rise to Power*. New York: Metropolitan Books, 2020.

Michaels, David. *Doubt Is Their Product: How Industry's Assault on Science Threatens Your Health*. New York: Oxford University Press, 2008.

Miller, Carl. *The Death of the Gods: The New Global Power Grab*. London: Windmill Books, 2018.

Mitnick, Kevin D. *The Art of Deception: Controlling the Human Element of Security*. New York: Wiley, 2003.

Nichols, Tom. *The Death of Expertise: The Campaign Against Established Knowledge and Why It Matters*. Oxford: Oxford University Press, 2017.

O'Connor, Cailin, and James Owen Weatherall. *The Misinformation Age: How False Beliefs Spread*. New Haven, CT: Yale University Press, 2019.

Oreskes, Naomi, and Erik Conway. *Merchants of Doubt*. New York: Bloomsbury, 2010.

Otis, Cindy L. *True or False: A CIA Analyst's Guide to Spotting Fake News*. New York: Feiwel and Friends, 2020.

Pariser, Eli. *The Filter Bubble: What the Internet Is Hiding from You*. New York: Penguin Press, 2011.

Patrikarakos, David. *War in 140 Characters: How Social Media Is Reshaping Conflict in the Twenty-First Century*. New York: Basic Books, 2017.

Petty, Richard E., and John T. Cacioppo. *Communication and Persuasion: Central and Peripheral Routes to Attitude Change*. New York: Springer-Verlag, 1986.

Pfaltzgraff, Robert, and Richard Shultz, eds. *War in the Information Age*. Washington, D.C.: Brassey's, 1997.

Pomerantsev, Peter. *Nothing Is True and Everything Is Possible: The Surreal Heart of the New Russia*. New York: Public Affairs, 2014.

Pomerantsev, Peter. *This Is Not Propaganda*. New York: Public Affairs, 2018.

Pratkanis, Anthony R., and Elliot Aronson. *Age of Propaganda: The Everyday Use and Abuse of Persuasion*. Rev. ed. New York: Henry Holt, 2001.

Rabin-Havt, Ari. *Lies, Incorporated: The World of Post-truth Politics*. New York: Anchor Books, 2016.

Rid, Thomas. *Active Measures: The Secret History of Disinformation and Political Warfare*. New York: Farrar, Straus and Giroux, 2020.

Robinson, Linda, Todd C. Helmus, Raphael S. Cohen, Alireza Nader, Andrew Radin, Madeline Magnuson, and Katya Migacheva. *Modern Political Warfare*. Santa Monica, CA: RAND Corporation, 2018.

Rosenblum, Nancy L., and Russell Muirhead. *A Lot of People Are Saying: The New Conspiracism and the Assault on Democracy.* Princeton, NJ: Princeton University Press, 2019.

Sammut, Gordon, and Martin W. Bauer. *The Psychology of Social Influence.* New York: Cambridge University Press, 2021.

Segal, Adam. *The Hacked World Order: How Nations Fight, Trade, Maneuver, and Manipulate in the Digital Age.* New York: PublicAffairs, 2016.

Shifman, Limor. *Memes in Digital Culture.* Cambridge, MA: MIT Press, 2014.

Shultz, Richard H., and Roy Godson. *Dezinformatsia: Active Measures in Soviet Strategy.* New York: Pergamon-Brassey's, 1984.

Singer, David. *The Perfect Weapon: Sabotage and Fear in the Cyber Age.* New York: Crown, 2018.

Singer, P. W., and Emerson T. Brooking. *LikeWar: The Weaponization of Social Media.* Boston: Houghton Mifflin Harcourt, 2018.

Singer, P. W., and Allan Friedman. *Cybersecurity and Cyberwar: What Everyone Needs to Know.* Oxford: Oxford University Press, 2014.

Smith, Sarah Harrison. *The Fact Checker's Bible: A Guide to Getting It Right.* New York: Anchor Books, 2004.

Stengel, Richard. *Information Wars: How We Lost the Global Battle Against Disinformation and What We Can Do about It.* Washington, D.C.: Atlantic Monthly Press, 2019.

Sunstein, Cass R. *Conformity: The Power of Social Influences.* New York: New York University Press, 2019.

Sunstein, Cass R. *Going to Extremes: How Like Minds Unite and Divide.* New York: Oxford University Press, 2009.

Taylor, Kathleen. *Brainwashing: The Science of Thought Control.* Oxford: Oxford University Press, 2004.

Uscinski, Joseph E. *Conspiracy Theories and the People Who Believe Them.* Oxford: Oxford University Press, 2019.

Watts, Clint. *Messing with the Enemy.* New York: HarperCollins, 2018.

West, Mick. *Escaping the Rabbit Hole: How to Debunk Conspiracy Theories Using Facts, Logic, and Respect.* New York: Skyhorse, 2020.

Whyte, Christopher, A. Trevor Thrall, and Brian M. Mazanec, eds. *Information Warfare in the Age of Cyber Conflict.* London: Routledge, 2020.

Winn, Denise. *The Manipulated Mind: Brainwashing, Conditioning, and Indoctrination.* Los Altos, CA: Malor Books, 2000.

Woolley, Samuel C., and Philip N. Howard, eds. *Computational Propaganda: Political Parties, Politicians, and Political Manipulation on Social Media*. New York: Oxford University Press, 2018.

Zimbardo, Philip G., Ebbe B. Ebbesen, and Christina Maslach. *Influencing Attitudes and Changing Behavior*. 2nd ed. New York: Random House, 1977.

SCHOLARLY JOURNAL ARTICLES AND BOOK CHAPTERS

Bradshaw, Samantha. "Disinformation Optimized: Gaming Search Engine Algorithms to Amplify Junk News." *Internet Policy Review* 8, no. 4 (December 2019). DOI: 10.14763/2019.4.1442.

Bradshaw, Samantha, and Philip N. Howard. "The Global Organization of Social Media Disinformation Campaigns." *Journal of International Affairs* 71, no. 1 (2018): 23–32. https://www.jstor.org/stable/26508115.

Briant, Emma L. "Leave.EU: Dark Money, Dark Ads, and Data Crimes." In *The Sage Handbook of Propaganda*, edited by Paul Baines, Nicholas O'Shaughnessy, and Nancy Snow, 532–48. London: Routledge, 2019.

Byrne, David. "The Echo Chamber." In *The Oxford Handbook of Social Influence*, edited by Stephen G. Harkins, Kipling D. Williams, and Jerry M. Burger, 457–60. Oxford: Oxford University Press, 2017.

Cotton, John L., and Rex A. Heiser. "Selective Exposure to Information and Cognitive Dissonance." *Journal of Research in Personality* 14, no. 4 (1980): 518–27.

De Grey, Aubrey. "Society's Parlous Inability to Reason about Uncertainty." In *What Should We Be Worried About?*, edited by John Brockman, 289–91. New York: Harper, 2014.

Delwiche, Aaron. "Computational Propaganda and the Rise of the Fake Audience." In *The Sage Handbook of Propaganda*, edited by Paul Baines, Nicholas O'Shaughnessy, and Nancy Snow, 105–24. London: Routledge, 2019.

Donath, Judith S. "Identity and Deception in the Virtual Community." In *Communities in Cyberspace*, edited by Peter Kollock and Marc Smith. London: Routledge, 1998.

Douglas, Karen M., Robbie M. Sutton, and Aleksandra Cichocka. "The Psychology of Conspiracy Theories." *Current Directions in Psychological Science* 26, no. 6 (2017): 538–42.

Effron, Daniel A., and Medha Raj. "Misinformation and Morality: Encountering Fake-News Headlines Makes Them Seem Less Unethical to Publish and Share." *Psychological Science* 31, no. 1 (2020): 75–87. https://doi.org/10.1177/0956797619887896.

Fazio, Lisa, Nadia M. Brashier, B. Keith Payne, and Elizabeth J. Marsh. "Knowledge Does Not Protect Against Illusory Truth." *Journal of Experimental Psychology* 144, no. 5 (2015): 993–1002. https://www.apa.org/pubs/journals/features/xge-0000098.pdf.

Fisher, Ali. "Swarmcast: How Jihadist Networks Maintain a Persistent Online Presence." *Perspectives on Terrorism* 9, no. 3 (June 2015): 3–20. https://www.universiteitleiden.nl/binaries/content/assets/governance-and-global-affairs/isga/perspectives-on-terrorism/2015-3.pdf.

Flaxman, Seth, Sharad Goel, and Justin M. Rao. "Filter Bubbles, Echo Chambers, and Online News Consumption." *Public Opinion Quarterly* 80, no. 1 (2016): 298–320. https://5harad.com/papers/bubbles.pdf.

Gaffney, Amber M., and Michael A. Hogg. "Social Identity and Social Influence." In *The Oxford Handbook of Social Influence*, edited by Stephen G. Harkins, Kipling D. Williams, and Jerry M. Burger, 259–77. Oxford: Oxford University Press, 2017.

Gaudette, Tina, Ryan Scrivens, Garty Davies, and Richard Frank. "Upvoting Extremism: Collective Identity Formation and the Extreme Right on Reddit." *New Media and Society* (September 2020). https://doi.org/10.1177/1461444820958123.

Heft, Annett, Eva Mayerhöffer, Susanne Reinhardt, and Curd Knüpfer. "Beyond Breitbart: Comparing Right-Wing Digital News Infrastructures in Six Western Democracies." *Policy and Internet* 12, no. 1 (March 2020): 20–45. https://doi.org/10.1002/poi3.219.

Hodges, Bert H. "Conformity and Divergence in Interactions, Groups and Cultures." In *The Oxford Handbook of Social Influence*, edited by Stephen G. Harkins, Kipling D. Williams, and Jerry M. Burger, 87–105. Oxford: Oxford University Press, 2017.

Hogg, Michael A. "Self-Uncertainty, Social Identity, and the Solace of Extremism." In *Extremism and the Psychology of Uncertainty*, edited by Michael Hogg and Danielle Blaylock, 19–30. Malden, MA: Wiley, 2012.

Hogg, Michael A. "Uncertainty-Identity Theory." In *Handbook of Theories of Social Psychology: Volume 2*, edited by Paul A. M. van Lange, Arie W. Kruglanski, and E. Tory Higgins, 62–80. London: Sage, 2012.

Hughes, Michael G., Jennifer A. Griffith, Thomas A. Zeni, Matthew L. Arsenault, Olivia D. Cooper, Genevieve Johnson, Jay H. Hardy, Shane Connelly, and Michael D. Mumford. "Discrediting in a Message Board Forum: The Effects of Social Support and Attacks on Expertise and Trustworthiness." *Journal of Computer-Mediated Communication* 19, no. 3 (April 2014): 325–41.

Ingram, Haroro J. "The Strategic Logic of State and Non-state Malign 'Influence Activities': Polarizing Populations, Exploiting the Democratic Recession." *RUSI Journal* 165, no. 1 (2020): 12–24. https://doi.org/10.1080/03071847.2020.1727156.

Kahne, Joseph, and Benjamin Bowyer. "Educating for Democracy in a Partisan Age: Confronting the Challenges of Motivated Reasoning and Misinformation." *American Educational Research Journal* 54, no. 1 (February 2017): 3–34.

Kirby, Aidan, and Vera Zakem. "Jihad.com 2.0: The New Social Media and the Changing Dynamics of Mass Persuasion." In *Influence Warfare*, edited by James J. F. Forest, 27–48. Westport, CT: Praeger Security International, 2009.

Kruger, Justin, and David Dunning. "Unskilled and Unaware of It: How Difficulties in Recognizing One's Own Incompetence Lead to Inflated Self-Assessments." *Journal of Personality and Social Psychology* 77, no. 6 (1999): 1121–34. https://www.ncbi.nlm.nih.gov/pubmed/10626367.

Kruglanski, Arie W., and Edward Orehek. "The Need for Certainty as a Psychological Nexus for Individuals and Society." In *Extremism and the Psychology of Uncertainty*, edited by Michael Hogg and Danielle Blaylock, 3–18. Malden, MA: Wiley, 2012.

Lazer, David, Matthew A. Baum, Yochai Benkler, Adam J. Berinsky, Kelly M. Greenhill, Filippo Menczer, Miriam J. Metzger, Brendan Nyhan, Gordon Pennycook, David Rothschild, Michael Schudson, Steven A. Sloman, Cass R. Sunstein, Emily A. Thorson, Duncan J. Watts, and Jonathan L. Zittrain. "The Science of Fake News." *Science* 359, no. 6380 (March 2018): 1094–96.

Lewandowsky, Stephan. "Disinformation and Human Cognition." *Security and Human Rights Monitor* (August 13, 2019). https://www.shrmonitor.org/disinformation-and-human-cognition/.

Lewandowsky, Stephan, Ullrich K. H. Ecker, and John Cook. "Beyond Misinformation: Understanding and Coping with the 'Post-truth' Era." *Journal of Applied Research in Memory and Cognition* 6, no. 4 (December 2017).

Lord, Carnes. "The Psychological Dimension in National Strategy." In *Political Warfare and Psychological Operations: Rethinking the US Approach*, edited by Carnes Lord and Frank R. Barnett, 19–33. Washington, D.C.: National Defense University Press, 1989.

Messing, Solomon, and Sean J. Westwood. "Selective Exposure in the Age of Social Media." *Communication Research* 41, no. 8 (2014): 1042–63. https://doi.org/10.1177/0093650212466406.

Nezlek, John B., and C. Veronica Smith. "Social Influence and Personality." In *The Oxford Handbook of Social Influence*, edited by Stephen G. Harkins, Kipling D. Williams, and Jerry M. Burger, 53–68. Oxford: Oxford University Press, 2017.

Nickerson, Raymond. "Confirmation Bias: A Ubiquitous Phenomenon in Many Guises." *Review of General Psychology* 2, no. 2 (1998): 175–220. https://www.researchgate.net/publication/280685490_Confirmation_Bias_A_Ubiquitous_Phenomenon_in_Many_Guises.

Pennycook, Gordon, and David Rand. "Lazy, Not Biased: Susceptibility to Partisan Fake News Is Better Explained by Lack of Reasoning Than by Motivated Reasoning." *Cognition* (June 2018): 39–50. https://doi.org/10.1016/j.cognition.2018.06.011.

Piret Pernik. "Hacking for Influence." *Concordiam: Journal of European Security Defense Issues* 10, no. 1 (2020): 46–51.

Sagarin, Brad J., and Lynn Miller Henningsen. "Resistance to Influence." In *The Oxford Handbook of Social Influence*, edited by Stephen G. Harkins, Kipling D. Williams, and Jerry M. Burger, 437–56. Oxford: Oxford University Press, 2017.

Sanger, Larry. "Internet Silos." In *What Should We Be Worried About?*, edited by John Brockman, 401–2. New York: Harper, 2014.

Strickland, April, Charles Taber, and Milton Lodge. "Motivated Reasoning and Public Opinion." *Journal of Health Politics, Policy, and Law* 36, no. 6 (2011): 89–122. https://doi.org/10.1215/03616878-1460524.

Wanless, Alicia, and Michael Berk. "The Audience Is the Amplifier: Participatory Propaganda." In *The Sage Handbook of Propaganda*, edited by Paul Baines, Nicholas O'Shaughnessy, and Nancy Snow, 85–103. London: Routledge, 2019.

GOVERNMENT AND INTERGOVERNMENTAL ORGANIZATION REPORTS

Bay, Sebastian, and Rolf Fredheim. *Falling Behind: How Social Media Companies Are Failing to Combat Inauthentic Behaviour Online*. Brussels: NATO Strategic Communications Centre of Excellence, 2019. https://www.stratcomcoe.org/how-social-media-companies-are-failing-combat-inauthentic-behaviour-online.

Bay, Sebastian, NATO StratCom COE, and Singularex. *The Black Market for Social Media Manipulation*. Brussels: NATO Strategic Communications Centre of Excellence and Singularex, 2018. https://www.stratcomcoe.org/black-market-social-media-manipulation.

Flore, Massimo, Alexandra Balahur-Dobrescu, Aldo Podavini, and Marco Verile. *Understanding Citizens' Vulnerabilities to Disinformation and Data-Driven*

Propaganda. Technical Report, Joint Research Center, European Commission Science and Knowledge Services. Luxembourg: Office of the European Union, 2019. https://ec.europa.eu/jrc/en/publication/understanding-citizens-vulnerabilities-disinformation-and-data-driven-propaganda.

Hwang, Tim. *Deepfakes: Primer and Forecast*. Brussels: NATO Strategic Communications Centre of Excellence, 2020. https://www.stratcomcoe.org/deepfakes-primer-and-forecast.

Ireton, Cherilyn, and Julie Posetti. *Journalism, "Fake News," and Disinformation*. Paris: UNESCO, 2018. https://en.unesco.org/fightfakenews.

Mueller, Robert S., III. *Report on the Investigation into Russian Interference in the 2016 Presidential Election*. Washington, D.C.: U.S. Department of Justice, 2019. https://www.justice.gov/storage/report.pdf.

Sharp, Walter L. *Information Operations*. Joint Publication 3–13. Washington, D.C.: Office of the Chairman of the Joint Chiefs of Staff, 2006. https://www.hsdl.org/?view&did=461648 and at https://www.globalsecurity.org/intell/library/policy/dod/joint/jp3_13_2006.pdf.

United States Director of National Intelligence. *Background to "Assessing Russian Activities and Intentions in Recent U.S. Elections": The Analytic Process and Cyber Incident Attribution*. Washington, D.C.: Office of the Director of National Intelligence, 2017. https://www.dni.gov/files/documents/ICA_2017_01.pdf.

United States of America v. Internet Research Agency LLC a/k/a/ Mediasintez LLC et al. Criminal No. (18 U.S.C. SS 2, 371, 1349, 1028A). United States District Court for the District of Columbia (filed February 26, 2018). https://www.justice.gov/file/1035477/download.

United States Senate, 116th Congress. *Russian Active Measures Campaigns and Interference in the 2016 U.S. Election*, Volume 1: *Russian Efforts Against Election Infrastructure*. Report of the Select Committee on Intelligence. Washington, D.C.: United States Senate, 2019. https://www.intelligence.senate.gov/sites/default/files/documents/Report_Volume1.pdf.

United States Senate, 116th Congress. *Russian Active Measures Campaigns and Interference in the 2016 U.S. Election*, Volume 2: *Russia's Use of Social Media*. Report of the Select Committee on Intelligence. Washington, D.C.: United States Senate, 2020. https://www.intelligence.senate.gov/sites/default/files/documents/Report_Volume2.pdf.

United States Senate, 116th Congress. *Russian Active Measures Campaigns and Interference in the 2016 U.S. Election*, Volume 3: *U.S. Government Response to*

Russian Activities. Report of the Select Committee on Intelligence. Washington, D.C.: United States Senate, 2020. https://www.intelligence.senate.gov/sites/default/files/documents/Report_Volume3.pdf.

United States Senate, 116th Congress. *Russian Active Measures Campaigns and Interference in the 2016 U.S. Election*, Volume 4: *Review of the Intelligence Community Assessment*. Report of the Select Committee on Intelligence. Washington, D.C.: United States Senate, 2020. https://www.intelligence.senate.gov/sites/default/files/documents/Report_Volume4.pdf.

United States Senate, 116th Congress. *Russian Active Measures Campaigns and Interference in the 2016 U.S. Election*, Volume 5: *Counterintelligence Threats and Vulnerabilities*. Report of the Select Committee on Intelligence. Washington, D.C.: United States Senate, 2020. https://intelligence.senate.gov/sites/default/files/documents/report_volume5.pdf.

Vilmer, Jean-Baptiste J., Alexandre Escorcia, Marine Guillaume, and Janaina Herrera. *Information Manipulation: A Challenge for Our Democracies*. A Report by the Policy Planning Staff (CAPS, Ministry for Europe and Foreign Affairs) and Institute for Strategic Research (IRSEM, Ministry for the Armed Forces). Paris: Republic of France, 2018. https://www.diplomatie.gouv.fr/en/french-foreign-policy/manipulation-of-information/article/joint-report-by-the-caps-irsem-information-manipulation-a-challenge-for-our.

Vitto, Vincent. *Report of the Defense Science Board: Task Force on Strategic Communication*. Washington, D.C.: Office of the Under Secretary of Defense for Acquisition, Technology, and Logistics, 2004. https://apps.dtic.mil/dtic/tr/fulltext/u2/a476331.pdf.

Wardle, Claire, and Hossein Derakhshan. *Information Disorder: Toward an Interdisciplinary Framework for Research and Policy Making*. Council of Europe, September 27, 2017. https://rm.coe.int/information-disorder-toward-an-interdisciplinary-framework-for-researc/168076277c.

RESEARCH CENTER AND THINK TANK REPORTS

Atlantic Council Digital Forensic Research Lab. *Confronting the Threat of Disinformation: The Problem*. Google Jigsaw Data Visualizer, February 2020. https://jigsaw.google.com/the-current/disinformation/dataviz/.

Barrett, Paul M. *Tackling Domestic Disinformation: What the Social Media Companies Need to Do*. Stern Center for Business and Human Rights, New York

University, April 3, 2019. https://www.nyu.edu/about/news-publications/news/2019/april/tackling-domestic-disinformation—what-the-social-media-companie.html.

Bodine, Barbara K. et al. *The New Weapon of Choice: Technology and Information Operations Today*. Working Group Report, Institute for the Study of Diplomacy, Georgetown University, October 21, 2020. https://isd.georgetown.edu/2020/10/21/isd-launches-new-report-on-information-operations/.

Bradshaw, Samantha, and Philip N. Howard. *Challenging Truth and Trust: A Global Inventory of Organized Social Media Manipulation*. Working Paper 2018.1, Computational Propaganda Research Project, Oxford Internet Institute, July 20, 2018. http://comprop.oii.ox.ac.uk/wp-content/uploads/sites/93/2018/07/ct2018.pdf.

Bradshaw, Samantha, and Philip N. Howard. *The Global Disinformation Order: 2019 Global Inventory of Organised Social Media Manipulation*. Computational Propaganda Research Project, Oxford Internet Institute, July 2019. https://comprop.oii.ox.ac.uk/wp-content/uploads/sites/93/2019/09/CyberTroop-Report19.pdf.

Bradshaw, Samantha, and Philip N. Howard. *Troops, Trolls, and Troublemakers: A Global Inventory of Organized Social Media Manipulation*. Working Paper No. 2017.12, Computational Propaganda Research Project, Oxford Internet Institute, July 17, 2017. https://demtech.oii .ox.ac.uk/research/posts/troops-trolls-and-troublemakers-a-global-inventory-of-organized-social-media-manipulation/.

Bradshaw, Samantha, Hannah Bailey, and Philip N. Howard. *Industrialized Disinformation: 2020 Global Inventory of Organized Social Media Manipulation*. Program on Democracy and Technology, Oxford Internet Institute, January 13, 2021. https://demtech.oii.ox.ac.uk/research/posts/industrialized-disinformation/.

DiResta, Renee, Carly Miller, Vanessa Molter, John Pomfret. *Telling China's Story: The Chinese Communist Party's Campaign to Shape Global Narratives*. Stanford Internet Observatory and Hoover Institution, Stanford University, July 20, 2020. https://cyber.fsi.stanford.edu/io/news/new-whitepaper-telling-chinas-story.

DiResta, Renee, Kris Shaffer, Becky Ruppel, David Sullivan, Robert Matney, Ryan Fox, Jonathan Albright, and Ben Johnson. *The Tactics and Tropes of the Internet Research Agency*. New Knowledge, Tow Center for Digital Journalism, and Canfield Research, 2019. https://digitalcommons.unl.edu/senatedocs/2/.

Dotto, Carlotta, and Sebastien Cubbon. *How to Spot a Bot (or Not): The Main Indicators of Online Automation, Co-ordination, and Inauthentic Activity.* First Draft, November 28, 2019. https://firstdraftnews.org/latest/how-to-spot-a-bot-or-not-the-main-indicators-of-online-automation-co-ordination-and-inauthentic-activity.

Douglas, Karen, Robbie Sutton, Jim Ang, Farzin Deravi, Joe Uscinski, and Türkay Nefes. *Why Do People Adopt Conspiracy Theories, How Are They Communicated, and What Are Their Risks.* Center for Research and Evidence on Security Threats, United Kingdom, 2019. https://crestresearch.ac.uk/projects/conspiracy-theories/.

Fletcher, Richard. *The Truth Behind Filter Bubbles: Bursting Some Myths.* Reuters Institute, University of Oxford, January 22, 2020. https://reutersinstitute.politics.ox.ac.uk/risj-review/truth-behind-filter-bubbles-bursting-some-myths.

François, Camille. *The IRA CopyPasta Campaign.* Graphika, October 21, 2019. https://graphika.com/reports/copypasta/.

Grossman, Shelby, Khadeja Ramali, and Renee DiResta. *Blurring the Lines of Media Authenticity: Prigozhin-Linked Group Funding Libyan Broadcast Media.* Stanford Internet Observatory, March 20, 2020. https://cyber.fsi.stanford.edu/io/news/libya-prigozhin.

Grossman, Shelby, Khadeja Ramali, Renée DiResta, Lucas Beissner, Samantha Bradshaw, William Healzer, and Ira Hubert. *Stoking Conflict by Keystroke: An Operation Run by IRA-Linked Individuals Targeting Libya, Sudan, and Syria.* Stanford Internet Observatory, December 15, 2020. https://cyber.fsi.stanford.edu/io/news/africa-takedown-december-2020.

Gu, Lion, Vladimir Kropotov, and Fyodor Yarochkin. *The Fake News Machine: How Propagandists Abuse the Internet and Manipulate the Public.* TrendLabs, Oxford University, 2017. https://documents.trendmicro.com/assets/white_papers/wp-fake-news-machine-how-propagandists-abuse-the-internet.pdf.

Howard, Philip N., Bharath Ganesh, Dimitra Liotsiou, John Kelly, and Camille François. *The IRA, Social Media, and Political Polarization in the United States, 2012–2018.* Project on Computational Propaganda, Oxford University, 2018. https://demtech.oii.ox.ac.uk/research/posts/the-ira-and-political-polarization-in-the-united-states/.

Insikt Group. *The Price of Influence: Disinformation in the Private Sector.* Report CTA-2019-0930. Recorded Future, 2019. https://go.recordedfuture.com/hubfs/reports/cta-2019-0930.pdf.

Jack, Caroline. *Lexicon of Lies: Terms for Problematic Information*. Data and Society, August 9, 2017. https://datasociety.net/library/lexicon-of-lies/.

Kalenský, Jakub. *A Change of Tactics: Blurring Disinformation's Source*. Disinfo Portal, June 6, 2019. https://disinfoportal.org/a-change-of-tactics-blurring-disinformations-source/.

Krasodomski-Jones, Alex, Josh Smith, Elliot Jones, Ellen Judson, and Carl Miller. *Warring Songs: Information Operations in the Digital Age*. Demos, 2019. https://demos.co.uk/wp-content/uploads/2019/05/Warring-Songs-final-1.pdf.

Lehman, Joseph G. *An Introduction to the Overton Window of Political Possibility*. Mackinac Center for Public Policy, April 8, 2010. https://www.mackinac.org/12481.

Lewis, Rebecca. *Alternative Influence: Broadcasting the Reactionary Right on YouTube*. Data and Society, September 2018. https://datasociety.net/library/alternative-influence/.

Marcellino, William, Kate Cox, Katerina Galai, Linda Slapakova, Amber Jaycocks, and Ruth Harris. *Human-Machine Detection of Online-Based Malign Information*. RAND Corporation, 2020. https://www.rand.org/pubs/research_reports/RRA519-1.html.

Martin, Diego A., and Jacob N. Shapiro. *Trends in Online Foreign Influence Efforts*. Woodrow Wilson School of Public and International Affairs, Princeton University, July 8, 2019. https://scholar.princeton.edu/jns/research-reports.

Martin, Diego A., Jacob N. Shapiro, and Julia G. Ilhardt. *Trends in Online Influence Efforts*. Empirical Studies of Conflict Project, Princeton University, 2020. https://esoc.princeton.edu/publications/trends-online-influence-efforts.

Marwick, Alice, and Rebecca Lewis. *Media Manipulation and Disinformation Online*. Data and Society, May 15, 2017. https://datasociety.net/pubs/oh/DataAndSociety_MediaManipulationAndDisinformationOnline.pdf.

Mitchell, Amy, Jeffrey Gottfried, Jocelyn Kiley, and Katerina Eva Matsa. *Political Polarization and Media Habits*. Pew Research Center, October 21, 2014. https://www.journalism.org/2014/10/21/political-polarization-media-habits/.

Nimmo, Ben, Camille François, C. Shawn Eib, Léa Ronzaud, and Joseph Carter. *GRU and the Minions*. Graphika, September 2020. https://graphika.com/reports/gru-and-the-minions/.

Nimmo, Ben, Camille François, C. Shawn Eib, Léa Ronzaud, Rodrigo Ferreira, Chris Hernon, and Tim Kostelancik. *Secondary Infektion*. Graphika, June 2020. https://secondaryinfektion.org/downloads/secondary-infektion-report.pdf.

Nimmo, Ben, and Alec Toler. *The Russians Who Exposed Russia's Trolls*. Atlantic Council Digital Forensics Lab, March 8, 2018. https://medium.com/dfrlab/the-russians-who-exposed-russias-trolls-72db132e3cd1.

Paul, Christopher, and Miriam Matthews. *The Russian "Firehose of Falsehood" Propaganda Model*. RAND Corporation, 2016. https://www.rand.org/pubs/perspectives/PE198.html.

Pernik, Piret. *Hacking for Influence: Foreign Influence Activities and Cyberattacks*. International Center for Defense and Security, Estonia, February 2018. https://issuu.com/disinfoportal/docs/hacking_for_influence.

Phillips, Whitney. *The Oxygen of Amplification*. Data and Society, May 22, 2018. https://datasociety.net/library/oxygen-of-amplification/.

Pruszkiewicz, Katarzyna, Wojciech Ciesla, and Konrad Szczygiel. *Undercover at a Troll Farm*. Investigate Europe, November 1, 2019. https://www.investigate-europe.eu/undercover-at-a-troll-farm/.

Romero, Alex. *An Ecosystem of Mistrust and Disinformation*. Disinfo Portal, June 2019. https://disinfoportal.org/an-ecosystem-of-mistrust-and-disinformation/.

Silverman, Craig. *Lies, Damn Lies, and Viral Content*. Tow Center for Digital Journalism, Columbia Journalism School, February 10, 2015. https://www.cjr.org/tow_center_reports/craig_silverman_lies_damn_lies_viral_content.php.

Smith, Victoria, and Natalie Thompson. *Survey on Countering Influence Operations Highlights Steep Challenges, Great Opportunities*. Partnership for Countering Influence Operations (PCIO), Carnegie Endowment for International Peace, December 7, 2020. https://carnegieendowment.org/2020/12/07/survey-on-countering-influence-operations-highlights-steep-challenges-great-opportunities-pub-83370.

Stanford Internet Observatory. *Analysis of an October 2020 Facebook Takedown Linked to U.S. Political Consultancy Rally Forge*. SIO Cyber Policy Center, Stanford University, October 8, 2020. https://cyber.fsi.stanford.edu/io/news/oct-2020-fb-rally-forge.

Tucker, Joshua, Andrew Guess, Pablo Barberá, Cristian Vaccari, Alexandra Siegel, Sergey Sanovich, Denis Stukal, and Brendan Nyhan. *Social Media, Political Polarization, and Political Disinformation: A Review of the Scientific Literature*. Hewlett Foundation, March 2018. https://papers.ssrn.com/sol3/papers.cfm?abstract_id=3144139.

Wardle, Clare. *First Draft's Essential Guide to Understanding Information Disorder*. First Draft, October 2019. https://firstdraftnews.org/latest/information-disorder-the-techniques-we-saw-in-2016-have-evolved/.

Woolley, Samuel C., and Douglas R. Guilbeault. *Computational Propaganda in the United States of America: Manufacturing Consensus Online.* Working Paper No. 2017.5, Computational Propaganda Research Project, Oxford Internet Institute, 2017. http://comprop.oii.ox.ac.uk/wp-content/uploads/sites/89/2017/06/Comprop-USA.pdf.

INDEX

acid rain, 73–74, 75
advertising profit model, 16–21
affinity fraud, 41, 148
Alba, Davey, 24
Alethea Group, 45
algorithms: confirmation bias and, 115, 120; deepfakes and, 162; disinformation and, 162; echo chambers and, 141–42, 144–45, 150–51, 153; fake online personas and, 38; targeting data and, 7, 32–33, 102, 156
al-Qaeda, 26–28
Amazon, 65
American Cancer Society, 72
American Petroleum Institute (API), 76
American Pundit, 45
America's Last Line of Defense (Facebook page), 5
Anglin, Andrew, 51
Anonymous (hacker collective), 25
API (American Petroleum Institute), 76
Archimedes Group, 16

Arendt, Hannah, 78
Armstrong, Matt, 68–69
Aronson, Elliot: *Age of Propaganda*, 124; on bandwagon effect, 128; on cognitive dissonance, 112–13; on collective identity, 124; on commitment escalation strategies, 118–19; on echo chambers, 145–46; on factoids, 88, 89; on propaganda, 84; *The Social Animal*, 107
astroturfing, 49
attention economy, 1, 21, 28–29, 142, 157
attention hacking, 50–51
attribution theory, 132
autism fraudulently linked to vaccines, 75, 95

backfire effect, 115, 120
bandwagon effect, 128, 143
Bannon, Steve, 34, 36, 155–56
Barnes, Susan, 31
Bartlett, Bruce, 51, 52
Bateman, Jon, 164

BBC: on climate change science, 76; on news consumption guidelines, 167
Bearded Patriot, 45
Berger, J. M., 100–101, 124, 131, 144
Bhargava, Rohit, 62, 63
Blair, Christopher, 5, 7, 19
Bodanis, David, 132
Borel, Brooke: *The Chicago Guide to Fact-Checking*, 167
bots and botnets, 20, 37–38, 94
Bradshaw, Samantha, 55
brainwashing, 67
Brandenburg, Steven, 99
Breitbart, 4, 115, 150, 152, 162
Brexit, 35
Briant, Emma, 35; *Propaganda Machine*, 36–37
bribery, 8
Brooking, Emerson, 14, 26–27, 37, 49, 53, 158
Brown, Scott, 49
Buzzfeed on Macedonia's digital influence mercenaries, 34
Byrne, David, 150–51

Cacioppo, John T., 83
Cadwalladr, Carole, 34
Cali, Frank, 98
Cambridge Analytica, 8, 34–37, 145
Camerota, Alisyn, 87–88
Canon, Lance, 110
Capitol insurrection (2021), 149, 163
CDC (Centers for Disease Control and Prevention), 90
central processing of information, 83–85
CFCs (chlorofluorocarbons), 74, 75
cheapfakes, 42
Chesney, Robert, 43, 92

Cialdini, Robert, 118, 127
Cieśla, Wojciech, 37
CISA (Cybersecurity and Infrastructure Security Agency), 164–65
Citizen Lab, 55
Citron, Danielle Keats, 43, 92
clickbait, 29, 43–44, 82
client-services profit model, 7–16, 157–58
climate change, 73–74, 76–77
cognitive bias, 33, 57–58, 108–9, 136, 140, 166
cognitive dissonance: echo chambers and, 139, 140; exploiting target's desire to avoid, 70, 111–13; information processing by humans and, 84
Cohen-Watnick, Ezra, 49
Cold War, 73
Coler, Jestin, 3–4, 7, 19, 42, 113
collective identity, 123–37; echo chambers and, 146–47; exploitation of, 125–29; in-group conformity and, 130–35
Colt Ventures, 34
Combs, Cindy, 28
Comello, Anthony, 98
commitment escalation, 118–21
confirmation bias, 103–22; cognitive dissonance avoidance and, 111–13; collective identity and, 132, 137; commitment escalation and, 118–21; conspiracy theories and, 94–95; echo chambers and, 140, 148, 150, 153; exploitation of, 29–30, 111–18; in-group conformity and, 132; lazy reasoning and, 116–18; motivated reasoning and, 114–16; pride and, 107–11

INDEX 237

conformity: collective identity and, 126–29; echo chambers and, 148, 152; exploitation of, 130–35

conspiracy theories, 82–102; collective identity and, 137; echo chambers and, 143–44; factoids and, 88–92; fear and, 22; information processing capabilities of humans and, 83–85; in-group conformity and, 131–32; profiting from, 92–101; truth and, 85–88; uncertainty and, 22

Consumer Reports, 65

Conway, Erik, 73, 74; *Merchants of Doubt*, 72

Coppins, McKay, 80

COVID-19 pandemic: anti-science discourse and, 75–76; conspiracy theories and, 95–96, 98, 149; disinformation campaigns and, 10, 101, 161–62; uncertainty created by, 59–60; vaccine provocation campaigns, 46, 96, 99, 161

credibility: client-services profit model and, 14; collective identity and, 128; confirmation bias and, 104, 107; conspiracy theories and, 97; deepfakes and, 158; disinformation and, 52, 55; echo chambers and, 147; targeted attacks on, 55, 155; uncertainty and, 74, 79

Cruz, Ted, 35, 36

cyberbullying, 54, 159

Cyber Command (U.S.), 165

Cybersecurity and Infrastructure Security Agency (CISA), 164–65

Daily Caller, 115

data analytics, 31–33

Data & Society report on trust in media, 62

data mining, 8, 33–37

DDoS (distributed denial-of-service) attacks, 55

DeepFaceLab, 43

deepfakes, 24, 42–43, 158–60, 162

deep state conspiracy theories, 97, 98–99

De Grey, Aubrey, 65

dehumanization of out-group, 132

denial-of-service (DoS) attacks, 55

Denning, Dorothy, 53

Department of Homeland Security, 164–65, 167

deplatforming, 163, 165–66

Digital Forensic Research Lab, 167

digital influence mercenaries: client-services profit model, 7–16; derivation of term, 1; future of, 156–60; landscape of, 1–30; methods of, 31–57; online advertising profit model, 16–21; responses to, 160–68; rise of, 5–24; YouTube and, 22–24

digital vigilantes, 25–28

Direct Mailers Group, 45

Disinfomedia, 3–4

disinformation: COVID-19 pandemic and, 10, 101, 161–62; doubt created about verifiable information by, 85; echo chambers and, 143–44; media amplification and, 50–53, 167–68; as method of digital influence, 41–44; profitability of, 3–5; sources of, 16, 66, 105; on YouTube, 23

Donath, Judith, 47

dopamine, 110, 118

DoS (denial-of-service) attacks, 55

Douglas, Karen, 90, 92

doxing, 54

Dunning-Kruger effect, 109–10, 116
Duterte, Rodrigo, 47

echo chambers, 138–54; exploitation of, 145–47; filter bubbles and, 139–45; polarization and, 147–52; uncertainty and, 66
8Chan, 97, 100
8kun, 100
election of 2016, 35–36, 164
election of 2020, 39, 100
elective affinity, 140
Endchan, 100
Erbschloe, Michael, 13, 25
expertise, 62, 87, 153

Facebook: conspiracy theories and, 96; deepfakes on, 43, 160, 162; digital influence mercenaries operating on, 9, 16; echo chambers and, 139, 140, 142, 151; fake online accounts on, 40; polarization of content on, 150; QAnon and, 98; responses to digital influence mercenaries, 161–65, 167; targeting data and, 34–36
Faceswap software, 43
FactCheck.org, 167
factoids, 88–92
FakeApp software, 43
fake news: distribution strategy, 17, 23; sources of, 2. *See also* disinformation
false equivalence, 78
Farid, Hany, 46, 149, 160–61
Farrakhan, Louis, 162
Fauci, Anthony, 75, 96, 99
FBI (Federal Bureau of Investigation), 98
fear: cognitive dissonance and, 112; collective identity and, 126; confirmation

bias and, 109, 132; conspiracy theories and, 22; gaslighting and, 69; in-group conformity and, 132, 134; provocation and, 44–45, 46; uncertainty as driver for, 59–64, 68, 84
Federal Bureau of Investigation (FBI), 98
feedback loops, 105
Festinger, Leon: *A Theory of Cognitive Dissonance*, 111
FIEs (foreign influence efforts), 11
filter bubbles: echo chambers and, 139–45; exploitation of, 145–47; polarization and, 147–52
Fischer, Sara, 37–38
flaming, 46–47
Fletcher, Richard, 141, 143
foreign influence efforts (FIEs), 11
4Chan, 43, 97, 100
Fox News, 4, 78, 150
Francis (pope), 2
Freelon, Deen, 137
Fukuyama, Francis, 116

Gab, 160, 162
Gaffney, Amber, 124, 130
Gainous, Jason, 139, 152, 153–54
Garcia, Laura, 142, 167
gaslighting, 69–71, 80, 85, 104
Gates, Bill, 96
Gateway Pundit, 4, 162
George C. Marshall Institute, 74, 76
Georgetown University, 158
Gingrich, Newt, 87–88
Gleicher, Nathan, 67
Global Health Security Network, 99
Goebbels, Joseph, 104
Gore, Al: *The Assault on Reason*, 64
Gorka, Sebastian, 27

Graphika, 39
greenhouse gases, 76
group identity. *See* collective identity; in-group; out-group
group think, 135. *See also* collective identity
Guardian: on Cambridge Analytica, 34, 36; on Macedonia's digital influence mercenaries, 34
Gully, Andrew, 11–12

Harris, Cameron, 4, 7, 19, 113
hashtags, 3, 48, 50
Hayden, Michael, 61
Heartland Institute, 76
Heritage Foundation, 74
Hodges, Bert, 109, 126
Hogg, Michael, 124, 130
Holiday, Ryan, 24
homophily effect, 138
Howard, Philip: on botnets, 20, 38; on commitment escalation, 118; on confirmation bias, 108; on echo chambers, 142, 145; on fake digital personas, 15; on profit models of digital influence mercenaries, 7, 8, 13–14; on selective exposure, 140; on social media takedown strategies, 55; on targeting data, 33
Hussein, Amr, 3

identity politics, 129
Inclusive Conservation Group, 40
information processing capabilities of humans, 83–85
InfoWars, 22, 115, 162
in-group: collective identity and, 124–25, 129; confirmation bias and, 119; conformity and, 130–35; conspiracy theories and, 100–101; echo chambers and, 140–41, 144–48, 153; polarization and, 28. *See also* echo chambers
insecurity, 59–60, 68, 84, 123. *See also* fear; uncertainty
Insikt Group, 12
Instagram: echo chambers and, 139, 142; fake online accounts on, 40; responses to digital influence mercenaries, 162, 163, 165
Institute for the Study of Diplomacy, 158, 164
Internet Research Agency (IRA): client-services profit model of, 7, 8–9, 13; fake online accounts and, 39, 40; provocation campaigns by, 45; sanctions against, 165; targeting data and, 34; trolling by, 47–48
Investigate Europe, 37
Iran, media amplification campaigns in, 53
Islamic State, 26–28
Israel, digital influence mercenaries in, 16

Jigsaw, 11–12, 167
Jones, Alex, 22, 107, 162

Kaiser, Brittany, 35–36; *Targeted*, 36
Kakutani, Michiko, 63, 79, 80, 102; *The Death of Truth*, 60
Kalenský, Jakub, 25
Kaplan, Alex, 99
Kaplan, Lisa, 20
Katz, Elihu, 123
Kavanagh, Jennifer, 63, 64
Keen, Andrew: *The Cult of the Amateur*, 138
Kennedy, Ted, 49

Kessler, Gladys, 73
Khan, Sadiq, 28
Kianpour, Suzanne, 53
Kiely, Eugene, 167
Kirk, Charlie, 10, 27
Knight, Will, 160
Koch Foods, 45
Kogan, Aleksandr, 34
Kolbert, Elizabeth, 108–9, 110, 136–37
Kovach, Bill: *Blur: How to Know What's True in the Age of Information Overload*, 167
Kruglanski, Arie, 124
Kyoto Protocol, 76

LaFrance, Adrienne, 97
Lazarsfeld, Paul, 123
Lazer, David: "The Science of Fake News," 104
lazy reasoning, 116–18
Leave.EU campaign, 35
legends, 15, 39
Levitin, Daniel: *Weaponized Lies: How to Think Critically in the Post-truth Era*, 103, 167
Lewis, C. S., 106
Lewis, Rebecca, 50–51, 62
"liar's dividend," 92
Lifton, Robert, 117, 135
Limbaugh, Rush, 20–21, 90, 107
Linvill, Darren, 147

Macedonia, digital influence mercenaries in, 2–3, 34
Mackey, Douglass, 164
Mailer, Norman, 88
Manheim, Jarol, 31, 83, 113, 119
Martin, Diego, 11

Marwick, Alice, 50–51, 62
Massoumi, Cyrus, 4, 103–4
Mathis, Joel, 95–96
Mazarr, Michael, 43, 87, 118, 158
McCain, John, 117
McIntyre, Lee: on anti-science discourse, 76; on "both sides" strategy, 79; on cognitive dissonance avoidance, 112; on collective identity, 136; on confirmation bias, 109–10, 121; on echo chambers, 153; on fake news, 4; on motivated reasoning, 114; on polarization, 148; on postmodernism and truth, 60; *Post-truth*, 77–78, 86, 114; on uncertainty created by social media, 81
McMaster, H. R., 49–50
McNamee, Roger, 153
McRaven, William, 117
media: attention economy and, 28; collective identity and, 135, 136; confirmation bias and, 114, 115; conspiracy theories and, 94, 97; disinformation in, 50–53, 167–68; echo chambers and, 150–52; fake outlets, 42; gatekeeping function of, 154; trust in, 62; uncertainty and, 62–63, 72, 79. *See also specific media outlets*
Mercer, Rebekah, 36
Mercer, Robert, 34, 36
MetaFilter, 43
methods of digital influence, 31–57; crafting of credible fake online personas, 37–41; disinformation, 41–44; engagement deception, 48–50; media amplification, 50–53; provocation, 44–48; targeted attacks, 53–56; targeting data, 33–37
MeWe, 162

Mikovitz, Judy, 96
Miller, Carl, 6, 33, 167
Mishra, Pankaj: *Age of Anger*, 84–85
misinformation, 41–44. See also disinformation
Moreno, Eduardo, 99
motivated reasoning, 111, 114–16, 120–21
MSNBC, 78
Mueller, Robert, 36
Murray, Patrick, 149

National Endowment for Democracy, 114
NATO: on client-services profit model, 7, 11; on DDoS attacks, 55; on digital influence mercenaries, 5–6, 156; on online advertising profit model, 17, 29; Strategic Communications Centre of Excellence, 7
negative campaign strategies, 8
Newark, Craig, 164
Newsmax, 115, 150
New Waves (digital marketing company), 3, 7
New Yorker on Macedonia's digital influence mercenaries, 34
New York Times: on Cambridge Analytica, 34; on Heartland Institute, 76
Nichols, Tom: *The Death of Expertise*, 61–62
Nietzsche, Friedrich, 117
Noelle-Neumann, Elisabeth, 126
Nyhan, Brendan, 115

Obama, Barack, 93
objective truth: conspiracy theories and, 86–88, 92, 101; uncertainty and, 69, 77, 79

O'Connor, Cailin: *The Misinformation Age*, 107
Office of the U.S. Director of National Intelligence, 8, 9
OII (Oxford Internet Institute), 6, 16, 20, 24, 47, 157
Omar, Ilhan, 28
Ong, Jonathan Corpus, 16
online advertising profit model, 16–21
Orehek, Edward, 124
Oreskes, Naomi, 73, 74; *Merchants of Doubt*, 72
Organized Crime and Corruption Reporting Project, 3
Orwell, George: *1984*, 87
othering, 125, 147–48
Otis, Cindy: *True or False*, 167
out-group: collective identity and, 124–25, 129; confirmation bias and, 118; conformity and, 130–35; conspiracy theories and, 100–101; dehumanization of, 132; echo chambers and, 138, 144, 147–48
overconfidence, 103–22; cognitive dissonance avoidance and, 111–13; commitment escalation and, 118–21; exploitation of, 111–18, 160; lazy reasoning and, 114–16; motivated reasoning and, 116–18; pride and, 107–11; uncertainty and, 67
Oxford Internet Institute (OII), 6, 16, 20, 24, 47, 157

Pariser, Eli, 141
Parler, 160, 162
Patrikarakos, David, 138
PBS Newshour, 4
Pennycook, Gordon, 114, 115, 116

peripheral processing of information, 83–85
Petty, Richard E., 83
Pew Research Center: on polarization of politics, 148; on trust in information sources, 149
Phillips, Whitney, 51–52
Pizzagate conspiracy theory, 94, 99
Plandemic (video), 96
Poland, digital influence mercenaries in, 14–15
political entrapment, 8
Pomerantsev, Peter, 39, 87, 91
Posobiec, Jack, 26
postmodernism, 61, 78, 87
Pragmatico, 16
Pratkanis, Anthony R.: *Age of Propaganda*, 124; on bandwagon effect, 128; on cognitive dissonance, 112–13; on collective identity, 124; on commitment escalation strategies, 118–19; on echo chambers, 145–46; on factoids, 88, 89; on propaganda, 84
pride and confirmation bias, 107–11
Prigozhin, Yevgeny, 8, 9, 10, 52–53
Prim, Jessica, 99
Princeton University, 157
privacy paradox, 31
propaganda: "both sides" strategy and, 78; confirmation bias and, 104–5; information processing capabilities of humans and, 84
provocation: gaslighting and, 69–70; in-group conformity and, 134; as method of digital influence, 44–48
psychographic modeling, 36
Psy-Group, 8, 34
Public Health Service (U.S.), 71

public relations, uses for digital influence mercenaries, 24–25
Putin, Vladimir, 8

QAnon, 96, 97–100, 131–32, 162–63

Rabin-Havt, Ari, 77
Rahuba, Adam, 4
Rally Forge (marketing firm), 10, 13, 27, 40, 49, 165
RallyPAC, 13
RAND Corporation: on collective identity, 128; on cyberbullying, 159; on deepfakes, 43, 158; on digital influence mercenaries, 157; on objective knowledge, 87; on tobacco industry's strategy, 72; on truth decay, 63–64, 110
Rand, David, 114, 115, 116
rationalization trap, 84
Reader's Digest survey on trust in government, 62
Recorded Future, 12
Reddit, 43, 130
Reifler, Jason, 115
Rich, Michael, 63, 64
RICO (Racketeer Influenced and Corrupt Organizations) Act, 73
Rid, Thomas, 8
Rightside Data, 45
Robertson, Lori, 167
Romero, Alex, 67
Roose, Kevin, 150
Rosenstein, Rod, 8
Rosenstiel, Tom: *Blur: How to Know What's True in the Age of Information Overload*, 167
RT (formerly Russia Today), 9–10, 68, 92
RT America TV, 9–10

Rumble, 160
Russia: digital mercenaries in, 8–10; election interference by, 68. *See also specific organizations and individuals*

salami slicing, 70–71, 80
sanctions against digital influence mercenaries, 165
SCL Group (Strategic Communications Laboratories), 34
secondhand smoke, 90
selective exposure, 140
Shadloo, Farshad, 100
Shapiro, Jacob, 11
Silverman, Craig, 5, 15, 19, 100
Singer, Fred, 74
Singer, P. W., 14, 26–27, 37, 49, 158
Slyman, Alpalus, 99
Smith, Sarah Harrison: *The Fact Checker's Bible*, 167
smoking: secondhand smoke, 90; tobacco industry's strategy for manufacturing uncertainty, 71–77, 115
social capital manipulation, 146, 153
social media: client-services profit model and, 10–16; collective identity and, 123, 127, 128; confirmation bias and, 120; conspiracy theories and, 98, 102; disinformation campaigns on, 2–3, 12, 17; echo chambers and, 139, 141–42, 150, 153–54; engagement deception and, 48, 50; fake online personas and, 37, 39, 40; future of digital influence mercenaries and, 156–57, 160, 162–66; online advertising profit model and, 16–19, 24; provocation strategies and, 44, 46–48; rise of digital influence mercenaries and, 5, 7–8, 27–29, 56–57; targeted attacks and, 55; targeting data and, 31–33; uncertainty and, 81. *See also specific social media platforms*
social proof: collective identity and, 127–28, 136; confirmation bias and, 121; echo chambers and, 143, 146; engagement deception and, 48; illusion of, 18; uncertainty and, 70
sockpuppets (fake identities), 14, 39–41
Solberg, Erna, 53
Soufan Center, 1
Southfront, 10
Special Counsel Investigation (U.S.), 8–9
Stamos, Alex, 6
Stanford Internet Observatory, 6, 9, 52–53, 166
Starbird, Kate, 138
Stengel, Richard: *Information Wars*, 67
Stitcher, 40
Strategic Communications Laboratories (SCL) Group, 34
Strategic Policy Institute, 53
Suleimani, Qassim, 53
Sunstein, Cass: *Going to Extremes*, 143
Sykes, Charlie, 68

Targeted Victory, 35
Taylor, Kathleen, 84, 129, 132, 134
TheSoul Publishing, 20
Tobacco Industry Research Council (TIRC), 72
tobacco strategy for manufacturing uncertainty, 71–77, 115
TripAdvisor, 65
trolling, 26, 46–48, 50, 54, 96, 165
Trudeau, Justin, 95
true believers, 6, 26–28, 93, 130–31
Trump, Donald: "both sides" strategy

and, 79; Cambridge Analytica and, 35–36; collective identity and, 133, 135; confirmation bias and, 107, 115–16, 117; conspiracy theories and, 100; COVID-19 response and, 75–76; echo chambers and, 149; fake news creation and, 2–3, 19; false or misleading claims by, 101; overconfidence and, 109; QAnon and, 97
Truth Examiner (Facebook page), 4
Truth Monitor (Facebook page), 4
Tucker, Patrick, 140
Tumblr, 43
Turning Point Action, 10, 13, 27, 40, 165
Twitter: conspiracy theories and, 96; deepfakes on, 43, 160; echo chambers and, 139, 142, 151; fake online accounts on, 40; provocation campaigns on, 45; QAnon and, 98; responses to digital influence mercenaries, 161, 162–63

Ukraine, digital influence mercenaries in, 16
uncertainty, 58–81; "both sides" strategy, 77–79, 87; conspiracy theories and, 22; discomfort of, 29, 66–67, 104, 112, 123; as exploitable vulnerability, 64–67; false equivalence and, 77–79; fear created by, 59–64, 68, 84; gaslighting and, 69–71; in-group conformity and, 132, 134; salami slicing and, 70–71; strategies that manufacture and enhance, 67–79; tobacco strategy for manufacturing, 71–77; trust and, 59–64
uncertainty-identity theory, 124
UNESCO: on deepfakes, 158; on digital influence mercenaries, 5; on disinformation's goal, 85; on online advertising profit model, 17; on public relations uses for digital influence mercenaries, 24–25
University of California, 162
U.S. Cyber Command, 165
U.S. Public Health Service, 71
U.S. Special Counsel Investigation, 8–9

vaccines: autism fraudulently linked to, 75, 95; conspiracy theories and, 96, 99; COVID-19, 46, 96, 99, 161
voter disengagement tactics, 36

Wagner, Kevin, 139, 152, 153–54
Wakefield, Andrew, 75, 95, 108
Walker, Robert, 39, 49, 69–70
Wall Street Journal on echo chambers, 142
Ward, Kelli, 13
Wardle, Claire, 51, 52, 54, 168
Warner, Anthony Quinn, 99
Warner, Judith, 77
Warren, Patrick, 147
Washington Post: on conspiracy theories, 91–92; on Trump's disinformation, 101
Watts, Clint, 10, 13
Weatherall, James Owen: *The Misinformation Age*, 107
Welch, Edgar Madison, 94, 98
WhatsApp, 160
White, Paula, 134
WHO (World Health Organization), 90, 162
Wikileaks, 25
Winn, Denise: on collective identity, 126–27; on confirmation bias, 114; on echo chambers, 140; on in-group conformity, 134; *The Manipulated Mind*, 107; on uncertainty exploitation, 66

Wired on Macedonia's digital influence mercenaries, 34
Wolf of Washington, 45
World Health Organization (WHO), 90, 162
Wright, Matthew Philip, 98
Wylie, Christopher, 35

YouTube: conspiracy theories and, 96, 100; digital influence mercenaries operating on, 22–24; fake online accounts on, 40; QAnon and, 98; responses to digital influence mercenaries, 161–62

Zimbardo, Philip, 166